The Artists' Guide
to the GIMP

Michael J. Hammel

Published by:
Specialized Systems Consultants, Inc. (SSC)
PO Box 55549
Seattle, WA 98155
Phone: +1-206-782-7733
Fax: +1-206-782-7191
E-mail: info@ssc.com
URL: http://www.ssc.com/

ISBN: 1-57831-011-3

Table of Contents

Preface

Many people have worked to make the GIMP the powerful tool that it is, and many are listed in the program itself, under the *About* dialog from the File menu in the Toolbox. My name is actually included in that list, although I really didn't do much in the development of the code for the 1.0 release (I ported John Beale's Sparkle code into the 0.54 version of the GIMP, long before the major architectural changes for the 1.0 version). It would be difficult to list them all. However, a few people deserve special recognition, not just for their work on the GIMP, but for their contribution to my general knowledge of computer graphics, the sort of contribution that went far in leading me to write this book.

Of course, there are the original authors of the GIMP, Spencer Kimball and Peter Mattis. At the time of the GIMP's original release, they were undergraduate students at the University of California at Berkeley working with the XCF—the Experimental Computing Facility. The story goes something like this: Spencer and Peter were working on a senior project that just wasn't going well, and they had only a couple of weeks left before it had to be turned in. They quickly ran through some possible alternative projects before deciding that a Photoshop-like tool for UNIX systems would be a fun thing to do. Not long after, a Motif-based version was released, the 0.54 release, and the project was taking shape. I'm not certain that's the right story, but it's the one I remember reading about on one of the mailing lists.

I first got hold of the GIMP while working for X Inside, Inc. (now Xi Graphics, Inc.). A co-worker, Jeremy Chatfield, with whom I have worked at several other companies, knew of my interest in computer graphics, and suggested I take a look at it. I loved it, if for no other reason than that it gave me the opportunity to learn about why things worked and not just how to get them to do what I wanted. I was never that great at low-level work, like with X servers, but I understood how applications worked, and the GIMP was using the same set of facilities I had taught myself long ago, the X Window System API, to do something more interesting to me than providing a graphical windowing interface to more mundane functions.

I played with the early releases and quickly found the plug-in API. The early releases used a very simple API, and I found it quite easy to learn, especially with the help I was getting from the GIMP Developers list. However, I didn't know enough about creating effects to write my own plug-in. I needed an algorithm I could simply port. That's where John Beale comes in. He had written a number of tools for creating a variety of effects, both as stand-alone applications and as hooks for other tools. One tool of his caught my eye: his Sparkle program. I grabbed it and ported it to the 0.54 API in the GIMP. I was so proud. Of course, porting is actually the easy part in these situations. The algorithms are the important things.

Well, it's been quite some time since all that happened. In fact, it's been at least two years—closer to three now. The 0.54 GIMP is no more, except on a few die-hard systems. I actually still have a copy of the 0.60 version installed on my box. I guess I'm just a sentimentalist.

That leads us to the present. The 1.0 release is here. During its long development process, one of the items in which no one seemed to take much interest (at least not until very late in the development) was documentation. I had taken on the task earlier of doing documentation for the GIMP as a project in itself, going so far as to work on some SGML templates for plug-in authors to use. But few coders like to write documentation, so that just fell by the wayside. Later, I wrote a series of articles on the GIMP for *Linux Journal*. I had also written a bit about it in my "Graphics Muse" column for the *Linux Gazette*. The publisher of *Linux Journal*, SSC, Inc., found my articles quite good (at least that's what they told me) and asked if I'd like to do a book on the subject.

The rest, as they say, is history.

This book took me close to a year to write. I kept it quiet for most of that time. I had coauthored another text, the *UNIX Web Server*, a year previously and found that working with a team of writers just didn't fit my style. I don't seem to fit well in the popular Bazaar model that the GIMP has grown up in. But even I don't exist in a vacuum. Federico Mena Quintero, known as Quartic to many GIMP, GTK and GNOME developers, was an excellent resource for information about the internal workings of the GIMP. Adrian Likins, Miles O'Neal and a cast of thousands on the GIMP User and GIMP Developer mailing lists offered quick and direct answers to questions, not just from me but from the ever increasing throng of GIMP users. Andreas Dilger and Larry Gritz offered lots of help when I first ventured into graphics using three-dimensional tools such as POV-Ray and BMRT. This help was a catalyst to get me even more involved in graphics, eventually leading me to the GIMP. And although we didn't discuss the book directly, I have to thank Zach Beane for his willingness to work as an editor for the book. I now know of at least one person who actually read the whole thing. Thanks, Zach! Others who deserve mention include Wayde Allen of the Boulder Linux Users Group, Chip Richards, Bill Marrs and Chris Cason (my three IRTC compatriots), and Michael Sweet for information on the Print Plug-In.

Of course, not all the help I received was just computer or graphics help. Much of it has been help in becoming a writer—a real writer, not a guy who does his own web pages for free. My biggest thanks probably belong to Margie Richardson at *Linux Journal*. She encouraged me to write first for the *Linux Gazette* and then later for *Linux Journal*. Her consistent encouragement eventually led to my doing two covers for *Linux Journal* and writing a four part series on the GIMP. That series then led SSC, Inc. to ask me if I'd be interested in doing this book. So, as you see, none of this would have gone anywhere without that first push from Margie. Thanks, Margie!

As the book progressed, I came in contact with a number of people at SSC. The last two I owe a great deal of thanks to are Clarica Grove and Carlie Fairchild. Clarica handled editing issues for me and Carlie handled just about all the rest, including useful feedback on the cover (which was done using the GIMP, of course). For a time I was getting a bit burned out, not only with working on the book but with computers in general. Carlie's phone calls and upbeat attitude helped keep me motivated.

Some of the information you'll find in this book is taken from my articles for *Linux Journal*, while other information was gathered from various net-based resources, including the GIMP User and GIMP Developer mailing lists. I never joined in on the GIMP IRC chat rooms—on-line chatting lost its appeal to me long ago, after spending far too many hours on the Bitnet Relay system (how many of you remember that bit of history?). All of the images in the book were created by me either specifically for this book, or previously for no particular reason. All of the photos scanned for use in the book are photos I've taken or have had for many years. The hardest part of doing this book was finding photos that were decent enough for use as source images for doing the examples. I have lots of photos, I just don't have lots of good photos. Maybe that will be my next project—learning to become a better photographer.

I hope you find this text useful. It is meant to be a reference guide for non-technical users—people who want to use the GIMP to do real work. I expect that the next version will have more information on developing plug-ins and writing Script-Fu scripts. That depends on how much of an expert I become in those topics between now and then. In any case, I know the GIMP has opened a whole slew of new doors for me. I hope this text helps open doors for you as you explore the wonders of computer graphics that you can find when you use the GIMP.

Michael J. Hammel
October 1998

Chapter 1 - Introduction

What Is the GIMP?

The GIMP is the **GNU Image Manipulation Program**, a tool for manipulating graphics images that borrows its look and feel from the popular Macintosh and Microsoft Windows program from Adobe called Photoshop. It is used for all varieties of image processing, photo retouching and image composition. Built-in features such as scripting make it very easy to create logos for web pages and magazine cover art, and the plug-in API provides a convenient mechanism for extending the very rich standard feature set. Support for a large number of input and output file formats is provided, including support for reading Photoshop files. The GIMP offers such advanced features as layered editing, a gradient editor, channel operations and alpha blending. All of this is provided through an easy-to-use interface to users of a variety of UNIX-based platforms.

Linux and UNIX systems in general are often thought of by the general public as systems that sit in some far-off office or closet and handle file and network serving tasks. Except for using high-end Silicon Graphics systems to do detailed three-dimentional graphics work, one would suppose that no self-respecting digital graphic artist would ever consider using a UNIX-based system to do web page design or cover art for magazines, CD covers, or any other sort of print media. The common myth is that UNIX systems are for system administrators to write Perl scripts and for web administrators to design CGI scripts. They aren't for everyday routines.

That myth is about to be put to rest. Linux, a UNIX-like system for PCs, Macs, Digital Alphas and other hardware platforms, has become a cost-effective solution not only for many system and web administrators, but also for the average user who expects and needs a graphical interface. Beyond serving files on a network, Linux provides a viable solution to desktop productivity. Already there are office automation tools such as word processors and spreadsheets available for free and from commercial vendors, including Corel's WordPerfect and Applix's popular Applixware suite of office tools. Linux is a desktop solution. And the GIMP is about to bring that fact into the limelight of the graphic arts world.

The GIMP makes very good use of many features, such as shared memory, that well-designed, POSIX-compliant, UNIX operating systems provide. Even though this book is geared toward the desktop world that Linux is opening to UNIX users, you shouldn't feel that other UNIX systems have been left out of the world of the GIMP. On the contrary—the GIMP has been ported to most of the more popular flavors of UNIX, including Sun Solaris, SGI IRIX, FreeBSD and HP/UX. In fact, many of the publicly provided plug-ins that are now part of the base distribution of the GIMP have come from graphics experts using SGIs and other high-end systems. The GIMP is for anyone with access to almost any UNIX system.

Who Is This Book For?

The primary audience for this book is the large group of people who now use Linux on their desktops. However, since the GIMP is not Linux-specific, every effort will be made to keep discussions platform-independent. If it becomes necessary to cite platform dependencies or nuances, a note will be made stating that the information may not apply to all situations. In general, you can assume that unless otherwise noted, the information provided is applicable to all supported platforms.

Book Organization

This book follows a format which is a combination of the formats of some of the better texts on Photoshop which I've read over the past few years. The majority of the chapters contain a series of images. The images are captioned to associate them with the portions of the text to which they are relevant. Images without captions are used as examples and any relevant text will accompany the image directly beneath it.

Although my original intent for this book was to be oriented toward artistic design rather than general use, it is impossible to ignore the fact that the GIMP is new. There simply are no other texts available to explain how to use individual features or how to navigate through the myriad menus, buttons, and dialog windows. This lack of other reference material requires this text to be split into two parts. The first part, the Guided Tour, contains 11 chapters which explain what the window features and basic tools look like, how to use them, and to some extent, why you'd want to use them. The second part, Filters and Script-Fu Effects, discusses the plug-ins available for the GIMP. It is hoped that the flow of the book will lend itself not only as a reference guide but as a general classroom guide for creating digital graphic effects.

The sections and chapters in the book are outlined below:

Part One - Guided Tour

- Chapters 1 and 2 are introductory in nature, explaining basic graphics terminology and general use and feature descriptions of the GIMP.

- Chapters 3 through 5 cover the basic layout of the windows and how selections are used.

- Chapter 6 introduces the concept of layers and provides details on how to use them, along with their companion feature—channels.

- Chapter 7 explains the use of color and text in images.

- Chapter 8 is a discussion on drawing and painting with the GIMP.

- Chapter 9 introduces the reader to transforms and explains how they are used.

- Chapter 10 covers gradients, the flow of color along a line in one or more directions.

- Chapter 11 talks about scanning, printing and print media.

Part Two - Filters and Script-Fu Effects

Each chapter in this section is relatively terse, giving brief descriptions and examples of usage for most, but not all, of the filters available from the given menu hierarchy.

- Chapter 12 - Artistic filters

- Chapter 13 - Blur filters

- Chapter 14 - Filters that deal with colors

- Chapter 15 - Distorts filters

- Chapter 16 - Edge-Detect and Combine filters

- Chapter 17 - Enhancement filters

- Chapter 18 - Glass Effects filters

- Chapter 19 - Light Effects filters

- Chapter 20 - Map and Miscellaneous filters

- Chapter 21 - Noise filters

- Chapter 22 - Render filters

- Chapter 23 - Some Script-Fu examples

Throughout the book are references to World Wide Web sites (URLs) which contain additional information and/or programs that can be used in conjunction with the GIMP.

X and Window Managers

UNIX systems use the *X Window System* to provide graphical displays. This is roughly the equivalent of Microsoft Windows for DOS systems, but much more sophisticated. The X Window System is very configurable, allowing users to define all sorts of default display settings. One of the most common items users can choose is the Window Manager. Window Managers are the programs which control the frames, border, title bars and buttons that surround windows. They also handle how windows can be positioned on (and off) the screen as well as how and where window icons are placed.

Many distributions of Linux now come with the FVWM95 window manager because it gives Linux a look and feel very similar to Windows95. Other window managers include (but are not limited to) FVWM2, which is a variation of the FVWM95 window manager, mwm (the Motif Window Manager), Afterstep (a NeXTStep clone), CDE, and a new desktop project called GNOME. All of these work similarly, but each offers a slightly different look to the frames and buttons they place around windows. Experienced users may have replaced the default window manager on their system with any of these or a host of other window managers. Don't let this variety confuse you. I use FVWM2 on both my Linux systems at home and Solaris and SGI's at work. Because of this, the screen shots of GIMP windows that will be presented might look slightly different than yours, but only around the edges of the windows. The functionality of the GIMP is not affected. This is true no matter which UNIX OS you are working on.

Hardware and Software Requirements

The GIMP can run on just about any UNIX system, but like most graphics packages, it benefits greatly from the addition of lots of memory, lots of disk space, and high-end graphics hardware. On the other hand (unlike some packages), the GIMP is fairly well suited to many graphic arts tasks without any additional software. There are a few minimums to consider in either case.

Hardware Requirements

CPU

If you have workstation CPUs, such as an SGI Indigo or O2, you're pretty well covered. Same goes for PowerPC and DEC Alpha-based Linux/UNIX systems. On the low end, 386-based PCs running Linux will also work with the GIMP, although computer graphic manipulation can be very CPU-intensive and faster is generally considered better.

At a minimum, I recommend a 486 CPU running at least at 66 Mhz. Any slower than this and the tile-based scheme used in the GIMP may take more time, even on modestly sized images, than the average user might tolerate. A more reasonable system would be a Pentium 133 Mhz-based system or its equivalent. I run the GIMP on a Cyrix P166, which is a 133 Mhz CPU rated to run as fast as a Pentium 166 Mhz CPU. At these speeds, you will find the bottleneck is less likely to be from your CPU than from too little memory or swap (disk) space.

Disk Space

The version of the GIMP which I used for this book, the initial 1.0 release, required approximately 45 MB[1] of disk space for the runtime files. This includes about 6 MB for the binary (not stripped, you can cut it to under 1 MB if you run "strip gimp"[2]), 15 MB for the various plug-ins, and about 24 MB for the libraries and data files such as patterns, brushes and so forth. The source code takes up approximately 17 MB uncompiled, plus 5 MB for the Extras package. If you plan on building the source yourself and then installing it, consider that you'll probably need close to double this space, maybe even just a bit more. If you are installing a binary-only release, you'll probably need only around 50 MB of disk space for the runtime system. This is just for the program and its datafiles. You're going to find you need a lot more disk space than that for image files and swap space.

Working with images is very disk space intensive—this means that you're going to want to have lots of disk space for all the images you will be creating and manipulating. Don't think that the space you'll need will just be the size of the images you create. You will also need room for variations of images, photos from archives which you will use as starting points for creating your images, and a number of copies of the same image in different formats. Managing all the files alone could be a full-time job (and in large media shops it is a full-time job), so be aware that in the long run you may want and/or need to add hard disk space. You should also consider large off-line media storage, such as Jaz drives or high-end DAT tapes to which you can migrate older work.

Another area of disk space you will need to be concerned with is swap space. The GIMP uses what are called *tiles* to manage memory and disk space efficiently. Tiles are rectangular regions of the image that can be swapped between disk and memory. By using tiles the GIMP can better manage very large images, upwards of 10,000x10,000 pixels and

---

1. Built on a Linux 2.0.13 system. Building on other Unix systems will probably have very different results.
2. If you build the GIMP from the source distribution it will, by default, include debugging symbols which are useful for debugging crashes and other problems. If you aren't concerned with this and don't plan on trying to report or track crashes (which are fairly uncommon with the 1.0 release) then you can reduce the size of the program to less than 1 MB by running "strip gimp" (you need to be in the directory where the GIMP binary lives). The usefulness of doing this is debatable, but it can help reduce both disk and memory usage to a minor extent.

beyond. Such images are often used by print media for large print posters and in film and video effects. The size of these tiles is computed based roughly on the number of colors available multiplied by a 64x64 square. For small images, the tiles can cause excessive thrashing between memory and the swap files. Fortunately, there is a configurable option in the startup file, the `gimprc` file, which you can modify to help reduce thrashing or to make the GIMP use more memory when it is available.

Memory

Although the GIMP's tile-based memory management provides a mechanism to run the GIMP even on memory limited systems, the basic truth is that the more memory you have, the better performance you'll get. Take a look through some of the popular computer graphics magazines and you'll find galleries of artwork along with the system configurations the artists used to create those images. More often than not, you'll see systems with 64 MB, 128 MB, even 512 MB of memory and more. Computer graphics are resource hogs—unlike many other applications for computer software, better performance actually can happen by throwing more hardware at the problem.

So what is the minimum you need to use the GIMP? First, let us look at the underlying recommendations for your X Windows configuration. Most of the systems which run X Windows recommend 16 MB as a minimum amount of memory. This amount suffices for simple tasks like text editing and simple X-based applications and small databases. However, throw a web browser on and the system can begin to bog down. Add the GIMP and you're looking at free time to make dinner while you wait for windows to be updated.

A more reasonable minimum is 32 MB. This will work for doing graphics for web pages which generally don't need to be much larger than 400x400 pixels in size. If you plan on running other applications like Applixware, a web browser, and perhaps even a three-dimensional rendering tool like POV-Ray or BMRT, you'll start to look beyond even this minimum. I use 64 MB on my system and find it reasonable for most of the graphics I work on. While working on the cover art for the November 1997 issue of *Linux Journal*, however, I often wished for another 64 MB. Large images like cover art (in my case the images were about 2100x2800 pixels in size) can chew up memory pretty quickly.

Another reason to consider adding lots of memory is the GIMP's support of *layers*. Layers allow an artist to create and manipulate images as if they were stacked sheets of transparencies. Each layer can be added, subtracted, and otherwise blended with the layers below it. If a particular layer needs to have its color hues modified, the changes will affect only that layer while all the other layers maintain the original settings. This powerful feature of the GIMP can also place additional requirements for memory on your system. The more layers you have, and the more complex each layer is, the more memory you'll need. Layers can work with memory-limited systems because of the GIMP's use of tiles, but excessive swapping can slow how you view images as you edit them. The moral is: the deeper into computer graphics you get, the greater your memory requirements will be.

Video Requirements

The GIMP is not hardware specific, since it makes use of the low-level X11 interface provided by Xlib through its own X toolkit, gtk+ and its low level interface to X, glib. The GIMP's toolkit, gtk+, does not rely on either the Xt toolkit or Motif. This allows the X server to handle the actual screen drawing and lets the GIMP provide the computational work for what is to be displayed. Consequently, the GIMP will work with all of the well-known X servers for Linux (Metro Link, Xi Graphics, and XFree86) as well as with any of the X servers provided by high-end UNIX workstations. Like any high-end software graphics tool, you'll have better results with the higher quality graphics adapters.

I use a Matrox Mystique with 4 MB of on-board video memory displaying at a resolution of 1152x900, which allows up to 16 million colors. As with system memory, the more video memory you have the better performance you can expect when working with graphical applications like the GIMP.

Linux users: be sure to check the server documentation or vendors' marketing material to find out if the video adapter you will be using is supported by the X server you choose.

One extension to the X Windows protocols that most modern X servers support is the *MIT Shared Memory Extension*. This extension provides a method for an X application to make use of the shared memory resources of the operating system without having to go through the Xlib interprocess communication channel. What this means is that the processing of large images by the low-level X routines can be done much faster. The GIMP makes use of this feature to help provide speed enhancements. Unfortunately, not all X servers provide support for this extension. Many older versions of these X servers do not support the MIT Shared Memory Extension. The gtk now knows how to determine the existence of this extension, so users don't have to worry about checking whether they have it.

Note that all three of the major X server vendors for Linux (Metro Link, Xi Graphics and the XFree86 Project) currently provide servers for Linux that support this extension. However, older versions of these servers may not. Some of the popular (but older) X terminals from NCD also do not support this extension.

Other Hardware

The GIMP does not have built-in support for external devices like flatbed or hand-held scanners, or video capture boards, but does support pen devices and drawing tablets. Some of these are supported through plug-ins that are not part of the main distribution package but can be found at the GIMP Registry or other web sites. Drawing tablets are supported through the use of the X Input Extension. Users of UNIX workstations from manufacturers such as Silicon Graphics and Sun Microsystems can usually contact their vendor for both hardware and software that can make use of these sorts of external video-related hardware.

Even though these devices are not directly supported by the GIMP, Linux users can make use of them through external drivers. The following information is specific to Linux users, although some information may be applicable to other UNIX systems.

Scanners

There are a variety of scanners for which Linux drivers have been written. The first place to look is the SANE Project. This is an effort to provide a generic interface for external input devices like scanners, QuickCams, and other similar hardware. The SANE Project currently supports HP ScanJet scanners, Mustek flatbed scanners, and UMAX flatbed scanners.

The SANE Project is platform-independent and the SANE drivers have been ported to a variety of UNIX systems. See the SANE web site at `http://www.mostang.com/sane/`.

Drawing Tablets

Drawing tablets are commonly supported by X servers via another extension to the X Windows protocol known as the *X Input Extension*. This extension, like the MIT Shared Memory Extension, must be supported by the X server in order for applications which use the extension to access these devices. The GIMP is an application which supports tablets through the use of the X Input Extension.

Currently, both the XFree86 servers, starting from version 3.3 and later, and the Xi Graphics Accelerated X server, from version 4.1 and later, support this extension for PC-based UNIX systems such as Linux and FreeBSD. As such, those servers are the only ones which directly support drawing tablets with the GIMP. Most UNIX-based workstations have X servers which do not support this extension by default, although you can usually purchase additional servers that do. It should be noted that Wacom, a maker of a variety of drawing tablets from small 5"x7" tablets to large color LCD screens which act as drawing tablets, is an active supporter of the XFree86 project.

Metro Link, another maker of commercial X servers for PC-based UNIX systems, is reported to be working on support for this extension.

Once a server that supports the X Input Extension has been obtained, you can take a look at some of the plug-ins that make use of it. A number of contributors to the GIMP Developer mailing list have the Wacom ArtPadII working directly with XFree86 using stand-alone applications and GIMP extensions. Owen Taylor maintains a set of web pages describing how to use the GIMP with drawing tablets.

The XFree86 Web site is located at `http://www.xfree86.org/`.

Xi Graphics can be found at `http://www.xi.com/`.

Metro Link maintains a Web site at `http://www.metrolink.com/`.

X Input support for the GTK and the GIMP can be found at `http://www.gtk.org/~otaylor/xinput/`.

Video Capture Boards

Currently there is no direct support in the GIMP for video capture boards, also known as frame grabbers. These boards connect to video input like VCRs and camcorders and display directly to your monitor. There are, however, drivers for Linux available for a number of boards. Some of these display under X Windows and some display using the console drivers or the SVGA library. Since these boards do have drivers, it is possible to use them to first capture an image from a video source and then edit it later under the GIMP. The only thing you can't do is capture and edit interactively at the same time. Perhaps in the future one or more of these drivers will be supported under the GIMP directly or, possibly, through such projects as the SANE interface.

A short list of the video capture boards which have one or more drivers and front-end packages available from the Sunsite archives is given below:

- Pro MovieStudio card

- FAST Screen Machine II

- Cortex 1

- CX100

- Data Translation DT2851 Frame Grabber

- WinVision black and white video capture board

- Matrox Meteor

- Multech MV1000 PCI-framegrabber

- SVGAlib QuickCam viewer

- Video Blaster

The Sunsite Linux archives is one of the best places to look for applications, drivers, and new tools for Linux. See `http://www.sunsite.unc.edu/pub/Linux/`.

The Xi Graphics Accelerated X server also supports the X Video Extension for use with Matrox Marvel II, including a simple application for capturing single frames as X Pixmap files.

Software Requirements

Runtime Requirements

The CD which accompanies this text contains binary distributions of the GIMP for Linux, Sun Solaris 2.5, and SGI IRIX 6.4. Runtime distributions have certain requirements based upon how the program was created on those systems, but these requirements are generally the same for all three platforms: the runtime X11 library libX11.so. This is the low-level library often referred to as Xlib. The GIMP also makes use of *Toolkit libraries*, which are used to define the look and feel of the program (which happens to be very similar to the Motif look and feel). The GIMP Toolkit libraries, also known as the GTK libraries, were built with the GIMP as static libraries; that is, you don't need the shared versions of the GTK libraries. This makes the GIMP program a bit bigger but it also removes the requirement to install another set of libraries in order to use the GIMP.

If you wish to use versions of the GIMP from other sources, you may need to check whether the GTK shared libraries are needed. Binary versions are available from the GIMP web site as well as RPM versions at the Red Hat archives.

Building From Source

Of course, the GIMP is distributed in full source code, as well. The source distribution can be retrieved from the GIMP's web site. There are three files you'll need to build and install from the source: `gimp-1.0.tar.gz`, `gimp-data-min-1.0.tar.gz`, and `gimp-data-extras-1.0.tar.gz`. The first is the real source code and the latter two are the standard set of brushes, palettes, patterns and so forth that comes with the default source distribution. Be sure to install both the `gimp-data-min` and `gimp-data-extras` if you want to have a complete set of brushes, palettes, and patterns. Note that the actual version and release numbers might be different, so just look for the latest releases on the GIMP ftp site.

Originally the GIMP was distributed with the GIMP Toolkit, GTK, packaged together. During the latter part of the 1.0 development cycle these two packages were split apart. In order to build the 1.0 version of the GIMP, you will also need to grab the GTK library package. You should build and install the GTK package first. After that, you can build the GIMP package safely. Building the GIMP from source is only necessary if you plan on working on the base source code. If you plan on writing plug-ins, you generally don't need to build the source, as the binary distributions also include the libraries needed for plug-in development. Source for both the GIMP base distribution and the GTK libraries are included on the CD that accompanies this text.

Building from source should be a straightforward process:

• Unpack the archives

• Run `./configure`

• Run `make`

• Run `make install`

This process is required for both the source code and the data files archives. If you intend to install in the default locations under /usr/local you will need to be the root user to do the last step. If you wish to install in some other location, you can type ./configure -prefix=/your/path instead. There are a number of options available via the configure program. Check the INSTALL file first, and if you can't find what you need there, try running ./configure --help. And, as always, help is available from the GIMP Developer and GIMP User mailing lists.

The GIMP web site is the canonical location for GIMP information. You can find it on the Web at http://www.gimp.org/. *Information about the GIMP User and GIMP Developer mailing lists can be found here as well. Red Hat Software maintains archives of RPMs at its site:* http://www.redhat.com/.

Getting Started

The gimprc File

Once the GIMP has been installed, you're ready to start experimenting. Starting the program is simple: type gimp.

When the GIMP starts, it first reads a configuration file located in the .gimp directory located in your $HOME[3] directory. This directory is where user-configurable options and user-specific plug-ins, palettes, brushes and so forth are kept. A similar set of directories is kept in the system directories (by default under /usr/local/share and /usr/local/lib).

If the GIMP does not find the .gimp directory in the user's $HOME directory, it will create and populate it for the user. Since this process can potentially take longer than just a few moments, a window is displayed explaining what the program is doing. The user need not do anything during this time. When the initialization of the .gimp directory has completed, the program will open the main window and the user can begin to work. Future invocations of the application will

---

3. $HOME is an environment variable which you can set in your .profile, .bashrc, .cshrc, or .kshrc files. For users of the BASH or KSH shells you can use
    export HOME=/home/myhomedir
Users of CSH can use
    setenv HOME /home/myhomedir
Consult the man page for the shell you use for details on setting environment variables.

not trigger the creation of the `.gimp` directory unless that directory is removed between GIMP sessions.

The configuration file, `gimprc`, contains the specifications for where the GIMP is to find all of its files. In this way a user can, if desired, use a locally installed version of the GIMP instead of the one installed in the system directories. The `gimprc` file also defines the default settings for many of the features for the application. Items such as the speed at which the *marching ants* (the moving dashed line that denotes a selected region of an image) move around selected areas of an image, the number of colors to use or whether or not the GIMP should use its own colormap and setting the gamma correction are also defined in the `gimprc` file. This file is well commented, so you shouldn't have too much trouble understanding what the various configurable parameters will affect. You should probably take a look at this file at least once before starting the GIMP, although it may not be absolutely necessary for you to become familiar with it, especially if you are using a higher-end system with a high-end graphics adapter and lots of memory. The defaults provided will work well with high-end systems. Experienced users will find reasons to modify some settings to fit their particular hardware configurations and software installations.

See **Appendix A - The gimprc File** for details on the default settings for the `gimprc` file.

Temporary Directories and Files

The GIMP uses its own temporary and swap files for saving runtime data. Most temporary files get removed at the end of a GIMP session; however, some of these files, such as working color palettes, may remain after exiting. This directory should not be one that is cleaned up by the system automatically. It is recommended that the temporary directory be a directory that is specific to the individual user. The default location is the user's `$HOME/.gimp` directory and is defined in the `gimprc` file.

The swap file is a file separate from the other temporary files that can get very large due to the tile-based memory scheme the GIMP uses. Because of this, it is recommended that the swap file directory be `/tmp` or some other directory on a local filesystem with plenty of disk space. Filesystems mounted over NFS are not recommended for use with the swap file, as this would severely hamper swapping and negate any speed gains you may be able to realize with your system. The default location for the swap file is the user's `$HOME/.gimp` directory, although you may want to change this if that filesystem is limited in disk space. Also, swap files can become abandoned if the GIMP crashes for some reason. You may want to consider using a separate directory for the swap directory that you can clean up easily by hand or through an automated `cron` job.

Defaults for both the temporary files directory and the swap file directory exist in the `gimprc` file. You should verify these are appropriate for your use before doing any heavy image processing work.

One of the settings in the `gimprc` that you might want to change is the one for allowing the GIMP to use its own colormap. If you have a system with only 1 MB of video memory[4] and you want to run in a high resolution mode like 800x600 or 1024x768, you may only be able to run with a maximum of 256 colors. In this case, the GIMP (and many other applications, such as Netscape) will quickly run out of colors. In some cases, with smart applications, you'll get what is known as *color flashing*—where the color of windows and the background changes depending on which window currently holds the focus for keyboard and mouse input. Although a bit annoying, color flashing is the result of a little trick provided in X applications to help guarantee they each have enough colors for themselves. They do this by installing their own colormap. This process allows the images managed by the GIMP to display colors that more closely match the actual colors that will be saved to file. The GIMP allows you to enable the installation of a colormap in the `gimprc` file. However, this option is not turned on by default. If you have a low-end video system and run using an 8-bit (256 color) display, then you'll want to uncomment this option in the `gimprc` file before starting the GIMP.

If the color flashing that occurs is bothersome, there is another option for setting the color cube. Changing the values here, however, is a little trickier and should probably be done only if you understand what dithering colors is all about. In either case, installing a colormap or setting the color cube will result in at least some differences between what is visually displayed and the contents of the files to which images are saved. To avoid this problem, you should consider higher-end graphics adapters with more video memory.

---

4. Video memory, not system memory. The video memory is usually on the video adapter or, if the video card is integrated into your motherboard, is memory reserved for use only by the video subsystem.

Remote Displays

As with nearly all X applications, the GIMP supports the ability to run on one machine and display on another. Most X applications accept, through the Xt toolkit, the `-display` command line option to specify a remote host to display on. The GIMP accepts a similar command except that two dashes are required. Somewhere in the evolution of free software there was a migration from one to two dashes for command line options. I'm sure there is a valid reason for it, I just never figured out what it was. In any case, the command line option for displaying on a remote system is

```
--display <remote host>:<display number>.<screen>
```

For most users, the display number and screen will both be 0 (zero). The remote host should be one that can be resolved either in the `/etc/hosts` files or through a DNS lookup. Try running

```
nslookup hostname
```

to see if the host is known to your network before using the `--display` option with the GIMP.

Moving On

The next chapter will introduce some graphics basics necessary for understanding why things work with the GIMP. Understanding why things work also helps in understanding how to achieve the effects you really want in your images.

If you already understand how raster graphics work, how layers work, and do not need to know about the file formats supported by the GIMP, you can skip over the next chapter and start reading **Chapter 3 - GIMP Windows** for an introduction to the windows and dialogs you will encounter in the GIMP.

Chapter 2 - GIMP Basics

Raster Images and Pixels

The GIMP is a raster[1] graphics tool, meaning that it operates on images as a collection of individual points called *pixels,* or picture elements, which are displayed on a raster device—your monitor. Each pixel is made up of a number of *channels*. The number of channels depends on the image type being worked on. For example, RGBA images consist of four channels, one each for levels of Red, Green and Blue, and one called the Alpha channel which is used to determine the amount of *transparency* for a pixel. Transparency is used to allow other color information in an image to blend with the partially (or even fully) transparent pixel. Transparency for individual pixels becomes important when working with *layers*. Layers are a feature of the GIMP that allow an artist to work with an image as if it were made up of a stacked set of transparent sheets of paper. The pieces can be manipulated on their own without affecting other layers, yet laying them one atop another provides a complete, combined image of all the layers. This is useful, for example, when creating complex mosaics, image compositing and animations. The images on the covers for the November 1997 and June 1998 issues of *Linux Journal* had many layers. The text for the word "Graphics" on the November issue was made up of four layers, each combined with the layer below in a different way to create the final three-dimensional effect.

The image files you work with in the GIMP are rectangular. All of them. When you place them in a web page, using transparency, you can

---

1. Raster displays simply display information as a series of dots arranged in horizontal rows. The array of dots is called the *raster*. See Foley, et al., *Computer Graphics: Principles and Practice, 2nd ed.,* Addison Wesley.

simulate non-rectangular images, but while working on the image you deal with rectangular coordinates. The upper left corner is pixel 0. The bottom right pixel can be calculated using this method

```
(#rows * pixels per row) - 1
```

In an image that is 640x480 pixels in size you would have 307200 pixels, with the bottom right corner being pixel number 307199.

```
(640 * 480) - 1
307200 - 1
```

(Knowing the pixel numbers comes in handy when writing Script-Fu scripts for the GIMP, a topic for experts not covered in this book.)

Each pixel is made up of either a combination of varying levels of Red, Green, and Blue colors (commonly referred to as RGB), or equal amounts of each in varying intensities to produce grayscale images. Grayscale images are not strictly black and white images—those would be monochrome images—but are made up of varying shades of gray.

"Monochrome images" are two-color images: black and white. Pixels are either "on" (white) or "off" (black). This differs from grayscale images, because in grayscale images there are more than two levels that the pixel can be set to.

In fact, there are 256 levels for pixels in grayscale images.

Along with the RGB levels comes the transparency, referred to as Alpha. RGB images with transparency are often referred to as RGBA images. The color of a pixel in an image is computed by first combining the red, green and blue levels and then adding in the alpha level. Adding alpha to the pixel will fade the color, depending on what (if any) colors are beneath that pixel in the image.

RGB vs. CMYK, Indexed Color, Grayscale Images, and Channels

The images you work with in the GIMP are made up of pixels that are colored by combining different levels of red, green, and blue colors. The GIMP can maintain the information about the pixel's color in one of three ways: by maintaining information about each of the three primary colors as individual channels for every pixel, by keeping the combined colors in an indexed array called a *color palette*, or by using an indexed palette that maintains only a single level for all three colors which provides for grayscale images.

Channels are used with images which maintain information about all three colors for each pixel. These are known as RGB images and each color's channel (of the red, green and blue elements in this image type) has 256 distinct levels available. Computers can keep 256 values as a series of 8 bits (which is a convenient number for your computer, it being the same as one byte on the computers that most GIMP users are using), so having three channels gives 24 bits of information. You will often see images referred to as "24-bit images", meaning they contain 8 bits of color information for each of the red, green, and blue channels for each pixel in the image. With 24 bits per pixel, and a 640x480 pixel image having 307200 pixels, even small images can be over a megabyte in size! Needless to say, these images can take up a lot of memory and disk space.

An image can be manipulated through each of the channels independently. For example, it is possible to apply a mask (a sort of cardboard cutout) so that the colors for that channel are not used. You can use this technique to mask out stains in old photographs, for instance. Channel manipulation is discussed in **Chapter 6 - Layers and Channels**.

Indexed color images use palettes which can be thought of as a boxes with 256 compartments, each filled with a different color of paint. You can use any of the colors in the palette but if you need a different one, you must abandon one of the original colors. Indexed palettes are used for images which need to limit the number of colors they use. The World Wide Web makes use of palettes like this to help guarantee that browsers will be able to display images that use colors from only a particular palette. In general, you seldom work directly with indexed color images. It is more convenient to do most of your work in RGB images, then convert those images (using simple menu options) to indexed images. After the conversion has been done, a little touch-up may be needed to smooth the edges or sharpness of the image. Indexed color images use only a single channel in the GIMP. An example where you would probably want to work with only indexed color images, right from the start, would be animations. Working with a series of images for an animation in RGB mode and then converting each to indexed color mode independently may cause the colors in the images to vary noticeably. The animation may be smooth in movement but the colors in each frame (sequential individual images) won't match quite right, causing an unintentional flashing effect.

Another form of indexed images is known as grayscale images. These are just like indexed color images, except instead of an arbitrary collection of 256 colors, the colors are on a scale of 256 gray levels, ranging from white to black. There may be times you want to take an RGB image that has color and desaturate it so that the colors are reduced to their grayscale components. You can desaturate an RGB image, making it a appear as a grayscale image with 2^8 different levels of gray, but this is not the same as an indexed grayscale image. Like indexed color images, indexed grayscale images have only a single channel. Desaturated RGB images, although they appear to be grayscale, still contain enough information in them to be three channel color images. Don't let this distinction fool you. One way you can check if the image you are working on is an indexed grayscale image or a gray-appearing RGB image is to click on the *Channels* tab of the *Layers and Channels* dialog. This dialog is discussed in detail in **Chapter 6 - Layers and Channels**.

RGB images are called this because they use the RGB *color model*. Color models describe the composition of colors in a three-dimensional coordinate system. For RGB images, the coordinate system is a unit cube subset of the three-dimensional Cartesian coordinate system. There are many types of color models used for raster graphics systems such as YIQ (a recoding of the RGB color model, used for television transmissions; Y represents Luminosity, I is the In-phase color value containing orange-cyan color information, and Q is for the Quadrature color value, containing green-magenta information), HLS (Hue, Lightness and Saturation), and HSV (Hue, Saturation and Value). Another color model often used in tools like the GIMP is the CMY, or CMYK, color model. CMY stands for Cyan, Magenta, and Yellow. The K stands for Black. K is used to keep it from being confused with the B used for Blue in RGB. CMY and CMYK are color models for images used most often in printing. CMY images map almost directly to RGB images, but in printing you would often have to mix large amounts of cyan, magenta and yellow to get black, and that could lead to messy prints. One of the reasons for adding a black ink, the K component, is to help reduce the amount of ink being used.

Cyan, magenta and yellow are *subtractive colors*, meaning you subtract them from white light to get the color desired. If you think about how light reflects off paper, this makes sense. The more of CMY you add to the paper, the less reflective it is and the darker it appears. RGB colors are *additive colors*, meaning you add them together in order to get the color you want. This is how computer monitors and television sets work. Each pixel on the screen has three color phosphors, one for red, one for green and one for blue. The three color phosphors for each pixel are lit to different intensities and combine to give a final color.[2] A *phosphor* is a coating on the glass screen that is excited by the electron beam of an electron gun in a *CRT* (Cathode Ray Tube). Monitors and TV screens are generically referred to as CRTs because of their use of this design. Using the term "phosphors" for each of the red/green/blue dots is just a handy way of describing the individual points on the screen, since a pixel is actually made up of three phosphors. Without any of the phosphors lit, you would have black. With all three phosphors lit fully, you would see white.

Unfortunately, there are no facilities for handling CMY or CMYK colors directly from the GIMP. This means that when you print your images, you may find they don't quite match the colors or intensities you expected to see based on what you saw on your monitor. Support for the CMYK color model is a priority, and given the fast development of the GIMP, it should arrive before too long. In the meantime, you may want to experiment with printing small swatches of your image to verify the colors you are going to get before printing your final image.

Hue, Saturation, and Lightness

According to Foley, et al.:[3]

Hue distinguishes among colors such as red, green, purple, and yellow. Saturation refers to how far a color is from a gray of equal intensity. Red is highly saturated, pink is relatively unsaturated; royal blue is highly saturated; sky blue is relatively unsaturated. Unsaturated colors contain more white light than saturated colors. Lightness embodies the colorless notion of perceived intensity of a reflecting object.

Adjusting the hue in an image actually rotates colors around a color wheel. For example, setting the hue to 0 (ranging from -180 to 180) makes red a pure red. Its complete opposite is cyan (since white minus red is cyan). Adjusting the hue to +/-180 makes red appear as cyan. The lightness adjusts how faded the color appears. Adding lightness fades the color more, subtracting lightness makes the colors darker. Taking the example of red again, adding 100% light to red creates a near white shade of red. Subtracting 100% light creates a red that is like a deep, dark blood red.

---

2. It is actually more complex than that, but that is beyond the scope of this text.
3. Foley, et al.; *Computer Graphics: Principles and Practice.*

Saturation works by adjusting the amount of gray mixed with the base color. Higher settings reduce the amount of gray in a color, making the color appear more pure. Lower settings cause the colors to fade toward gray.

The GIMP provides the user with the ability to adjust the hue, saturation, and lightness via a single dialog box (See **Chapter 7 - Color and Text**). The pixels affected can include either the entire image or a region that has been selected using one of the numerous selection tools.

Drawing, Painting, Modeling, and Rendering

The GIMP was not originally designed to do line drawing or painting specifically. There are drawing tools and a collection of brush types that can be used, but their use is not as encompassing as, say, MetaCreation's ArtDabbler or Adobe's Illustrator. In spite of this, you can use the GIMP to do certain amounts of drawing and painting.

Drawing in the GIMP is the ability to make freehand lines or to trace paths with a computer pencil of some kind. Painting can encompass filling in a region with a specified color or pattern, or it can be a freehand design using a simulated paint or airbrush. The GIMP provides a pencil, a paintbrush, an airbrush and a paint bucket (for doing bucket fills of a specified color or pattern). Each of these has various options such as antialiasing or rate of flow of the "paint". All but the paintbucket can use a variety of brush types which are selectable via a special brush dialog window. It is also possible to design your own brush types using the GIMP's built-in brush file format, using nothing more than a simple *File->Save* operation. Drawing and painting tools are discussed in depth in **Chapter 8 - Drawing and Painting**.

Tracing a path is also possible and actually rather simple to do. Just create a selection using one of the various selection tools, choose a brush type, and select *File->Edit->Stroke* from the *Image* menus and a line will be painted following the edge of the selection. The colors used can also be set prior to setting the stroked path. Stroke paths are discussed in **Chapter 5 - Selections**.

Selections

One of the most important sets of tools you will want to use with the GIMP is the *selection* tools. These tools allow the user to select regions of an image using rectangular, round, and freehand styles, and even by colors. Once a region is selected, it can be manipulated in a way that does not affect areas outside of the selected region. Selections can be cut, copied, pasted, rotated and resized no matter what shape they may take. Selections are the basis for doing stroke paths, where the edge of the selection is used as a path to draw and paint lines.

Selections can also be *feathered* to varying degrees, allowing a region to have a fading effect into the region outside of the selection. Selections can be enlarged, reduced and even inverted. Inverting a selection allows you to select a region that normally might be difficult to select on its own. The area that is to be outside the chosen region is selected first, then the selection is inverted and you have the region that would have been harder to select.

Chapter 5 - Selections gives more complete descriptions of all the selection tools available in the GIMP.

Layers and Compositing

Images in the GIMP consist of one or more *layers*. A layer is like a clear acetate sheet—those transparent sheets often used with overhead projectors. The layer is opaque[4] where there is image information for that layer and transparent elsewhere. The layers are stacked and the image window displays what the currently visible layers will look like when combined in the final image. Each layer can be turned on or off; that is, you can make them visible and part of the overall image or turn them off so they are not used in calculating pixel values for the displayed image.

Each layer can be *composited,* that is, combined, with lower layers using a variety of *modes*. The default mode for a layer is *Normal* meaning that the pixels in the current layer are not combined with lower layer pixels that reside in the same location in the image. Layers can be added, subtracted, multiplied or have any one of more than a dozen

---

4. Opaque means that no light is allowed to pass through. For layers this means that since light is not passing through, it must be reflected by pixels in that layer and underlying layers cannot be seen. More simply, opaque is the opposite of transparent. The more opaque a layer is, the less transparent it is, and vice versa.

operations applied. The layer modes for compositing are separate from the overall opacity of the layer, which can also be set from 0 (fully transparent) to 100 (fully opaque).

One of the less obvious uses of layers is creating animations. A single initial layer can be created and duplicated. The duplicated layer can then be modified slightly and duplicated again. This process can continue on virtually indefinitely. The final set of layers can then be saved as a series of individual frames in an animated GIF.

Layers are discussed in detail in **Chapter 6 - Layers and Channels**.

Image Resolution

The GIMP displays images on your monitor in a best-fit manner. This means that the image is scaled to fit on your display, so that images you create which would normally be too large for the display can be viewed in their entirety. The image windows which display the images can be zoomed to view regions that may have been scaled too small to view important details. Startup configuration options in the `gimprc` file allow the user to have the GIMP resize windows during zoom operations as well.

Images are normally displayed based on a pixel resolution basis. For example, the default width of a new image window is 256 pixels wide by 256 pixels high. The size units can be changed from pixels to inches to centimeters in the `gimprc` start-up file.

An image's *resolution*, that is, the number of pixels in width by height, determines an image's file size. Since the GIMP uses layers, there is no direct correspondence between number of pixels and the file size for the native file format, `.xcf`. However, it is generally obvious that larger resolutions create larger files.

Often you will find that stock images that you read from a file or CD are not the resolution you require for the images you are creating. In this case, you will need to resize them. There are a number of methods for dealing with this issue. One is to select a sub-region of the image and then *crop* the image down to the selected area. This process doesn't change the resolution but does reduce the size of the file with which you are dealing. An alternative to this method is to *scale* the image. Scaling changes the dimensions of the image—scaling up will increase the width and height of the image. Scaling down reduces the width and height. Scaling changes the total number of pixels being used in the image. Finally, an image can be *resized*. This reduces the size of the viewable region of the image in the same manner that cropping the image works. Resizing affects the entire image or layer, whereas cropping generally is applied to a region of an image or layer.

The GIMP supports all three types of resolution and sizing options. The dialog window which provides for resizing also allows an interactive placement of the box which defines the cropped region. **Chapter 3 - GIMP Windows** provides a detailed look at using these features.

The GIMP and Desktop Publishing

Much of the material in this section is general information applicable to desktop publishing. You need to be acquainted with these topics to best utilize the GIMP in your art.

Computer displays are often discussed in terms of pixels to describe image resolution. Printers are often discussed in the more confusing terms of *dots per inch* (dpi), *lines per inch* (lpi) and *halftones*. Each of these is related to determining the mapping of a raster image to a printed one in a fairly straightforward manner. **Chapter 11 - Scanning, Printing, and Print Media** discusses these at length, along with issues related to creating graphics specifically for web pages. It also discusses the specific printers supported by the GIMP through the Print Plug-In.

Image File Formats

There are hundreds of different formats used for graphics images on computer systems.[5] Some of the more popular static (non-animated) formats are:

- GIF - *Graphics Interchange Format,* originally from Compuserve. GIF is a compressed 8-bit color format that is lossless and is good for synthetic images (line drawings, "cartoonish" images). GIF images don't uniformly compress well.

---

5. C. Wayne Brown and Barry J. Shepherd, *Graphics File Formats Reference and Guide*, Manning, 1995.

- JPEG - from the Independent JPEG Group. JPEG supports 24-bit color, is lossy, works well for realistic images (scanned photos, high quality anti-aliased renderings with smooth changes in color and shading, etc.) and compresses well.

- TGA - formerly from TrueVision in support of their Targa display adapter. The TGA format is normally used for 24-bit color images, but supports 8-, 16-, 24-, and 32-bit (24 bits for image data and 8 bits for alpha channel) images too. Does not use any form of compression.

- TIFF - *Tagged Image File Format*, originally developed by a consortium headed by Aldus, this format has lossless compression when using LZW compression and lossy compression when used with DCT compression.

- XBM - X Bitmaps (bitmaps—black and white images)

- XPM - X Pixmaps (similar to bitmaps, but with color information)

- PNG - *Portable Network Graphics*, from the PNG group, supports bit depths from 1 (mono) to 64 (super truecolor and alpha). PNG was developed because GIF's built-in compression was patented by Unisys and couldn't support 24-bit or alpha images. Compresses better in some situations than GIF, but not as well as JPEG in others.

The compressibility of an image depends heavily on its contents. The term *compression* refers to the file format's use of defined compression techniques, not to how the image file can be compressed using tools like `gzip` or UNIX `compress`. The compression, in other words, is built into the file format definition.

Lossy means that parts of the image data are discarded. So if an image format includes some form of lossy compression, some of the image data is lost during the compression that is used for that format. If the image is decompressed and compared to the original, there will be missing data. Generally, the data lost during compression is redundant information and doesn't affect the visual appearance of the image. However, at higher compression ratios the lost data is not redundant and the quality of the image degrades.

Lossless means that all image data is retained. TGA, XBM, XPM, and PNG are all lossless formats. However, TGA, XBM and XPM do not use any form of compression in the format itself.

Alpha refers to the transparency of images. A full alpha channel in an image allows for any level of transparency (from fully opaque to completely transparent) across the entire image. GIF and PNG support palette-based transparency where a single pixel value is the transparent color. However, with GIF the pixel color is either fully opaque or fully transparent. PNG supports a range of transparency for the transparent color index. PNG also supports, along with TGA, a full alpha channel.

There are not nearly so many animation formats, especially ones that are available for UNIX and Linux systems. A few of the more commonly known formats are:

• MPEG - from the *Motion Pictures Experts Group*

• FLI/FLC - originally from AutoDesk Animator, FLI supports 256 colors at 320x240 resolution and FLC supports 16-bit color at higher resolutions.

• AVI - from Microsoft, Windows video environment format

• QuickTime - from Apple Computer, Inc.

Each of these formats, both animated and static, is well suited for different situations. GIF and JPEG images are currently the only widely supported image types for web browsers. PNG was recently adopted by the WC3 consortium and has become another web standard graphic image format. Both Netscape Navigator and Microsoft Internet Explorer already support this format for in-line images. PNG is a portable format that was recently developed in light of copyright or patent issues for other formats. TGA provides 24-bit images without use of compression in the image file, which means the quality of the new image is likely to be nearly as good as the original when reducing the image size.

Which format you use is dependent on the environment in which you wish to use your images. If you're doing web page development, you will be working primarily with GIF, JPEG and PNG image types when integrating your images into your pages. However, you may find that creating the images will require some other format, such as TGA for three-dimensional images (depending on what three-dimensional tools you use). If this is the case, you will have to deal with image conversion tools to get your image into the right format or to use in the GIMP, if that specific format is not supported.

The GIMP supports all of the formats used by web browsers for in-line images (GIF, JPEG, and PNG). It also supports a number of other formats, which are described in the following sections.

Format	RGB Only	Indexed Only	Both	Uses
BMP			*	
FITS			*	Astronomy
CEL		*		KISS Paper Doll format
GBR	*			
GIF		*		Web page images, both static and animated
GIcon			*	GIMP icon files
HRZ			*	Amateur radio, slow-scan TV
Header	*			GIMP internal format
JPEG	*			
PAT	*			GIMP pattern files (for bucket fills)
PCX		*		
PIX	*			Alias/Wavefront files; also reads 8-bit .alpha, .matte, and .mask files
PNG			*	
PNM			*	
Post-Script			*	Cannot save images with alpha channel
SGI			*	
SUN-RAS			*	
TGA			*	
TIFF			*	Probably best for cross platform use
XWD			*	X Window System dumps (screen captures)
XPM	*			

Raster Formats

The 1.0 version of the GIMP directly supports the following formats for reading and writing. The types of images which can be used with each format are listed, along with some general uses for these formats.

Use of GIcon and Header formats isn't necessary unless you plan on doing development work on the GIMP source code.

The GIMP also supports reading and writing of PostScript/PDF files in both indexed color/grayscale and RGB formats, although PostScript is not a raster format.

The PhotoCD format popular on Microsoft and Macintosh platforms and used with many digital cameras is not directly supported by the GIMP. However, the hpcdtoppm *program will convert PhotoCD files to PPM format which the GIMP can read. The* hpcdtoppm *program is part of the NetPBM tools package, a copy of which (in source format) is available on the accompanying CD.*

The GIMP Native Format - XCF

As with most graphics programs, the GIMP has its own file format that it uses to save files. This format, known as the XCF[6] format, saves all information about a GIMP image including layers, channels, and guides. Although a fractal compression technique is used to reduce the size of the data saved for layers; .xcf files can be quite large.

Finally, there is one other format that the GIMP can read: Photoshop 4 files. At this time, support for this format is incomplete but may be available by the time this text reaches bookstore shelves.

PhotoCD and Digital Camera Formats

Kodak PhotoCD disks come with images scanned at five different resolutions for each image, six for the Pro PhotoCD format. The format for the files is actually called the Kodak Image Pac format. This format allows for digital processing of an image with higher levels of resolution using a single file. Some digital cameras are rumored to support this format. Often, these CDs are created by photofinishers at the time you develop your 35mm film prints.

---

6. XCF stands for the *Experimental Computing Facility*, the group at the University of California at Berkeley where the GIMP authors, Peter Mattis and Spencer Kimball, worked on their undergraduate and graduate degrees. See http://www.xcf.berkeley.edu/.

Support for PhotoCD files is not available with the standard 1.0 release of the GIMP. A plug-in was available at one time for an earlier, beta release of the GIMP but has not been ported to the 1.0 release. The current 2.0 beta release comes with a small plug-in (called `xpcd-gate`), which allows `xpcd` to pass images directly to the GIMP. The source for this plug-in should be available from the Plug-In Registry.

The Plug-In Registry is located at `http://registry.gimp.org/`.

Digital cameras are a relatively new technology available to the general public. Because of this, the formats used for the cameras may vary. Some digital cameras support JPEG formats while others may support PhotoCD, and some cameras may use other formats. The main advantage to using a digital camera is the quick access to the images— the cameras store the data as digital images so they do not require photo processing like film. Data is either saved to a diskette or in special memory chips in the camera, allowing the user user to simply download the images directly from the camera into his computer. However, digital cameras may not provide as high quality an image as ordinary film. The choice is currently one of convenience over quality.

How to Use WMF Files From CD-ROMs

One of the most common kinds of CD-ROM available from your local computer retail store is WMF image collections. WMF, the *Windows Meta Format*, is a vector format used on Microsoft Windows systems for creating drawings. It is commonly used to create icons or line art. WMF format files are not supported by the GIMP. In order to make use of these files, you must first find another program which reads the files and can export them to one of the supported raster file formats. There are many Microsoft Windows tools for doing this. On Linux and UNIX systems, a few commercial packages exist that can handle this conversion. The Applixware ApplixGraphics tool can read WMF files and export them to a number of formats, including JPEG, TIFF, and GIF.

There are no freely available tools for reading WMF files and exporting to raster format files, however.

Scanning Images

Scanners take a photograph or other hard copy image and digitize it for use on computers. Scanned images, like printed images, use their own resolution definitions. Samples per inch, pixels per inch (ppi) and dots per inch (dpi) are commonly used to refer to the resolution of a scanned image.

One option for getting images from hard copy into your computer that many beginners overlook is to have your pictures scanned for you by a *service bureau*, which is a commercial service that provides various prepress operations such as imagesetting and color proof printing. Many local print shops can also perform these types of services.

The latest version of the GIMP for which this book was written did not support scanners directly. However, a project known as SANE did have a plug-in for use with the GIMP. SANE is a project to develop a standardized interface for image acquisition devices like scanners and the Connectix QuickCam for UNIX systems. The project was reported to have been ported to a number of different platforms.

The SANE Web pages are located at:
`http://www.azstarnet.com/~axplinux/sane/.`

Although not directly supported by the GIMP, a number of scanner drivers are available to Linux users. A review of these can be found in the March 1997 issue of the Linux Gazette in the "Graphics Muse" column. The Linux Gazette can be found at `http://www.linuxgazette.com/.`

Undo/Redo - Fixing Goofs, Experimenting, and Saving Your Soul

The GIMP provides the very welcome ability to undo changes you've made to an image. This feature not only allows the undoing of the last change, but any number of changes up to the configured maximum. The `gimprc` file provides an option for specifying the maximum number of undo operations that can be done. Be aware, however, that the more undo levels you configure, the more memory your GIMP session will require.

Undoing an operation is simple enough—just select the *Undo* option from the *Edit* submenu in the *Image* pull-down menus. The Image pull-down menus can be opened by clicking with the right mouse button over an Image window.

Once you have undone an operation, you may find you really want it back after all. Who among us, after all, is absolutely decisive the first time? Guiltless experimentation is one of the greatest features of the GIMP. The seldom mentioned but often used *Redo* option is the counterpart to the Undo operation. It performs the last operation that was undone. The number of redo levels matches the number of undo levels (although there is no configuration item for redo levels in the gimprc). Redo will not perform the same operation that was just performed but which was not undone, however. That is a *repeat* operation, which is supported in another menu.

Moving On

This chapter has touched on just a few of the basics that you need to understand when working with digital images. In some places references were made to more detailed discussions in later chapters. Although not an absolute necessity, understanding the topics from this chapter will help you make better use of the GIMP.

The next chapter discusses the GIMP's windows.

Chapter 3 - GIMP Windows

This chapter introduces you to what the various windows for the GIMP look like, as well as some of the terminology associated with their use. You can use this as a quick reference section, along with the glossary, while you're working with the application.

The Toolbox

The GIMP Toolbox

The main window for the GIMP is called the *Toolbox*. This is the window which opens first every time you start the GIMP. It consists of a menu bar across the top and a set of buttons arranged in seven rows by three columns. Below the buttons are the foreground/background selection boxes. The menu bar has two options: File and Xtns. Under the *File* menu are options related to general GIMP operations such as opening an existing file, and opening a new, blank window. The *Xtns* menu holds GIMP extensions, such as the Script-Fu interface and the procedural database browser. For a detailed discussion of the Toolbox and all of its options, see **Chapter 4 - The Toolbox**.

The Image Window

The GIMP displays images in *Image Windows*. The visible parts of the Image Window consist of the image display area, the rulers across the top and left sides, and scrollbars across the bottom and right sides. Popdown menus and the Ruler Guides are not visible by default but are easy to access from the Image Window.

Rulers

A blank Image Window with rulers and guides displayed

By default, if the dimensions of an Image Window fit into the displayed screen area, the *rulers* are divided into units of 10 pixels. Major tick marks in the rulers are at intervals of 100 pixels. The other tick marks are by default those for units of 20 pixels. If the Image Window's dimensions are larger than the displayable screen area, then the GIMP will provide a window that uses major tick marks at intervals of 250 pixels. However, since the image would actually be larger than the screen, the Image Window does not display the image pixels one per display pixel. Don't let this confuse you. You can zoom in on your image to get pixel-level details. The GIMP is smart enough to know how to handle images that are too big for the display. This is useful for design work destined for print media.

The units represented by tick marks in the rulers are specified in the `gimprc` file (see **Appendix A - The gimprc File**). By default the units are in pixels, but this can be changed to inches or centimeters at the user's discretion.

Guides and Scrollbars

Guides are straight, dashed lines. The active (currently selected) guide's dashes alternate between red and black, while all other guides (not currently selected) alternate between blue and black. The guides extend from the left to the right edges of the Image Window's display area, or from the top to the bottom. To create a new guide, move the cursor over a ruler (top or left side), hold down the left mouse button and drag into the display area. (If you were using a different GIMP tool, this would change your active tool to the Move tool.) A new guide, parallel to the ruler from which you dragged the cursor, is created. When the cursor (with the Move tool chosen) is over the guide, it changes to a left-hand pointer (a hand with the index finger extended). Hold down the left mouse button to grab the guide and move it to a new location. To remove the guide, grab it and drag it back over the ruler and release the mouse button. Guides are useful for aligning objects or for snapping selections to specific areas. You can toggle selections[1] to snap to the guides from the Image Window's pop-down menu (*View->Snap To Guides*). Guides, although visible in the Image Window, are not saved to files of any image type except XCF. If you save a file to GIF or JPEG or TIFF for example, the guides will not show up in the image file.[2]

The *scrollbars* perform just as scrollbars do in any windowing application. Grab the slider while holding the left mouse button down to slide the image up/down (vertical scrollbar) or left/right (horizontal scrollbar). Click in the scrollbar outside of the slider (if the slider does not extend the length of the scrollbar) to page through the display area. Click on the arrow buttons on the ends of the scrollbar to increment or decrement your way through the display area.

Menus

The most important features of the Image Window are the pop-down menus. From these, you will have access to all of the GIMP's image processing capabilities. To post (i.e., display and leave open) the menus, place the cursor over the display area of an image window and click the right mouse button once. The top-level menu will open and stay open until you either click outside the menu windows, or select a menu option. Some of the options open submenus, which will also stay open if you simply click on those options. Clicking/dragging over the menus also works, although the menus will close if you drag the mouse off the menus and then release the mouse button.

The Image Window's pop-down menus are divided into the following categories. In the following list, references to "selections" can include an entire layer or image, depending on the existence of a selection or multiple layers.

---

1. See **Chapter 5 - Selections**.
2. Image formats were discussed in **Chapter 2 - GIMP Basics**.

File Menu

1. **New** - Opens a blank Image Window.

2. **Open** - Opens an existing image file.

3. **Save** - Saves the current image using the default image name.

4. **Save as** - Saves the current image via the file selection dialog window.

5. **Preferences** - Sets the various user-definable preferences via a pop-up dialog window. Some of these have to do with the way transparency is visually displayed in the Layers and Channels dialog. The number of levels of undo for the current GIMP session, temporary and swap directories, cache size, and enabling or disabling of tool tips can also be set from this option.

6. **Close** - Closes the current Image Window.

7. **Quit** - Quits completely from the GIMP.

8. **Mail Image** - Simple mail interface to send either a uuencoded or MIME encapsulated copy of the current image to another user. Requires the `uuencode` and `mail` programs be properly installed already. If `mail` uses `sendmail`, then this must also be properly configured.

9. **Print** - Prints the current Image Window contents.

Edit Menu

Most edit operations work on the current selection and the default selection buffer. Cut Named, Copy Named, and Paste Named all work with named buffers. When Cut Named or Copy Named are used, the selection is saved in both the named buffer and the default buffer. Undo and Redo work on a stack of operations, up to the configured number of undo operations. Undo adds to the top of the stack, Redo pops the top entry off the stack.

1. **Cut** - Cuts the current selection from the Image Window into the default selection buffer.

2. **Copy** - Copies the current selection from the Image Window into the default selection buffer.

3. **Paste** - Pastes from the default buffer into the current Image Window.

4. **Paste Into** - Pastes from the default buffer into the current selection. This differs from the generic paste in that the default buffer's contents are placed into the current selection and are clipped by the selection's region bounds.

5. **Clear** - Clears the current selection. This has the same effect as Cut, except the region removed is not saved into the default buffer. It can be retrieved only by using an Undo operation.

6. **Fill** - Fills the selected region with the background color.

7. **Stroke** - Draws a line which follows the selection outline using the foreground color and the currently selected brush shape.

8. **Undo** - Cancels the last operation, restoring the image to its previous state.

9. **Redo** - Performs the last operation canceled from an undo.

10. **Cut Named** - Cuts the current selection into a named buffer.

11. **Copy Named** - Copies the current selection into a named buffer.

12. **Paste Named** - Pastes a named selection into the current image.

13. **Copy Visible** - Copies the visible portion of an image window to the default buffer.

Select Menu

This includes Toggle, Invert, All, None, Float, Sharpen, Border, Feather, Grow, Shrink, Save To Channel, and By Color. Selections are covered in detail in **Chapter 5 - Selections**.

View Menu

1. **Zoom In** - View a close-up of the selected region or the entire image.

2. **Zoom Out** - Back away from the image.

3. **Zoom** - Provides a set of zoom ratios ranging from 16:1 (maximum zoom out) to 1:16 (maximum zoom in).

4. **Window Info** - Provides information about the Image Window, such as its dimensions, scale ratio, visual class and depth, and shades of colors for each channel.

5. **Toggle Rulers** - Hide or display the rulers. The default is to display them.

6. **Toggle Guides** - Hide or use guides. The default is to use them.

7. **Snap to Guides** - Snap selections to guides or disable snap to guides. The default is to snap to guides. This makes a difference only if you wish to make detailed selections very near guides (snap to guides toggled off) or if you wish to make selections based on the position of the guides (snap to guides toggled on).

8. **New View** - Opens another window on the current image. The new window will show all the changes of the first but from different zoom settings.

9. **Shrink Wrap** - Changes the size of the Image Window to fit the current zoom setting. If the zoom causes the image to be too large for the Image Window to display, shrink wrap will resize the window so the zoom stays the same but fits completely into the Image Window. If the image is too large for the physical display, then the shrink wrap does a best-fit guess for the new size of the Image Window.

Image Menu

Colors

1. **Equalize** - Redistributes current selection's light and dark values. This has the effect of brightening dark images or ones with poor contrast.

2. **Invert** - Inverts the colors in the selection. Colors are discussed in **Chapter 7 - Colors and Text**.

3. **Posterize** - Reduces the number of levels of color in a selection.

4. **Threshold** - Finds all pixels with intensity levels within the range specified. Creates a black and white image from the source selection.

5. **Color Balance** - Adjusts a selection's colors between RGB levels and CMY levels.

6. **Brightness - Contrast** - Sets the brightness and contrast levels for the current selection.

7. **Hue - Saturation** - Allows the setting of the hue, lightness, and saturation levels for a selection.

8. **Curves** - Allows the red, green, and blue channels to be adjusted so that each range flows along a curve instead of a straight line.

9. **Levels** - Adjusts the range of values covered by the individual red, green, blue and alpha channels.

10. **Desaturate** - Turns color images into "grayscale" images, although the image remains an RGB image. A desaturated image maintains information about all three red, green, and blue channels but changes each pixel so that all three channels for that pixel have the same value.

11. **Auto-Stretch Contrast** - Stretches the histogram of a layer or image to fit the complete range of contrast. Often used to remove unwanted tints from color images.

12. **Auto-Stretch HSV** - Same as Auto-Stretch Contrast, but works in HSV color space and preserves the hue in the image.

13. **Normalize** - Same as Auto-Stretch Contrast, except that it doesn't allow the color channels to normalize independently.

Channel Ops

1. **Duplicate** - Duplicates the current image, including all layers.

2. **Offset** - Offsets the current layer in the X and/or Y directions.

3. **Compose** - Combines previously decomposed images into a new, single image.

4. **Decompose** - Splits the current layer into its component channels. Supported decompositions include RGB, HSV, CMY, CMYK, and Alpha.

It is possible, using Decompose followed by Compose, to split an image into one set of channels and then recombine them as a different set of channels.

Alpha

1. **Add Alpha Channel** - Adds an alpha channel to a layer which does not already have one.

2. **Threshold Alpha** - Sets the maximum alpha level for the current layer.

RGB

If the current image is not in RGB format, this option will convert it to an RGB image. If the image is already an RGB image, this option will be grayed out.

Grayscale

If the current image is not in grayscale format, this option will convert it to a grayscale image. If the image is already a grayscale image, this option will be grayed out.

Indexed

If the current image is not an indexed format image, this option will convert it to an indexed image. If the image is already an indexed image, this option will be grayed out.

Resize

Crops the image based on the size and the location specified within the original image.

Scale

Changes the dimensions of the image, keeping the entire image within the bounds specified.

Histogram

Informational only; provides distribution, means, standard deviation, median and other useful statistics about the image and its various channels.

Save Palette

Saves the current palette for indexed images.

Transforms

Crops and rotates both layers and images.

Layers Menu

For a more detailed explanation on layers, see **Chapter 6 - Layers and Channels**.

1. **Layers and Channels** - Brings up the Layers and Channels dialog box.

2. **Raise Layer** - Raises the current layer above the next higher layer, if any.

3. **Lower Layer** - Lowers the current layer below the next lower layer, if any.

4. **Anchor Layer** - Anchors a floating layer to the current layer.

5. **Merge Visible Layers** - Merges the layers currently marked as visible. This does not affect any layers which are not marked visible.

6. **Flatten Image** - Composites all layers so they produce a single layer. The layer produced is the same as what was visually displayed in the Image Window associated with those layers prior to flattening.

7. **Alpha To Selection** - Converts the layer's alpha channel, if it has one, to a selection. This can be used by first creating a selection, then selecting this option. The result is a selection of the shape you first created that contains only the alpha channel for the current layer. You can then manipulate this the same way you do any other selection. Note that not all layers have alpha channels. The background layer, for example, does not by default contain an alpha channel.

8. **Mask To Selection** - Creates a selection based on the current layer's mask. If the current layer does not have a mask, this option is grayed out.

9. **Add Alpha Channel** - Adds an alpha channel to the current layer if it doesn't already have one.

10. **Align Visible Layers** - Permits the alignment of visible layers based on horizontal and vertical settings.

Tools Menu

Access to all the tools available from the Toolbox. Details on the Toolbox tools can be found in **Chapter 4 - The Toolbox**.

Filters Menu

The large set of image filters such as blurring, embossing, bump mapping, and many more are available, and are discussed in **Part Two**.

Script-Fu Menu

Provides access to all the various installed Script-Fu scripts. This menu is also available from the Toolbox Xtns menu.

Dialogs Menu

This provides a convenient way to open the various dialogs such as the Gradient Editor, the Layers and Channels dialog, the Color Palette, and the Brushes dialog.

1. **Brushes** - Allows selection of a brush for use with the Pencil, Paintbrush, Eraser, and Airbrush tools and the stroke edit option.

2. **Patterns** - Allows selection of any one of a set of patterns that can be used with the Bucket Fill tool.

3. **Palette** - Allows selection, creation and editing of color palettes. These allow a method of saving sets of frequently used or associated colors.

4. **Gradient Editor** - Selects, edits, and creates gradients for use with the Gradient tool.

5. **Layers and Channels** - Another method for accessing the Layers and Channels dialog, described in detail in **Chapter 6 - Layers and Channels**.

6. **Indexed Palette** - Shows the current indexed color palette for an indexed image. Palette entries can be edited and will affect the current image only. This option is not available for RGB or grayscale images.

7. **Tool Options** - Opens the tool options dialog for the currently selected tool. Also sets the tool options to be displayed for any tool until the current tools options dialog is closed. In a sense, this option toggles Tool Options on. To toggle them off, you simply close the currently opened Tool Options dialog.

Dialogs

It could be argued that all windows in the GIMP are dialogs except the Toolbox and Image Windows. If you are interested in the GIMP Toolkit, GTK, upon which the GIMP is built, then you would probably be interested in the validity of this argument. However, for our purposes, consider that all filters have their own windows and the dialogs are limited to the following major definitions:

- New Window

- File Selection

- Preferences

- Tool Options

- Brushes

- Patterns

- Palettes

- Layers and Channels

- Gradient Editor

- Procedural Database Browser

- Script-Fu

Each of these is discussed in detail below, or a reference is given to the chapter where more detailed information can be found.

New and Save

New Image dialog

Opening a new file is done with the *New Image* dialog. This is a small window which allows you to specify the height, width, and the image and fill types for the new window. The image type can be either RGB or grayscale. The default is to create a new RGB image. The fill type can be either white, the current background setting from the Toolbox, or transparent. The default is to use the current background setting.

Saving a file that was previously opened (not created using the New option) does not require a dialog box. The file will be saved using the fully qualified name (directory path and file name) which was used to open the file. The file will be saved in the same format in which it was opened. Be careful with this option—if you create new layers in the image after opening it and then save it using its original format, you may not save all the layer information. To save all layer information, change the file name extension to `.xcf` and use the *Save by extension* option menu in the *Save As* dialog.

Saving a file to a new name (or saving an image created from scratch using the New option) requires the use of the Save As dialog.

Open and Save As - the File Selection Dialog

File selection dialog

The same dialog is used for opening and saving files: the *Load Image* or *file selection* dialog. This dialog holds two list windows, one for directories and one for files. A text input field is included beneath these. To select a directory, you can either browse using the directory list or type in the name of the directory you want in the text input field, and click the OK button at the bottom of the dialog. Using the directory list requires only that you double click an entry to change to that directory.

You can also type in a directory name in the text input field and hit ENTER or the TAB key to go directly to that directory. The file selection dialog will be updated to show the contents of the new directory.

Files are selected from the list window on the right side of the file selection dialog window. Double clicking on a file in this list will close the dialog and perform the current operation—either save the file or open it. If you are saving a file and you double click on a file name in this way you will be prompted to verify that you want to overwrite the existing file.

The GIMP determines which file format to use when saving files by the extension used for the file name. Extensions traditionally use three characters, such as .jpg, .gif, or .xcf. When opening files, an additional menu option is available in the file selection dialog, allowing you to select either automatic file type determination (via these file name extensions) or by specifying the file type from the menu option.

Preferences

Preferences dialog

There are a number of configurable items which can be modified while using the program. All of these are available from the *Preferences* dialog. This dialog is opened from the Toolbox's File menu. Any settings made with this dialog are applied to the current GIMP session, and can be saved for future sessions as well. Note that changes made with this dialog are immediate and affect all Image Windows. It is recommended that you make changes to these options prior to beginning any other work with the GIMP.

The Preferences dialog is a notebook containing four pages:

1. Display

2. Interface

3. Environment

4. Directories

Each of these has a number of configurable options, described below.

Display

1. Image size and type - Sets the default dimensions and image type (RGB or grayscale) for Image Windows opened using the New option.

2. Preview size - Sets the size of the small images used in the Layers and Channels dialog. For an image with a large number of layers, it

may be useful to set this option to None. When this is set, the previews will contain either the letter L for layer or M for mask, but the image itself will not be displayed. This saves on memory and can speed up the GIMP quite a bit.

3. Transparency Type

> Light Checks - Light colored checkered pattern, alternating between dark and light.

> Mid-Tone Checks - The default; mid-toned gray checkered pattern.

> Dark Checks - Dark gray checkered pattern.

> White Only - Transparency represented as a white background.

> Gray Only - Transparency represented as a gray background.

> Black Only - Transparency represented as a black background.

4. Check Size - These options apply to the size of the checks used if one of Light Checks, Mid-Tone Checks, or Dark Checks are selected for the Transparency Type. They have no effect when a solid color is used for the Transparency Type.

> Small Checks

> Medium Checks

> Large Checks

Interface

1. Levels of undo - Sets the number of undo levels for the current GIMP session. Higher numbers use more memory. For very large images, this value should be kept low. On limited memory systems, and even on systems with reasonable amounts of memory but when working on very large images, it becomes possible that the swap files will grow so large as to use all available disk space. If this happens, the GIMP may exit unexpectedly without any errors. Reduce the number of levels of undo and, if possible, clean out some disk space before trying the operations again.

2. Resize window on zoom - Causes image windows to automatically resize when a zoom operation is performed. This occurs if the window can fit the zoomed image inside the display area of your monitor.

3. Disable cursor updating - Forces cursor to not change when application context changes, such as when saving a file. This feature may save some processing power for you if you run on a relatively low-end system.

4. Show tool tips - Enables the small yellow window that pops up beneath some parts of the GIMP and gives a brief description of the feature with which a button, slider, or other window component is associated.

5. Marching ants speed - Sets the speed at which the dotted outline of a selection moves around that selection. The value specified is in milliseconds. Note that the minimum value for this field is 50 milliseconds. Also, there is no way to disable the marching ants, although on low-end systems that use 8-bit displays you can use colormap cycling for the ants (see the next section under Environment).

Environment

1. Conservative memory usage - When set, causes the GIMP to trade speed for memory, freeing up memory but slowing down processing. Set this if you run on low-memory systems, for example those with less than 32 MB of memory.

2. Tile cache size (in bytes) - Higher values use less swap space but more memory. If disk space is at a premium you can set this to a lower value, but you should do this only if you can trade this off with more memory. If you have a system with large amounts of memory, say 128 MB or higher, and plenty of free disk space, you may want to increase this value from the default 10 MB to 32 MB or even 64 MB. If you leave it at 10 MB, then the GIMP will swap tiles more often and will not make efficient use of the available memory. Increasing this value will make better use of memory—but watch out! It can significantly impact the performance of other applications. If you plan on trying to run a number of applications while working in the GIMP, and you have a lot of memory, you will need to experiment a little to find a happy medium for Tile cache size.

3. Install colormap (for 8-bit displays only) - On low-end systems that support a maximum of only 256-color displays, this will allow the GIMP to install its own colormap. Doing so will provide for more accurate image displays in the GIMP, but can also cause color flashing, where other applications' colors become bizarre while keyboard focus is in the GIMP.

4. Colormap cycling (for 8-bit displays only) - Changes the way the marching ants are displayed around selections, from a dotted line pattern to one that uses colormap cycling. This effect works only with 8-bit displays.

Directories

These items determine where the GIMP will look for and save files of various types. It is not recommended that the Temp and Swap directories be placed on NFS mounted partitions due to the frequency with which the GIMP will need to access these directories. The Temp and Swap directories should also be on disk partitions with plenty of free space. The Swap directory, in particular, can take up large amounts of disk space while the GIMP is running.

1. Temp - Directory to use for temporary files.

2. Swap - Directory to use for swap files.

3. Brushes - Directories where brushes can be found. More than one directory can be specified, using a colon to delimit the paths.

4. Gradients - Directories where gradient files can be found. More than one directory can be specified, using a colon to delimit the paths.

5. Patterns - Directories where pattern files can be found. More than one directory can be specified, using a colon to delimit the paths.

6. Palettes - Directories where palette files can be found. More than one directory can be specified, using a colon to delimit the paths.

7. Plug-ins - Directories where plug-ins can be found. More than one directory can be specified, using a colon to delimit the paths.

Tool Options

The Toolbox tools have *Tool Options* dialogs that allow tool-specific configuration. The contents of the Tool Options dialog depend on the tool selected. Some tools, such as the Pencil tool, have no configurable options. In this case, the Tool Options window is simply a message dialog stating no options are available. Details on the Tool Options for each tool can be found in **Chapter 4 - The Toolbox**.

Although they might be considered tools, filters (aka plug-ins) do not have Tool Options dialogs associated with them. Filters have their own windows, which are specific to the individual filter's use.

Brushes

The *Brush Selection* dialog provides a simple mechanism for selecting the brush to use for drawing and painting operations. The dialog consists of a window of brushes, a mode option menu, an opacity slider, and a spacing slider. The brush modes operate in the same way as layer modes (see **Chapter 6 - Layers and Channels**). The opacity determines the amount of the brush "ink" to mix with the underlying image pixels. The spacing slider sets the frequency with which a new brush stroke is applied. A single brush stroke is a copy of the brush image selected in the brush window, so setting the spacing value higher will cause fewer brush strokes to be applied as you move the mouse around an image.

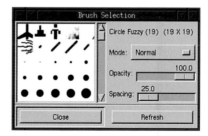

Brush Selection dialog

Brushes are used by the Pencil, Paintbrush, Eraser, Airbrush, Clone, and Convolver tools. They are also used to stroke a selection. A stroke is simply a brush applied to the outline of the selection.

All brushes are applied using the foreground color, which may be set before or after the brush is selected, but before the tool of choice is used. Brushes are defined in files using the `.gbr` suffix, and are located in the directories specified by the `gimprc` file (see **Appendix A - The gimprc File**). Directories can also be modified using the Preferences dialog. If new brush files are loaded into these directories after the GIMP has been started, you can use the Refresh button at the bottom of the dialog to load the new brushes into the dialog, and make them available for use in the current session.

Patterns

The *Pattern Selection* dialog is another fairly simple dialog, providing access to any configured pattern type for use with the Bucket Fill tool. Patterns are contained in any file with the `.pat` suffix, located in the directory specified for patterns in the `gimprc` file. Again, like the brush directories, these directories may be modified through the Preferences dialog. If new pattern files are loaded into these directories after the GIMP has been started, you can use the Refresh button at the bottom of the dialog to load the new patterns into the dialog and make them available for use in the current session.

Pattern Selection dialog

Color Palettes and Indexed Color Palettes

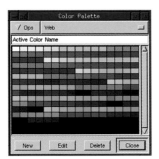

There are two *Color Palette* dialogs: one for saving collections of colors for future reference, and one for use with indexed images to edit the color palette for that image. In the first case, the Color Palette dialog, the window consists of an option menu labeled *Ops*, another option menu used to select the palette you wish to work with, a text field for setting and changing the current palette's name, a scrolled window of palette entries and a row of buttons along the bottom.

Color Palette dialog

To use this window, you first click on the Ops menu and select *New Palette*. This opens a smaller dialog allowing you to specify the name of the new palette. Enter a name for the palette and click the OK button. Now begin adding new palette entries by pressing the New button at the bottom. Since the default background for the palette entry's scrolled window is black, you may not be able to see the entry added to the palette the first time you do this. Immediately after clicking on the New button, press the Edit button. This will open the *Color Selection* dialog.

Choose a new color and click on the Color Selection dialog's OK button. The palette entry will change to the color you chose. From now on, any New entries added to the palette take on an initial color of the last palette entry. You can delete palette entries with the Delete button in the Color Palette window.

The Ops menu allows the creation of new palettes, merging of palettes, and deleting palettes. Closing the window can be done with either the Ops menu's Close option or with the Color Palette's Close button, at the bottom of the dialog window.

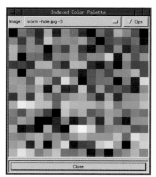

Indexed Color Palette dialog

The *Indexed Color Palette* window is similar to the Color Palette window, except it does not allow the creation of a new palette. It works on the existing palette for an indexed image. The dialog consists of an option menu for choosing an image, an Ops menu, a palette window and a Close button. The option menu for choosing an image will show only images which are in indexed color format. RGB and grayscale images will not be listed. The Ops menu provides only for closing the dialog, which is the same function provided by the Close button at the bottom of the dialog.

The palette window consists of up to 256 equally sized squares. Each square is a palette entry and each entry may be edited by clicking once within that entry's square. When an entry has been selected in this way, the Color Selection dialog will open. After changes have been made, click on the OK button in the Color Selection dialog. This will update the entry's color, as well as all pixels in the indexed image which contain this color. The update is immediate and may be undone using the Undo option.

Both palette dialogs are opened via the Image Window's menu from the Dialogs option.

Layers and Channels

Layers are like transparent acetate sheets, each one composited with those below in any one of a number of compositing modes. The compositing mode defines how the pixels of a given layer are combined with pixels from the layers below it. Layers can be added, subtracted, screened, or combined with lower layers based on their hue, saturation or color values.

Layers and Channels dialog

Channels are the component parts of pixels, such as their Red, Green, and Blue levels. Channels can also be created and used to save selections as masks. Masks are used to select which pixels will be visible in a layer and how transparent those pixels will be. The transparency is independent of the overall transparency of the entire layer, which can be set using the *Layers and Channels* dialog.

Layers and Channels are both accessed via the Layers and Channels Dialog. The Layers and Channels dialog is discussed in detail in **Chapter 6 - Layers and Channels**.

Gradient Editor

One of the more useful tools with the GIMP is the Gradient Fill tool. A gradient is a gradual blend of colors, as in a rainbow or sunset. By default, the Gradient Fill tool blends a region (either an image, a layer or a selection within a layer) from the foreground color to the background color using a linear blending technique. Custom gradients that flow through any number of colors including transparent are possible using the Gradient Editor. Users can also select Linear, Bi-Linear and Conical blends.

Gradients are discussed in more detail in **Chapter 10 - Gradients**.

Gradient Editor

Procedural Database and Script-Fu Dialogs

The GIMP provides a scripting interface which allows users and developers to combine a sequence of tools and plug-in operations into a single command. The command invokes a Script-Fu script. These scripts use a subset of the Scheme Language, known as SIOD, as their language for running the sequence of tools and filters, and even other scripts. The scripts may open dialog windows to query a user for initial values, such as text, fonts, colors and so forth. The format of the dialogs depends on the script.

Scripts work by accessing procedures within the GIMP and its filters that have been registered at run time in a database maintained by the GIMP. This database is known as the *Procedural Database*, often referred to simply as the PDB. You can browse the functions in the PDB via the DB Browser extension. This window consists of a scrolled list window of the registered procedures, a set of scrolled windows displaying relevant information for the currently selected procedure in the list, and a set of buttons along the bottom of the dialog.

In general, you can use the dialog to search for procedures that can be called by Script-Fu scripts. The information displayed includes a description of what the procedure is used for, its input and output arguments, author and other contact information.

Procedural Database Browser dialog

Cursors

The GIMP uses a number of different cursors to distinguish what you can do in different portions of the image when using different tools. A cross hair cursor is used by the Selection tools. This cursor is also used by the Color Picker, Bucket, and Blend tools. A double cross hair is used by the Crop tool. A pair of curved, point-to-tail arrows is used for the Transform tool. A two-pointed arrow (arrows on both ends) is used for the Flip tool. The Text tool uses the traditional I-beam cursor. The Move tool uses two two-pointed arrows, one pointing left/right and one pointing up/down. This is commonly referred to as a *fluer*. All other tools use a pencil cursor.

The cursor type also depends on whether a section of the image has been selected or not. For example, if a section of the image has been selected and the cursor is placed over that selection, then the cursor changes to match the context of the currently selected tool. If the Move tool is currently active, for example, then the cursor changes to the fluer cursor. If the Bucket Fill tool is selected, then when the cursor is over the selected region it changes to the crosshair cursor. For many of the tools, the cursor will be the traditional diagonal arrow over the unselected part of the image until the cursor is moved into the region that is selected. It takes a little work to become familiar with the currently active function based on the look of the cursor, but once you've worked with the GIMP for a short time you will become fluent in recognizing these changes.

The cursors will not change if the Interface/Disable Cursor Updating option is turned on in the Preferences dialog.

Moving On

Now that all the basics have been covered, it's time to move on to the details for the various tools available from the Toolbox. In the next chapter, we'll discuss each tool in depth, including the Tool Options dialog for each, and show examples for each tool.

Tutorial

Let's take a look at the various windows by opening and closing a few of them and creating a simple image in the process. First, when the GIMP starts, it displays the Toolbox. The first window we want to open is a new image. From the Toolbox menu, select the following:

File->New

You now see the New Image dialog. Just click on the OK button. A new Image Window with a solid white background now opens.

Press and hold the left mouse button over the ruler on the left edge of the Image Window. Now drag it to the right, into the Image Window background region. You've just created a new Guide! Try doing the same thing from the top ruler and dragging downward.

You've already seen the menus available from the Toolbox, so now let's take a look at the menus in the Image Window. Move the cursor inside the Image Window background region. Press and hold the right mouse button. The Image Window menu should be displayed. Find the *Window Info* submenu option. It's under the *View* menu option in the Image Window menu. This opens another dialog that gives some general information about the Image Window.

Take a look at the Image Window menu again, under the Image submenu. Notice the three options *RGB*, *Grayscale*, *Indexed*. Which one is "grayed-out" and cannot be selected? That's because the default Image Window type is RGB, so it wouldn't make any sense to allow access to that option. If it were there, it would convert the RGB image to ... another RGB image! No point in doing that, right? The other two options are used to convert the image to either grayscale or indexed types.

Now try the following from the Image Window menu:

File->Open

The file selection dialog opens. This should look familiar to you if you've used any sort of windowing system before, be it Microsoft Windows or Motif systems or even a Macintosh. Close that window. We won't need it for this particular tutorial.

Take a look at the *Dialogs* submenu. Open each of the dialogs presented there. You will become quite familiar with each of these over time, especially the Layers and Channels dialog.

Did you notice, when you opened the Layers and Channels dialog, that only one layer was displayed? We'll talk more about creating new layers and manipulating layers in a later chapter.

Now try this dialog:

File->Preferences

You can open this from the Toolbox File menu or Image Window File submenu. Here you will find some generic configuration items. Be sure to use the Save button in the Preferences dialog if you make changes that you want to take effect in all later GIMP sessions!

Now, what about those Tool Options dialogs? Let's see a few of those. First, double click on the Elliptical selection button (the middle button on the first row) in the Toolbox. This gives a typical example of a Tool Options dialog. Other tools have more complex dialogs; some have dialogs that simply say they don't have any options. A different kind of tool dialog is the Text Tool dialog. Click on the Text tool in the Toolbox. Now click once in the Image Window. Wait a few seconds for the Text Tool dialog to open. The amount of time it takes for the window to open depends upon how fast your X server is and how many fonts you have installed. The first time you open this dialog in the current GIMP session, you will see this delay. Thereafter the delay goes away. The GIMP simply has to query for all fonts the first time, thus the initial delay.

Now, during all this, did you notice the cursors? Play with a few of the tools from the Toolbox and see how the cursor changes. Experiment a little at this point, you won't break the computer if you do something "wrong"!

Chapter 4 - The Toolbox

The GIMP Toolbox

The *Toolbox* is the window which opens each time you start the GIMP. It is made up of a set of buttons (the tools) set in a seven-row by three-column box, with a menu bar across the top and a foreground/ background color selection box at the bottom. The menu bar holds a File menu similar to that of the pop-up menu in the Image Window (although with fewer options), and an Extensions menu. The tools are selected by a single left-button mouse click over the appropriate button. A double click will open the *Tool Options* dialog, which provides access to configurable options for the selected tool (if any). In the following discussion, the Tool Options dialog box for specific tools will be described with the tool with which it is associated.

Keep in mind that most tools and many other features in the GIMP are also accessible via keyboard accelerators, also known as keyboard shortcuts. This is an alternate way to implement a tool choice or GIMP command, through the keyboard rather than the mouse and menus. The default keyboard accelerators are given in the discussions that follow. Note that keyboard shortcuts are invoked only while the cursor is over the Image Window, not while the cursor is over the Toolbox. Also, not all features in the GIMP have default keyboard shortcuts.

Keyboard accelerators are configurable at run time by the user, and the changes can span GIMP sessions. See **Appendix B - Keyboard Shortcuts** for more details on setting your own keyboard shortcuts.

File and Extensions Menus

Toolbox menu

Across the top of the Toolbox is a menu bar. By default, there are two menus here: the File menu and the Extensions menu. The GIMP's built in extensibility permits developer extensions to place other menus here, but the default distribution has just these two.

The *File* menu consists of seven options. Each is described below:

- **New** - Opens a new Image Window. When selected, this option causes the New Image dialog to open. **Chapter 3 - GIMP Windows** discusses this dialog in detail. *Default keyboard shortcut: CTRL-n*

- **Open** - Opens an existing image file. This option uses the file selection dialog to choose the file to open, which is also discussed in **Chapter 3**. *Default keyboard shortcut: CTRL-o*

- **About** - A special dialog window that is a tribute to the many developers who have made the GIMP possible. *Default keyboard shortcut: none*

- **Preferences** - Opens the Preferences dialog, also discussed in **Chapter 3**. *Default keyboard shortcut: none*

- **Tip of the day** - Shows a random user's tip in a dialog window. *Default keyboard shortcut: none*

- **Dialogs** - Opens a submenu that provides quick access to dialogs that are applicable to any tool. The submenu consists of the following options. Each of these is discussed in detail in **Chapter 3**.

  1. **Brushes** - Opens the Brushes dialog. *Default keyboard shortcut: CTRL-SHIFT-b*

  2. **Patterns** - Opens the Patterns dialog. *Default keyboard shortcut: CTRL-SHIFT-p*

  3. **Palette** - Opens the Palette dialog. *Default keyboard shortcut: CTRL-p*

  4. **Gradient Editor** - Opens the Gradient Editor dialog. *Default keyboard shortcut: CTRL-g*

  5. **Tool Options** - Enables the Tool Options dialog. *Default keyboard shortcut: CTRL-SHIFT-t*

- **Quit** - Exits gracefully from the GIMP. *Default keyboard shortcut: CTRL-q*

As with most X applications, you should get in the habit of using the Quit option instead of the window manager's Close or Destroy options. Not all window managers are well behaved (nor all X applications), and the only way that one can be assured an X application will properly clean up or save session data is to have the user explicitly use the application's Quit option, if it has one.

The *Extensions* menu, shown as Xtns in the menu bar, is used primarily to access Script-Fu scripts. Script-Fu is the native scripting interface in the GIMP. Scripts allow you to run a series of plug-ins and other filters and tools in sequence to produce a specific result. Examples of scripting would be to create a logo with a drop shadow and text that results in a neon light effect. The GIMP can do this, but the effect requires a series of plug-ins to be run. Script-Fu lets you run this set of plug-ins as a single command.

By default, there are four options in the Extensions menu: *DB Browser, Screenshot, Script-Fu* and *Web Browser*. The first of these is a dialog used to look up information on procedures which can be called from scripts. This dialog is discussed in **Chapter 3 - GIMP Windows**. Screenshot allows the user to make a screen capture of their current X session. The user can either grab a single window (with or without window manager decorations) or the whole screen. The Script-Fu option leads to a series of categorized menus to provide access to the set of prepackaged scripts available from the main GIMP distribution. Web Browser opens a Netscape window and loads the appropriate web page based on the menu option selected. If Netscape is not running but can be found in one of the directories specified in the user's $PATH environment variable, then it will be started automatically. If not, then no action is taken by the GIMP with this menu option.

Another Xtns option which may have become part of the default distribution by the time this text reaches the reader is the *Waterselect* option. This option opens a dialog that allows users to select colors by swirling the mouse around a canvas, similar to mixing watercolor paints in a tray. This feature was not part of the 1.0 or earlier versions of the GIMP but should be available from the GIMP Registry.

The GIMP Registry is located at http://registry.gimp.org/.

Selection Tools

Selection tools

The first two rows of buttons are the *Selection tools*: *Rectangular, Elliptical, Free-hand, Fuzzy, Bézier* and *Intelligent Scissors*. Rectangular and Elliptical will draw the respective type of outline as you drag the cursor across the Image Window. Free-hand draws an outline which follows the path of the cursor as you move it. Fuzzy selects a region of an image, based on the colors in the region where you click with the left mouse button. The Bézier selection tool allows a region to be outlined in precise detail using combinations of straight lines and user-defined curves.

Rectangular Selection Tool Options

Elliptical Selection Tool Options

Free-hand Selection Tool Options

Fuzzy Selection Tool Options

Bézier Selection Tool Options

The selection tools available in the GIMP are:

Selection Type	Row/ Col	Icon	Description
Rectangular	1/1	a dotted-line square	Creates rectangular shaped selection areas.
Elliptical	1/2	a dotted-line circle or oval shape	Creates elliptical (i.e., circular) selection areas.
Free-hand	1/3	a cowboy's lasso	Creates free-form selection areas based on the path of the cursor around the Image Window.
Fuzzy	2/1	a magic wand	Selects a region based on a range of colors that are chosen by dragging the mouse through the Image Window. This sort of selection works best for images that do not contain gradients or wide ranges of colors over very small areas.
Bézier	2/2	an ink pen drawing a line	The Bézier tool can select both straight-line and curved regions. Clicking on the image creates an anchor point. Subsequent clicks create new anchor points that are connected to the previous anchor with a straight line. Clicking on an existing anchor point causes a handlebar to appear with a control box on each end. Clicking and dragging the control boxes will modify the straight line, creating a curve. Once a complete outline is selected, a single click on the inside of the selected region activates that region and the marching ants begin their dance around the selection's outline.

Note that all the selection tools have configurable options. Most support antialiasing and user-defined feathered regions.

Selection Tool Options Dialogs

All of the selection dialogs have configurable parameters that can be set using the Tool Options dialog. The table below describes the options found in the dialog for the various selection tools.

Selection Tool	Tool Option Dialog Contents
Rectangular	Feather toggle button - Turns feathering of selection on or off. Feather Radius slider - Sets width of feathered region.
Elliptical, Free-hand, Bézier	Antialiasing toggle button - Turns antialiasing of selection region on or off. Feather toggle button - Turns feathering of selection on or off. Feather Radius slider - Sets width of feathered region.
Fuzzy	Sample Merged toggle button - Turns sampling of underlying layers on or off for selected region. Antialiasing toggle button - Turns antialiasing of selection region on or off. Feather toggle button - Turns feathering of selection on or off. Feather Radius slider - Sets width of feathered region.

Chapter 5 - Selections gives more complete examples on creating and using selections.

Default keyboard shortcuts for selection tools—note that the keys used are case sensitive.

Selection Tool	Keyboard Shortcut
Rectangular	r
Elliptical	e
Free-hand	f
Fuzzy	z
Bézier	b

The last button of the second row is the Intelligent Scissors tool, another form of selection originally provided in the 0.54 release of the GIMP. It is primitively enabled in the GIMP 1.0 distribution, and improvements are planned for the 2.0 release.

Move

Move tool

Default keyboard shortcut: m

The first button of the third row in the Toolbox is the *Move* tool. This tool uses a *fluer*, a set of double ended arrows set perpendicular to each other, for an icon. The Move tool allows a selected region, layer or multiple layers to be moved. When the tool is enabled, the cursor changes to the fluer shape when it is moved over the currently selected region or layer. This allows the user to determine when a move will affect the selection or layer of interest.

The Move tool is more sophisticated than it might seem at first. When used with the Layers and Channels dialog, it becomes possible to select various pieces of an image to adjust them within the framework of the complete image. This is called *anchoring layers for a move* and is discussed in detail in **Chapter 6 - Layers and Channels**. The term *anchor* serves a dual purpose with respect to layers. The Move tool can also be used to *anchor floating selections*, that is, it can merge a floating selection with the current layer by overlaying the floating selection layer on top of the current layer. When the Move tool is selected, and the cursor is placed outside the marching ants of a floating selection, the cursor changes to a down arrow. The user can then click anywhere outside the marching ants and the floating selection will be anchored to the currently selected layer. This process is also discussed in **Chapter 6**. Floating selections are also discussed in **Chapter 5 - Selections**.

Moving layers can be a little tricky. When the Move tool is selected and the mouse is placed over the Image Window, the cursor will change to signify what action will take place when you click. If the cursor is the four-pronged fluer, then the current layer has a non-transparent pixel beneath the cursor. In this case, the current layer will be moved. If the cursor changes to a pointing finger, then there is non-transparent content in a pixel beneath the current layer, but the current layer is transparent at that pixel. When you click in this case, the active layer changes to the next layer with a non-transparent pixel, and the move operation will affect the newly selected layer.

The decision to use the current or some other layer is termed *pick correlation*. Since this sort of operation can be confusing when all you really want is to move the current layer, simply hold down the SHIFT key. This will disable pick correlation and allow you to move the current layer whether or not there is a transparent pixel beneath the cursor in that layer.

The Move tool can be used in conjunction with selections and keyboard modifiers such as the ALT and SHIFT keys, plus the arrow keys can be used to move a selection. All of these are also covered in **Chapter 5 - Selections**. There are no tool options for the Move tool.

Magnify

Magnify tool

Default keyboard shortcuts: = or -

The *Magnify* tool is used to zoom in and out of the image. This is useful for finding the edges of nearby objects in an image. At times you might wish to bucket fill a region, and the fill process covers more of the image than you expected. Using the zoom tool might show that a very tiny region of the fill area is not enclosed with colors different from the fill region, so the fill process "leaked" into adjoining regions. You may also wish to use a mask to make a cutout of an image, such as a face from a scanned photo. Zooming in to the edges of the face will help in making sure the mask doesn't overflow across the boundaries of the face, but still removes the background completely.

Magnify Tool Options

To use the Magnify tool, first select it from the Toolbox by clicking on its icon, a magnifying glass. Then click and hold the left mouse button in the Image Window and drag it to create an outline of the area into which you wish to zoom. When you release the mouse button, the image will be zoomed into the outlined region of the image. You can also do a simple zoom by clicking directly on a point of interest without dragging. The Image Window will zoom in one level and center itself on the pixel you clicked. Shift-clicking will zoom out one level.

There is a limit to how far you can zoom, but generally you will never need to zoom in extremely close. High zooms cause your image to look like a bunch of colored square tiles. These tiles are actually individual pixels and are the smallest modifiable piece of the image. You can change the colors of the individual tiles but you cannot apply a gradient to those tiles, since each is a single pixel with a single possible color value.

Zooming is also possible through the *View->Zoom* option from the Image Window menus. There are three options here: Zoom In, Zoom Out and a Zoom submenu. The Zoom In and Out options are also accessible by their keyboard shortcuts, = (the equal sign) and - (the minus sign) respectively. These two options provide 16 levels of zoom. The Zoom submenu offers the same depth to the zoom (a maximum of 1:16 and a minimum of 16:1) through a series of predefined zoom ratios. Pressing the "1" key in the image will reset the zoom level to 1:1, the original image setting. ("1" is the keyboard shortcut for resetting to this zoom level).

Zooming can also affect the size of the Image Window. If you have set the *Allow Resize Windows* option in the gimprc file (see **Appendix A - The gimprc File**) or set it via the Magnify tool's Tool Options dialog, then the Image Window will resize itself on zoom operations. The GIMP attempts to make the Image Window large enough to make the zoomed image completely visible, if possible. This feature can be both a bonus and a hindrance. Initially I found it interesting, but eventually it became annoying and I turned it off. I can resize the window on my own if I need to. When the Image Window size doesn't seem to match the image size, you can always use the Shrink Wrap option (CTRL-e) to fit the Image Window to the image size.

The Magnify tool's Tool Options dialog allows toggling of window resizes and is applicable to the current session only. More permanent changes should be made to the Allow Resize Windows option in the gimprc file.

Crop

Crop tool

Default keyboard shortcut: C (SHIFT-c)

The *Crop* tool is the right-most button of the third row in the Toolbox. The icon is that of a knife. In Adobe's Photoshop, this tool is known as the scissors tool. The Crop tool selects a region by boxing it out: hold down the left mouse button, drag, release and the region is selected. A dialog box will open, giving the dimensions of the selected region. At this point the region can be cropped. This means that the area outside the boxed region will be discarded and the Image Window will be resized to the area defined by the Crop tool. Click on the Crop button in the dialog, or click the left mouse button inside the boxed region in

Crop Information

X Origin:	66
Y Origin:	264
Width:	56
Height:	57

Crop	Selection	Close

Crop Information dialog

the Image Window to perform the cropping. All layers in the image will be cropped to the new dimension. Notice that the Image Window will resize itself to fit the cropped region even if Allow Reszie Windows has not been set in the `gimprc` file.

The crop box that outlines the region to be cropped can be changed at any time up until you perform the actual cropping. Simply click in a new location in the image and drag and release again.

Cropped regions can also be made to enclose a selection. Create a selection of any shape, then click on the Crop tool button in the Toolbox. Click in the image window to open the Crop Information dialog. The middle button of the dialog, labeled Selection, causes a crop border to be placed around the selection. The edges of the crop region align with the maximum and minimum X and Y values of the selected region.

Note that the Crop Information dialog is not the Tool Options dialog. The Crop tool has its own window which opens every time it is used, regardless of whether the Tool Options are turned on or not. Beside the Crop and Selection buttons, and the traditional Close button, the dialog shows the dimensions and location of the crop region. The X, Y origin values display the image location of the upper left corner of the crop border. Since this tool has its own window separate from the Tool Options, there are no additional options in the Tool Options dialog.

The Crop tool can be used with the arrow keys and with keyboard modifiers. In order to use the arrow keys, you must first select the region to be cropped using the mouse, as described earlier. The arrow keys can then be used to adjust the size and location of the crop border. The list below summarizes the effect the modifiers have on the arrow keys when used with crop borders.

No Key Modifiers

The arrow keys move the crop border up/down and left/right. The cropped region of the image is not affected by the movement of the crop border.

SHIFT Key Modifier

When the SHIFT key is held down, the arrow keys move the crop border in larger increments. The cropped region of the image is not affected by the movement of the crop border.

CTRL and ALT Key Modifiers

When the CTRL key is held down, the up/down arrow keys adjust the height of the crop region by moving the bottom line of the border. The left/right arrow keys adjust the width of the crop region by moving the right hand side of the crop border. The GIMP does not differentiate between the use of the right or left side CTRL keys, so both have the same effect.

The behavior of right or left CTRL keys ultimately depends on the X server setup. Some setups have the right CTRL key behave differently.

The ALT key has no effect when used with the Crop tool. Also, the keyboard modifiers have no effect when used with the mouse. The mouse is used solely to set the initial position of the crop border.

You should also note that there are image filters which can perform various forms of cropping. These are discussed briefly in **Part Two**.

Transform

Transform tool

Default keyboard shortcut: T (SHIFT-t)

Button one in row four of the Toolbox is the *Transform* tool. The icon for this button is a small window over the outline of a medium sized window, which in turn is over a larger window. A small arrow points to the bottom right corner of the largest window.

Transform Tool Options

The Transform tool has four options:

1. Rotation

2. Scaling

3. Shearing

4. Perspective

The default option when the GIMP starts is rotation. The Tool Options dialog for the Transform tool allows selection of any of these options using toggle buttons. Only one option can be set at a time. Once selected, an option remains in effect until it is changed with the Tool Options dialog or until the current session is exited. Once an option has been selected, you can click in the Image Window or in a previously created selection. For three of the options (rotation, scaling, and shearing) this causes a small dialog window to open showing the current status of the window or selection based upon the currently active Transform option.

For example, select a region of an image using any of the selection tools, and then click on the Transform tool button. Next, click inside the selected region. The area will be outlined with a rectangular bounding box and the corners will be outlined with small, wireframe boxes.[1] By default, the Transform tool is configured to perform rotations on the selected region. Click, hold and drag the mouse inside the selected region in order to perform the current transform. When you are done with the transform, click on another tool to remove the Transform tool's bounding box. The marching ants outline from the selection will remain. Notice that when transforms are performed that will change the shape of the selection, the selection outline is changed to match the transform changes. Also, transforms automatically cause floating layers to be created. The size of the layer is initially set to the size of the transform bounding box. If the transform causes the rectangular region that would bound the bounding box (i.e., the edges of the layer) to increase in size, then the layer increases in size. However, if the transform would allow the layer to shrink, the layer remains its current size. This distinction becomes important when you are trying to save memory, since each layer's size contributes to the overall amount of memory the GIMP is using.

The smaller dialog that opens for most of the transform options gives a current status on the operation. For rotations, this dialog shows the angle the bounding box has rotated from its initial position. For scaling, the dialog shows the original bounding box dimensions, the current bounding box dimensions, and the ratio of the original to the new dimensions. For shearing, the dialog box shows the magnitude of the shear. This is a measure of how far from the original bounding box the new shape has changed. The magnitude is measured in both the X and Y directions. For perspective transforms, there is no special dialog to show status.

 Double-clicking the Transform tool button brings up the Tool Options dialog, where you can choose one of the Rotation, Scaling, Shearing or Perspective options for the selected region or layer. Scaling will work with any selected area, but be aware that scaling of text or solid, filled selections can, if enlarged too much, cause aliasing (jagged edges) to occur. The smoothing option in the Tool Options dialog will lessen this effect, but excessive changes can still cause aliasing effects. The rule of

---

1. If the selection you made is not rectangular, then the bounding box for the transform will work much like the bounding box for the Crop tool—the selection's X,Y maximums and minimums will determine the width and height of the Transform's bounding box.

thumb here is to keep the transforms small, if possible, on images that have very defined edges. Gradients or blurred edges also exhibit this effect, but not to the degree seen when solid lines are transformed.

Rotational Transform

Rotational transforms can cause the corners of an image to extend beyond the edge of the Image Window. These areas are not lost if the layer is resized prior to flattening (see **Chapter 6 - Layers and Channels** for more on flattening of layers). However, once the image has been flattened or merged, these extended areas will be lost. If you find this has happened, and have not proceeded too far beyond when you flattened or merged the layers, you may be able to use the Undo feature to fix the problem. Also, the rotation transform does not provide a precise degree of rotation via keyboard input, so the rotation angle can only be approximated using the mouse and by watching the changes to the status dialog. Holding the CTRL key down while you drag the mouse will cause rotations in multiples of 15 degrees. There are also Image filters, accessible from the Image Window's menu under *Filters->Transform*, which provide exact rotations of from 90 to 270 degrees, in 90 degree increments, for selections, layers, and the whole image. Finally, there is a registered procedure available via the Script-Fu and plug-in interface in the Procedural Database called *gimp-rotate* which does allow arbitrary rotation amounts. This routine can be run manually, but to do so first requires an understanding of how to use the DB Browser.

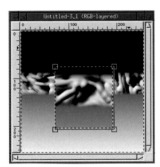

Scaled Transform

Scaling can be used with keyboard modifiers to provide more control. Without keyboard modifiers, the bounding box will scale with the upper right corner of the image or selection as the anchor point. The bounding box's dimensions can be changed in both the X and Y directions, and by any amount. If the CTRL key is held down, then the bounding box locks the X dimension and scales only in the Y dimension. Alternatively, the SHIFT key locks the bounding box in the Y dimension and scales only in the X direction. Holding both the CTRL and SHIFT keys down at the same time and dragging the cursor will cause the bounding box to scale by keeping the ratio of width to height equal.

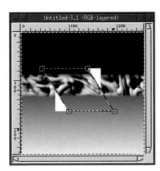

Sheared Transform

Shearing is like taking an empty cardboard box and pushing on one side so it slants the other way. You can shear the bounding box in either the X direction or Y direction, but only one direction at a time is permitted. Making a shearing change is done by clicking on one of the edges of the bounding box, continuing to hold down the mouse button, and dragging it (and the cursor). The side edges allow shearing in the X direction and the top/bottom edges allow shearing in the Y direction. For relatively small regions it may be hard to get the correct direction, so zoom in first for a closer view in these cases. Also, if you want to shear in both the X and Y directions, shear in the first direction, toggle a different transform

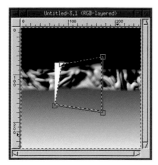

Perspective Transform

(any other transform, it doesn't matter which), then reselect shear and perform the second shearing operation. This will guarantee that the first transform has been set, and that the second transform doesn't cause the bounding box to reset to its original shape.

Perspective transforms will change the dimensions in both X and Y directions simultaneously. After clicking on the Image Window or selection, the bounding boxes are set around the region. Click and hold the left mouse button on a bounding box corner and drag the cursor to change the perspective view of the selection or image. This isn't really a perspective, it's a simple rectangular distortion; but with the proper adjustments to the control points on the corners of the bounding box, you can simulate perspective changes.

Chapter 9 - Using Transforms discusses the use of various methods of transformation within the GIMP in more detail.

Flip

Flip tool

Default keyboard shortcut: F (SHIFT-f)

To invert an image, either left-to-right or top-to-bottom, use the *Flip* tool. The middle button of row four in the Toolbox is the Flip tool. The icon is a double ended arrow pointing horizontally. Click on this button to flip a layer, image, or selected region either horizontally or vertically. The Tool Options dialog for this tool provides two toggle buttons, one for horizontal and one for vertical, to select the direction of the flip. The default direction is horizontal. A flip reverses the pixels of the selected region—the right-most pixels end up on the left-most side in a horizontal flip and the top-most pixels end up at the bottom in a vertical flip.

Flip Tool Options

Flipped regions can be used to mirror selections. For example, select a region of an image, using the Rectangular selection tool. Use *Edit->Copy* from the Image Window's menu to make a duplicate of this region. Now use *Edit->Paste* to create a new copy in a floating layer. Select the Flip tool from the Toolbox. Click on the image in the floating layer to flip the selection horizontally. Now use the Move tool to place the new layer so it appears side by side with the original selection in the Image Window. Create a new layer from the floating layer (see **Chapter 6 - Layers and Channels**). Now you have a mirror image of the original selection in a new layer.

Text

Text tool

Default keyboard shortcut: t

On the outside of the fourth row is the *Text* tool. Clicking once on this tool will enable the tool, but you need to click inside an Image Window to bring up the Text tool dialog. This dialog is used to select the font characteristics of the text you wish to insert in the image. The color of the text will match the current foreground color, so be sure you have set the foreground color before clicking on the OK button in the Text tool dialog. Once you click OK, the Text tool dialog closes and the text is inserted in the image with the marching ants dancing around the edges of the text. At this point, you can click on the Move tool to move the text to the desired location. Once you're familiar with the GIMP, you'll find that it's not necessary to click on the Move tool (notice the different cursor icon displayed over the inserted text). However, when first starting out, it is important to be familiar with the current mode the GIMP is operating in; to do this, you should explicitly select the tool you want.

Text tool dialog

An important note about adding text: text is inserted into an image as a floating selection. Floating selections have their own temporary layer in the Layers and Channels dialog. They require the user to select a disposition for them before any further work can be done on other layers. A floating selection's disposition can be one of *Anchor* or *New*. Anchoring a layer composites it with the current layer. Marking a floating selection as a new layer adds it to the top of the set of layers that make up the current image. You can learn more about layers in **Chapter 6 - Layers and Channels**.

One of the most common uses of text is creating logos for web pages and cover art. The text can be added easily enough, but the trick is manipulating the text after it has been added. Using the Text tool dialog to add text to your images and methods for processing it are discussed in more detail in **Chapter 7 - Colors and Text**.

The Text tool does not have a Tool Options dialog.

Color Picker

Color Picker tool

Default keyboard shortcut: o

Colors in the GIMP can be selected through the use of the Color Selection dialog which allows fairly detailed selection of the Red, Green, and Blue levels along with HSV (Hue, Saturation, and Value) levels. However, if you need to use a color that already exists in your image, the *Color Picker* tool, which resembles an eye dropper, is a much quicker way to set the foreground color to the desired color. The Color Picker button is the first one in the fifth row in the Toolbox. Click on the tool's button and then move the mouse over the pixel in the image window which contains the color you wish to use. Important note: be sure the layer in which that pixel lives is currently active! When you click in the image window the foreground color is set to the color of the pixel over which the mouse sits. The foreground color's setting is shown in the box at the bottom of the Toolbox. The two large boxes represent the current foreground (upper left) and background (lower right) colors.

Color Picker Tool Options

The Color Picker has only one Tool Option—a toggle button which allows the Color Picker to choose the color, based on a sampling of the merged layers at the specified pixel location. This is useful when you want to use the color you see displayed in the Image Window and not the color of a specific layer. It is possible, through the use of layer modes, that the colors in the layers are very different from what is displayed in the Image Window.

A small informational window opens when you click on a pixel with the Color Picker tool enabled. This window's contents depend upon the type of image being worked on. For RBG images, the small window will display the Red, Green, Blue, Alpha and Hex Triplet values for that pixel (or merged sample). The hex triplet can be used when specifying colors in HTML tags, for example bgcolor=#ffffff. The alpha value also can be given as N/A for RGB images that do not have an alpha channel (see **Chapter 6 - Layers and Channels**). For grayscale images, the window will show the Intensity and Alpha levels. For indexed color images, the window displays the palette index and the Alpha, Red, Green, and Blue levels associated with the selected pixel. For all values displayed in these windows, the number shown is in decimal and ranges from 0 to 255. For indexed images, the Alpha value is either 0 (for fully opaque) or 255 (for fully transparent).

Bucket Fill

Bucket Fill tool

Default keyboard shortcut: B (SHIFT-b)

Filling a region of the image with either a solid color or a pattern can be done using the *Bucket Fill* tool. The middle button of the fifth row in the Toolbox, the one with a bucket appearing to be poured, is the Bucket Fill tool. Bucket Fills, sometimes referred to as flood fills, can completely replace the existing pixels, be added to them, subtracted from them, or any number of other possible combinations using the Tool Options dialog.

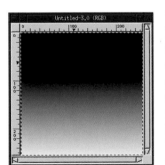

Bucket Fill Tool Options

Bucket fills can be used with selections, or to fill a region based on a threshold value. To use the Bucket Fill tool with a selection, select a region of an image using one of the Selection tools (or use CTRL-a to select the entire active layer). Next, click twice on the Bucket Fill tool button to bring up the Tool Options dialog. If you want a solid color to fill the selected region, click on the Color Fill toggle button. Now select a color for the foreground by double clicking on the foreground box at the bottom of the Toolbox. By default, the Bucket Fill tool will use the foreground color for its solid color. Once you've double clicked in the foreground color box, the Color Selection dialog will open. Set the color to red, for example, and then click on OK in the Color Selection dialog. Now you're ready to fill in the selected region. Simply click on the region within the Image Window. The GIMP fills it with a solid red shade. In this case, the fill is bounded by the marching ants which outline your selection. If you use selections and want the fill to fade out at the edges, you can set the selection to have a feathered radius. See **Chapter 5 - Selections** for more details on how to set and use selections.

You can also fill regions without selecting them, using the *Fill Threshold* slider in the Tool Options dialog for the Bucket Fill tool. The threshold option lets you specify the boundary of the fill operation based on the variation of color in the image itself. For example, if you have a gradient filled from top to bottom using the default black foreground and white background, then fill with a solid red using a threshold of 15 (the default setting) and click on the middle of the image, you will get a band of red, with soft (blurred) edges, across the middle of the image. The value in the threshold slider tells the GIMP to fill in pixels that are within 15 levels of intensity from the pixel upon which you clicked. Higher threshold levels will fill larger areas. Lower values fill smaller areas. Once the GIMP finds a pixel outside the range of the threshold value, it will not check for pixels beyond it, even if those pixels might fit within the threshold range.

Gradient filled Image Window before Bucket Fill

The selection method and the threshold method for using the Bucket Fill tool are mutually exclusive. If you have a selection in your Image Window (i.e., the marching ants are marching), then the threshold level will have no effect. If you don't have a selection, then the threshold level will be used to determine where the fill should stop.

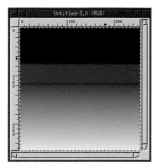

The Tool Options dialog for the Bucket Fill tool consists of a number of items:

- The Opacity slider

- The Threshold slider

- The blend Mode option menu

- The Fill Type toggle buttons

Image Window after Bucket Color Fill using default threshold of 15

- The Sample Merged toggle button

The threshold slider we've already discussed. The *Opacity* slider tells the GIMP how much the new pixels should be mixed with the existing pixel. Higher values mean more of the new pixel will be used. Lower values mean less of the new pixel will be used. Similarly, the *blend mode* options tell the GIMP how to blend the pixels. Blend modes are used in various places, but in each case their use is the same. For a complete discussion of blend modes see **Chapter 6 - Layers and Channels**.

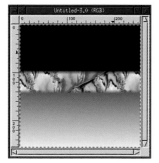

Bucket Fill using Ice pattern and default threshold of 15

The *Fill Type* can be either Color Fill or Pattern Fill. These toggles are mutually exclusive—only one can be set at a time. The *Color Fill* toggle will fill using the foreground color. Pattern Fills are possible using a pattern from the Patterns dialog. A host of default patterns are available with the GIMP. To choose a pattern, you first click on the *Pattern Fill* toggle in the Tool Options dialog for the Bucket Fill tool, then select the Image Window which will be filled, and type CTRL-SHIFT-p to open the Patterns dialog. Click on one of the patterns to select it. Now you can click in the Image Window to have the GIMP fill it with the pattern you selected. If you create an interesting PAT that you want to use for future Pattern Fills, you can save it as a PAT file from the Save Image dialog. Be sure to run the Refresh option in the Patterns Dialog window to update the set of available patterns to include your new pattern!

Whether you use the Color Fill or Pattern Fill options, the Bucket Fill will operate in the same manner. Bucket Fills on a selection using a Pattern Fill will fill only the selected region. Bucket Fills using the threshold will fill only those pixels which fit within the threshold setting.

The *Sample Merged* toggle will operate in the same manner as the toggle for the Color Picker. With the toggle turned off (the button looks raised), the Bucket Fill operation is applied only to the current layer. With the toggle enabled (the button looks recessed), the operation is applied to the current layer based on the merge of the current layer and all layers below it.

Gradient Fill

Gradient Fill tool

Default keyboard shortcut: l

The last tool in the fifth row of the Toolbox is the *Gradient Fill* tool, sometimes referred to as the Blend tool. This tool is used for filling a region with a blending or gradiation of colors in a direction the user specifies. The colors used can be blended from foreground to background, foreground to transparent, or with a custom gradient provided by the *Gradient Editor*. The Gradient Editor can be opened from the Image Window's pop-down menu as *Dialogs->Gradient Editor*. A number of default gradients come with the distribution, as well as some that have been created or collected by the Gradient Editor's author, Federico Mena Quintero.

Federico Mena Quintero's web pages are considered, along with the gimp.org site, to be a primary source for finding information related to the GIMP. His web pages are at http://www.nuclecu.unam.mx/~federico/gimp/el-the-gimp.html .

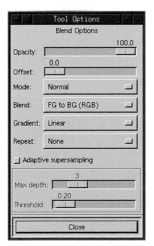

Gradient Fill Tool Options

The Gradient Fill tool, whose icon is a square which is filled with a gradient that runs from black on the left to white on the right, is used by clicking in the Image Window and dragging the mouse cursor to some other location. A straight line traces the path from the initial click point to the current cursor location. When you let go of the mouse button, the gradient is filled in, starting with the foreground color at the point you first clicked and running to the background color where you released the mouse button. The use of the foreground and background colors is only the default configuration, however. Creating a gradient can be done by a number of other possible methods. The level of color used in the fill can also be set by the length of the straight line between start and stop points of the drag.

The Gradient Tool Options dialog contains several options. Gradients can be offset slightly, made partially or fully transparent when combined with existing pixels, and blended with the existing pixels using modes similar to the Bucket Fill and Layer modes. The Gradient Fill tool is quite sophisticated. Gradients and blend modes modes are discussed in **Chapter 10 - Gradients**.

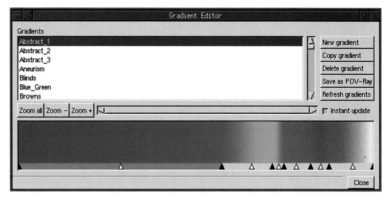

Gradient Editor

Pencil

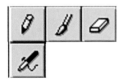

Pencil, Paintbrush, Eraser, and Airbrush tools

Default keyboard shortcut: P (SHIFT-p)

The next four buttons are the closest thing to *drawing tools* that the GIMP provides. They are, in order: the Pencil tool, the Paintbrush tool, the Eraser tool, and the Airbrush tool. The icons for the Pencil, Paintbrush and Eraser are fairly obvious and take up the buttons across the sixth row of the Toolbox from left to right. The Airbrush button has what looks like another pencil with a squiggly line behind it. This is the first button of the seventh row in the Toolbox.

Each of these tools requires that a brush type be set (there is a default setting, but you'll want to change this fairly often). The *Brush Selection* dialog allows the selection of the brush type. Once selected, the brush type is applicable to each of the drawing tools. The *Pencil* tool draws solid lines that follow the shape of the brush, using hard edges. Using a brush such as the Duck or Guitar, the effect is like using a stencil. This effect can seem strange when used with soft edged brushes. For example, the GIMP Brush (a 63x63 pixel soft-edged brush selectable from the Brush Selection dialog) has a soft, somewhat faded or blurred edge around what appears to be a circular brush. When used with the Pencil tool, however, the brush creates a solid square. Some brushes will paint solid squares, others solid patterns in the shape of the brush. There is no intuitive way to know which brushes will have what effects with the Pencil, so it will benefit you to play with the various brushes with the Pencil tool selected to see what each effect will actually be.

The Pencil tool does not have any configurable options available from the Tool Options dialog.

The Brush Selection dialog and all the drawing and painting tools in the GIMP are discussed in more detail in **Chapter 8 - Drawing and Painting**.

Paintbrush

Paintbrush Tool Options

Default keyboard shortcut: p

The *Paintbrush* works in a manner similar to the Pencil except that the edges of the stencil are not drawn using solid lines. This means that all brushes will appear just as they appear in the Brush Selection dialog window.

The Tool Options dialog for the Paintbrush contains a single slider, labeled *Fade Out*, which sets the speed at which the Paintbrush runs out of ink. If you set the Fade Out slider to 0, the special "never runs out of ink" value applies, and all brush strokes are equivalent in color intensity. If you set the Fade Out to 1, the Paintbrush runs out of ink almost immediately, and higher values will increase the amount of "ink" available for each brushstroke. As you move the brush around the Image Window, the brush strokes become lighter and lighter.

Eraser

Default keyboard shortcut: E (SHIFT-e)

The *Eraser* tool works in the opposite manner than the Pencil and Paintbrush tools, in that the shape of the brush is used to remove the underlying pixels. Note that this does not always mean the new color for the pixels is the background color. Instead, the pixels become transparent. If the Eraser is working on a layer that is not the bottom layer, and the layers below are not transparent, then the pixels in the lower layers which are in the same location that the Eraser is working on will show through. The shape of the brush determines which pixels are turned to transparent. If a pixel is not white in the brush shape, then that pixel will be set to transparent. Darker shades in the brush shape determine the amount of transparency applied; darker shades cause higher transparency, lighter shades cause less transparency.

The Eraser tool's Tool Options dialog contains two toggle buttons: Hard Edge and Incremental. The *Hard Edge* toggle will cause the eraser to act more like the Pencil as it erases using hard edges on the brush. With it disabled, the Eraser works more like the Paintbrush, with soft edges. The *Incremental* toggle allows you to erase over the same spot multiple times, removing more of the pixels with each pass. This effect is only noticeable if you have set the Opacity of a brush to less than 100. If the Incremental toggle is not set and the brush Opacity is less than 100, then repeated erasures will not completely erase the region over which the cursor is moved, no matter how many times you go over that region. With this toggle set, eventually the region could be completely erased. Think of using the Incremental toggle to force the eraser to act like the eraser on a pencil—the more you use it, the more you erase.

Airbrush

Default keyboard shortcut: a

Airbrush Tool Options

The *Airbrush* tool works in a manner similar to that of the Paintbrush, but acts as if the color or pattern is being blown onto the canvas at a given rate and with a certain pressure applied. The effect would be like using the brush as a stencil and then using an airbrush to blow paint through it. If you turn the airbrush on high, you get more paint through the stencil and the brush stroke looks darker.

The Airbrush uses two sliders in its Tool Options dialog: one for Rate and one for Pressure. The *Pressure* slider sets the amount of ink to flow for each brush stroke that comes from the Airbrush. Higher values cause darker brush strokes. Lower values give lighter brush strokes. The *Rate* slider works much like the Spacing slider in the Brush Selection dialog, although the two are not exactly the same. Setting a higher rate will cause brush strokes to be applied more often, at a quicker pace. Lower values will cause brush strokes to be applied at a slower pace. Think of the Airbrush as being driven by pulsed air and that the Rate slider adjusts how fast the pulses are, whereas the Pressure slider determines how much ink is blown with each pulse. Note that the pace for applying a brush stroke is independent of how fast you move the cursor around the image.

Clone

Clone tool

Default keyboard shortcut: c

Aside from the Airbrush tool, the bottom row of the Toolbox also contains the *Clone* tool, represented by a rubber stamp icon in the Toolbox. This handy tool allows you to use one part of an image or pattern to paint over another part of an image. This is useful, for example, for removing the edges between pasted objects, or for cleaning up the edges in a *tileable image*. Tileable images are ones which, when repeated side by side and top to bottom, have no seams between the images, thus creating the illusion of a solid image. Tileable images are often used as background images for web pages.

To use the Clone tool, click on the middle button on the bottom row of the Toolbox. Now, place the mouse over the Image Window on the spot you wish to use as the beginning source location. Hold down the CTRL key and press the left mouse button over this spot. A cross hair is displayed beneath the mouse pointer to signify that the source has been selected. Release both the button and the CTRL key. Now move the mouse to where you wish to begin cloning. The distance and angle between the source and destination points will remain constant as you hold down the left mouse button and drag it around the image. The area used as the source will be the same size and shape as the current brush type, so you will probably want to set this before beginning the cloning operation. When removing edges in an image you will probably want to use a brush type with soft edges, that is, edges that fade from black to white. The Nova brush is good for this sort of work. Note that the Clone tool can also use a pattern type, just like the Bucket Fill tool.

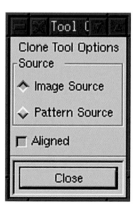

Clone Tool Options

The use of the pattern or the image as the source can be selected from the Clone tool's Tool Options dialog. There are two mutually exclusive toggle buttons in the Tool Options dialog for the Clone tool to specify from which source to work. The first is an *Image Source*. When this toggle is selected, you will need to use the CTRL-left-mouse-button-click combination to specify the source location. The source image you use does not have to be the same one in which you apply the clone operation.

The second toggle button, *Pattern Source*, will set the GIMP to use the currently selected pattern type from the Patterns dialog as the source for the clone operation. You can change the current pattern at any time, either before or after you set this toggle or actually begin the cloning. Cloning from a pattern works a little differently than from an image. When using a pattern as a source, the pattern repeats over the height and width of the layer or image to which the cloning is being applied. Using an image as the source limits the width and height of the clone operation to the boundaries of the clone image—the clone image source does not repeat the height and width of the destination layer.

The third toggle button in the Tool Options dialog for the Clone tool is the *Aligned* option. When this button is set, the source is used as a continuous feed so that the clone operation, when completed, will look just like the clone source. This is true even if you release the mouse button and then start cloning again. The cloned pieces stay aligned. If the button is not set then this alignment is not set and repeated clone operations will overlap. The best way to see this is to try cloning a pattern into a blank (white background) image window with the Aligned button set first, then unset. Make sure you do multiple clone operations in both modes, that is, click and hold the mouse button, then release it, then do it again, etc., then change the Aligned button setting and repeat.

Convolver

Convolver tool

Default keyboard shortcut: v

The last tool in the Toolbox is the *Convolver* tool. This tool can be used to sharpen or blur areas of an image, the choice of which is made from the Convolver tool's Tool Options dialog. Just select the tool from the Toolbox, and then start dragging the mouse around the area of the image you wish to sharpen or blur. The operation is not very obvious using the default Pressue setting of 50 (which can be seen and changed in the Tool Options window), so play with it a little to get the hang of how much dragging is required for the desired effect. Increasing the Pressure setting will cause the blurring to be more obvious with less work on your part. The Convolver along with the Clone tool can be used to clean up smudges or remove unwanted lines and streaks from images.

Convolver Tool Options

The Convolver Tool Options dialog contains a slider for setting the pressure level and two toggle buttons. Setting the *Pressure* slider to higher values will cause the Convolver to blur or sharpen at a higher rate. Lower values cause more gradual changes. The two toggle buttons are mutually exclusive. One sets the Convolver to the blur option, the other sets it to the sharpen option.

Sharpening with the Convolver is similar to using the Sharpen filter in the *Filters->Enhance* menu from the Image Window, except that the Convolver's *Sharpen* option causes a more grainy effect. It works well for small areas which need a touch-up, say around a person's nose or ears when they appear a bit out of focus, but does not work well for changing the focus of the entire image. The same is true of the *Blur* option. It functions similarly to the various blur filters (*Filters->Blur*), but is best when applied to small regions. Again, an example application might be to smooth the skin on a face that was scanned in and which had text or lines from the underside of the paper bleed through during the scan.

Foreground/Background

Foreground/Background color selectors

Default keyboard shortcut: none

At the bottom of the Toolbox window, you'll find the *Foreground/Background* color selection box. This box contains two large boxes, a two-ended arrow, and two smaller boxes. The large boxes are the foreground color and background color (top left to bottom right, respectively). Clicking on either selects that box as the current active box. When active, the box appears depressed (the inactive box appears raised). Clicking the active box again will open the *Color Selection* dialog, allowing you to set the color for that box. The two ended arrow allows you to swap the foreground and background colors. Simply click on the arrows to swap the colors. The currently active box does not change when you do this. The smaller boxes below the foreground color box reset the colors to their default values. This also does not change which box is active.

The foreground color is generally used for drawing, painting and fill operations. The background color is used in creating new windows or layers in the current window and when selections are cut or the Eraser tool is used. If a layer has no alpha channel (which is the default for the automatic background layer in all new windows), then a cut operation fills the cut region with the background color. Similarly, without the alpha channel, the Eraser erases the pixels by replacing them with the background color. If the layer does have an alpha channel, then both cut operations and the Eraser will change pixels to transparent.

Most operations that don't use patterns use the foreground color for fill, paint, and drawing operations. The color should be set prior to clicking on the tool of interest, or the results may be unexpected. New layers and windows can be created using a white background, a transparent background, or the current background color. If you use the current background color for these new windows or layers, be sure you've chosen the color you want prior to creating them.

Moving On

You've now seen the Toolbox and its tools. If you are so inclined, you can begin to experiment on your own, since you have enough information to get started. However, there are still quite a few details with which you'll need to become familiar in order to make real use of the GIMP. One of these is the use of selections. In the next chapter we'll look at all the methods for creating, manipulating, saving and using selections.

Tutorial

Using the Blend tool set with a Radial gradient, create a blend that runs from the top left corner of an Image Window to the bottom right. You can set the type of gradient using one of the menu options in the Blend tool's Tool Options dialog. Now use the Bucket Fill to create a red arc that starts along the top of the window and ends along the left side. Hint: you don't have to do any mouse drags for this except to create the original blend. Set the Threshold level in the Bucket Fill Tool Options dialog to some reasonable number, such as 15 (if you're using a default 256x256 pixel Image Window, this should be sufficient).

Create a text selection with a color blend. First, select the Text tool. Now click in an Image Window. When the Text tool dialog is open, type in some text and select a font. Click on the OK button. The text will be displayed in the Image Window with marching ants. Select the Move tool and move the text so you can see all of it (in case any of it is off the edge of the window). Now click on the Blend tool. Select a Linear gradient. That should be the default, although you may have changed it in the previous tutorial. Drag the mouse from left to right over the text. Now select *Layers->Anchor* from the Image Window menu. Voilà! Blended text!

Open the Brush Selection dialog and choose the Nova brush (it looks sort of like a star burst with many flares extending from its center). Open a new window. Verify the foreground and background colors are set to their defaults. Select the Pencil. Draw a line near the top of the image window. Select the Paintbrush. Draw a line through the middle of the Image Window. Select the Airbrush. Draw a line near the bottom of the window. Why are the three lines so different?

What feature of the Image Window can you use to create a rectangular selection that is exactly 100 units wide by 200 units tall? Hint: try using the Guides.

What is the difference between the Clone tool and the Convolver tool? Open an existing image of some kind and try them out.

Click on the Text tool in the Toolbox. Now type "r" to enable the Rectangular Selection tool. What happens?

Which selection tools might you use to select irregularly shaped regions? Hint: consider the use of keyboard modifiers. It's not as obvious as you think!

Which tool offers shearing and perpective changes? What is the difference between shearing and perspective changes to a selection? Try it! Experimentation costs as much as the GIMP does—nothing!

Place the cursor over the Toolbox. Hit the ENTER key. Hit the TAB key a few times. Hit ENTER again. It's a little known, and probably seldom used, feature of the GIMP—you can select tools using the TAB and ENTER keys!

So which selections can make irregularly shaped regions? Why, all of them, of course! By combining different selections and using keyboard modifiers to remove parts of selections, you can make pretty much any selection shape you can imagine!

Chapter 5 - Selections

One of the most important features of any tool like the GIMP is the ability to select regions of an image to be processed. Knowing the types of selections that are available and how to use them will greatly enhance your use of the GIMP.

Selection tools available from the GIMP Toolbox

The Toolbox offers six basic selection methods: Rectangular, Elliptical, Free-hand, Fuzzy, Bézier and Intelligent Scissors. For those of you who have used Adobe Photoshop, the rectangular and elliptical selections are accessed from Photoshop using a single tool called the Marquee. The Free-hand selection tool in the GIMP is referred to as the Lasso in Photoshop. All of these work basically the same as in Photoshop, although the Tool Options dialogs in the GIMP look different than their Photoshop counterparts.

The GIMP also offers a variety of other selection types from the Image Window menus. Some options create new selections, while others modify existing ones. The menu options are all accessible via keyboard shortcuts. Selections can also be modified while they are created by using keyboard modifiers. Modifiers are like shortcuts except they are keys that are held down right before a mouse click or during the mouse drag to change the way a selection is created. In the discussions that follow, the keyboard shortcuts for all selection options along with all possible modifiers will be given. The default keyboard shortcuts are also listed in **Appendix B - Keyboard Shortcuts**.

Selections are denoted by a moving dashed line that flows around the perimeter of the selected region. This line is often referred to as *marching ants*, as it resembles a single line of ants dutifully marching one by one.

Selections can be moved, rotated, flipped, filled, cut, pasted and have nearly any filter applied to them. A selection is created relative to the active layer, but a selection can be made in one layer and processed in another layer by simply changing layers. Layers are discussed in **Chapter 6 - Layers and Channels**.

Select All and Select None

The simplest selection is the one which selects the entire current layer. This particular selection can be done either via the Image Window menus (*Select->All*) or by using the CTRL-a keyboard accelerator. Once selected, the region is surrounded by the marching ants. Once a region is selected, it is important to know how to turn off the selection. One method is to click on one of the selection tools in the Toolbox and then click the left mouse button in the Image Window. You can also turn off the selection using the Image Window menus and keyboard accelerators. The Image Window menu option *Select->None* (CTRL-SHIFT-a) turns off the selection.

*Selections can be made on any one layer image or layer mask and used on another layer image or mask simply by clicking on a different layer thumbnail! For more on layers and masks, see **Chapter 6.***

Modifiers

There are no modifiers which affect the Select All and Select None selection types.

Rectangular and Elliptical Selections

Rectangular selection tool

Elliptical selection tool

A *rectangular* selection is one where parallel sides are equal in length. The perpendicular sides are not necessarily the same length, however. *Elliptical* selections are simply round regions, either ellipses or circles. The simplest way to use these is to click the left mouse button somewhere in an Image Window and drag the cursor through the Image Window to create a selection outline. However, a single rectangular region or a single elliptical region is seldom all you want to encompass with your selection. Using these selection types in conjunction with their modifiers can allow you great flexibility in creating selections.

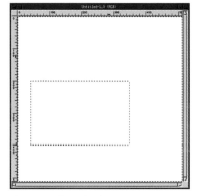

A rectangular selection.

Another rectangular selection, which we want to combine with the first.

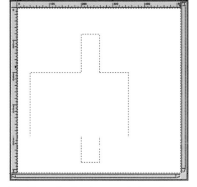

The first selection is created, then the second is created with the SHIFT key held down so the two selections get combined.

Modifiers

Several keys can be used to modify the behavior of the Rectangular and Elliptical selection tools. These keys can also cause different behaviors, depending on whether the key is pressed before or after the mouse button is pressed. Photoshop users will recognize these, since they work the same in both Photoshop and the GIMP. The following table summarizes the available modifiers:

Modifier	Mode	Shape
None (default)	Replace any existing selections	Not constrained
SHIFT	Add to current selection	Constrain new selection
CTRL	Subtract from current selection	Create new selection using click point as center of selection
CTRL-SHIFT	Intersect with current selection	Constrain new selection and center it on initial click point

The modifiers are overloaded, meaning their use is very much dependent on the order in which a click and the keystroke occur. For example, if you make a rectangular selection, then press the SHIFT key and click/drag, you'll get a constrained square. Now if you release the SHIFT key without releasing the mouse button and continue to drag, the rectangle is no longer constrained. When you finally release the mouse button, the new rectangle will be added to the existing one. If you had released the mouse button before you released the SHIFT key, you would have ended up with a square selection that replaced the original selection. The key to using these modifiers is to think of their use in two steps: setting the mode, then setting the shape. In most cases, this simply means:

Set the mode:

1. Press the modifier key and hold it.

2. Press and hold the mouse button.

3. Release the modifier key—you have now set the mode.

Set the shape:

4. While still holding the mouse button, press a modifier key and hold it—this sets the shape.

Finally, start your drag operation. While you drag, the selection shape you are creating will be based on the shape you set in step four. When you release the mouse button, the new selection will be combined with any existing selections based on the mode you set.

Of course, you don't have to set a mode or shape. You can take the defaults for either. If you only wanted to set the shape, without changing the default mode, you would press and hold the mouse button, then press the appropriate modifier key. The key here is to make sure you press the mouse button before you press the modifier key. If you wanted to set a mode but use the default shape, simply do steps one to three, and skip step four.

Normally, one corner of the selection's bounding box is anchored to the point you click on in the image. The bounding box is rectangular, which means for rectangular selections the bounding box is the same as the selection. For ellipses, the bounding box marks the maximum and minimum X and Y values for the ellipse. If you use the CTRL or CTRL-SHIFT modifiers after you've pressed the mouse button, you can cause the initial click point to be the center of the selection.

Free-hand Selections

*Free-hand
selection tool*

When the *Free-hand* selection tool (the lasso icon in the Toolbox) is selected, the mouse cursor will leave a trail as it is dragged. The trail becomes the outline for the new selection. The GIMP will connect the starting point of the outline with the end point, using a straight line. The outline can overlap itself. If the outline overlaps, the GIMP uses an even/odd calculation to determine if a region is inside the selection or not. This means that if you were to trace a row of pixels from left to right, a pixel is determined to be inside the selection if, as you travel across the row, you have crossed an odd number of selection outlines. If you have passed an even number, then the pixels are not in the selection.

We can show this even/odd methodology with a couple of examples. First, consider a simple circular region (not necessarily a perfect circle, just round). Pick a row in the image and start on the left hand side of the image. Initially, the pixels in that row are not in the selection because you have not yet crossed the selection outline. When you cross the left side of the circular outline, an odd number of 1, the pixels are considered inside the selection. Finally, when you cross the next outline, the second (even) time, the pixels are considered outside.

Now draw the outline as an exaggerated heart shape.[1] In the example image, we've crossed the outline upon itself in the center of the heart. Now follow a row through the center of the selection region and count the times you cross the selection outline. Part of the region is considered inside the selection, and part outside, even though the overall area is encompassed by the outline.

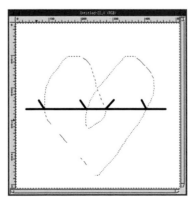

*Free-hand selection, showing
even/odd lines.*

*Same selection, filled to show inside
and outside regions.*

---

1. Okay, so it isn't very heart-shaped. You get the idea.

This inside/outside situation becomes much easier to see if you move the mouse cursor from left to right over the selection. Notice the cursor changes from a cross hair to a fluer (double-ended arrows, like the Move icon) as the mouse moves inside the selection region. When you move to an area outside the selection region, the fluer changes back to the cross hair.

Creating selections using the Free-hand selection tool can be difficult using the mouse. The Free-hand selection tool acts sort of like a pencil to draw the outline, but the mouse isn't designed for that sort of drawing. However, this tool works quite well if you're fortunate enough to have a tablet configured.

Modifiers

The Free-hand selection tool uses the same keyboard modifiers as the Rectangular and Elliptical selections, except that only the mode modifiers have any effect. There is no constraint mechanism for the Free-hand selection tool, so you cannot use the keyboard modifiers to define the shape for this selection.

Fuzzy Selections

Fuzzy selection tool

You can achieve some very interesting selections using the *Fuzzy* selection tool. This tool operates by determining a range of pixel values throughout the image to include in the selection. This differs from the other selection tools in that with the other tools, you select the outline which will encompass the selection region. With the Fuzzy selection tool, you are selecting any pixels in the image which have values that fall within the selected range of pixel values. Selections of these types tend to be discontinuous in nature—they don't generally enclose a single, solid region, though they can in cases where the selection is being done on a smooth gradient.

The range of pixel values is determined by dragging the cursor while holding the left mouse button down. This sets the range or *threshold* value. If you don't drag the mouse, but simply click once in the image, the Fuzzy selection will choose the pixels that have the same pixel value, plus or minus 15 units, as the one over which you clicked in the image. By default, the threshold of values is +/- 15 units from the current pixel's value. The default is set in the `gimprc` file.[2] If you click and hold the mouse button down for a second, a solid outline of the selection region will be displayed. While holding the mouse button down, drag the mouse up to reduce the threshold. This makes the selection smaller. Drag the mouse button down to increase the threshold, increasing the selected region. Once you've changed the threshold amount by dragging, the GIMP will remember the new threshold and use it the next time you use the Fuzzy selection tool. You cannot reset the threshold to its default value except by exiting and restarting the GIMP, so you may find it helpful to manually reset it to a smaller threshold after using Fuzzy selection once.

Modifiers

The Fuzzy selection tool uses the same keyboard modifiers as the Free-hand selection. Like the Free-hand selection tool, there is no constraint mechanism for the Fuzzy selection tool, so you cannot use the keyboard modifiers to define the shape for this selection.

Bézier Selections

Bézier selection tool

The *Bézier*[3] selection tool in the GIMP is similar to the *paths* feature of Photoshop. In the GIMP, the user creates paths for the selection using the tools in much the same manner as the Free-hand tool is used, except that *control points,* sometimes called *anchor points,* are used to refine the outline of the selection. Using Bézier selections, you can create very accurate selections using curves of any size or shape and/or straight lines.

The control points of a Bézier selection are created by clicking on pixels in the image. As each new control point is created, it is connected with the previous control point by a straight line. The GIMP represents the control points as small filled circles. These circles can be moved after they have been placed, and they can be used to adjust the shape of the lines between the control points.

---

2. See **Appendix A - The gimprc File**.
3. Named after Pierre Bézier.

Bézier control points have been placed around the outline of the lion's face.

The control points have been adjusted so that the curves between them more closely match the outline of the lion's face. Note the splines on the control point on the right side of the image.

To use the Bézier tool, you first need to place the control points around the region to be selected. Don't use too many—you only need one on each end of any given curved segment. Place the last control point over the first one to close the outline. At this stage, you have the straight line outline and control points, but you don't quite have a selection. To turn the outline into a real selection, with the now familiar marching ants, you must click inside the Bézier outline. Remember, if the outline you created overlaps itself, the inside/outside methodology discussed with Free-hand selections applies.

Before starting to add control points you should determine where they will go. This is necessary because the GIMP does not currently allow you to remove control points once they have been set. Also, once you begin editing the control points, the use of CTRL-z to undo changes does not work. Undo will remove all control points or the selection if you've already converted the Bézier curves into a selection. Guides can be used to approximate where the control points will go. They can be moved later if they are not exactly where you want them in the first place.

Now the selection you just created is not quite the exact outline you might have hoped for—it lacks the curves for which Bézier selections are famous. To create curved outlines, you need to adjust the lines between control points. Before doing this, adjust the position of the control points by clicking inside a control point's circle to select it. Then, while holding the CTRL key and the left mouse button down, drag the control point by moving the mouse. A common problem is to not have the control point properly selected first. Be sure to click inside the control point once to be sure it is selected. You can tell it is selected when the circle is an outline and not filled. Another problem arises when the CTRL key is not pressed before the mouse button. Pressing the mouse button first will cause the control point's handles to appear. To clear these, click inside another control point, then back in the original and attempt the drag operation again.

Now you are ready to adjust the lines between control points. Select a control point by clicking in it. Now drag the mouse from inside the control point out, while holding the left mouse button down. The adjusting handles, known as *splines*, appear. The splines are two lines stretching from the control point out in a straight line (at least initially) with small boxes on the ends. These boxes are used to adjust the curves between control points. One spline controls the curve to one side of the control point, the other spline controls the line on the other side. These handles can be moved together or independently and can remain displayed while moving the control point (using the CTRL key).

Using the handles is fairly easy:

1. Click on one of the spline's boxes.

2. While holding the left mouse button down, move the box around to adjust the curves on both sides of the control point. In this case, both splines will move and the curves on both sides of the control point will be modified.

To adjust only the side associated with the box selected, hold down the SHIFT key while you follow these steps. The angle between the handle boxes changes when moved independently; however, once moved they will revert back to being a straight line (and therefore change the curves between control points) if you attempt to move them again without holding the SHIFT key down.

Splines can also be used to flatten or raise a curve. Dragging the splines out from the control point, extending the spline, will flatten the curve. Shortening the spline will raise the curve, making it more pronounced.

Adjusting the curves between control points using the splines can actually be done as you create the control points. You don't have to close the outline of connecting control points first.

Bézier selections are rather difficult to master. It takes practice to know where control points should go and how many there should be. Since you cannot add or remove control points once you've closed the loop, you will need to plan ahead before placing them on the image. Despite this, Bézier curves are still the best tool available for highly accurate selections around regions without distinct color boundaries. The Freehand selection is close, but takes a much more accurate and steady hand, and does not allow editing of the selection.

Modifiers

The Bézier tool uses the SHIFT and CTRL keys to modify the actions associated with mouse movements. SHIFT allows modification to either end of the handlebar (the splines). CTRL allows a control point to be moved after it has been placed.

Intelligent Scissors

*Intelligent
Scissors tool*

Intelligent Scissors are similar to the Free-hand selection tool. Both tools allow you to draw the outline of your selection with the mouse. However, when you finish your selection using Intelligent Scissors, your selection is adjusted by the program, finding edges and curves in the image that match the selection you drew. A stable Intelligent Scissors option is a late addition to GIMP 1.0, and while it doesn't crash, the option doesn't always yield useful results. This tool should improve as the GIMP is further developed.

Selecting by Color

Aside from the Bézier selection tool, selecting by color may be the most useful selection available. Unlike Bézier, Fuzzy, Rectangular, Elliptical and Free-hand selections, selection by color is not available from the Toolbox. The Image Window menu *Select->By Color* opens a dialog that contains a preview window, a fuzzy threshold slider, and a set of toggle buttons that determine how a color selection is combined with any existing selections.

*Select By Color dialog with preview window
example.*

The preview window displays a grayscale version of the selection, where all pixels that are not black are part of the selection. Choosing the Replace toggle will cause the new selection to replace any existing selection. You can experiment with different levels for the fuzzy threshold slider, using *Replace* to see which areas would be selected. Alternatively, if you already have a selection created, for example, with the Rectangular selection tool, then you can use the *Add* toggle to extend the selection using the new areas covered by the color selection. Similarly, the *Subtract* toggle will remove the color selection from the existing selection, reducing the initial selection wherever the two overlap. Finally, the *Intersect* toggle acts in an opposite manner from the Subtract. Any areas which overlap between the new and old selections remain, and the rest of the selection is discarded. Keep in mind that what is discarded is simply the selection area, not the image pixels. Modifying the selection only changes what area is encompassed by the selection path(s). It doesn't actually modify the image itself.

Select By Color Tool Options

Like the Toolbox-based selection tools, the *By Color* menu option has a Tool Options dialog. The dialog contains three toggle buttons and a slider. The toggle buttons consist of: a *Sample Merged* toggle, which will select colors based on the visible color and not just the current layer's color; an *Antialiasing* toggle, which allows for the selection to include computations for antialiasing; and a *Feather* toggle. The Feather toggle will cause an automatic feathering to be applied to the edges of the selection, which means that the selection will include semitransparent pixels around the edge of the selection. This causes a feathered appearance around the edges of the selection when an *Edit->Copy* operation is performed using that selection.

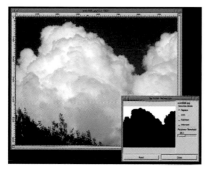

The sky in this picture is selected using the Select by Color dialog settings shown. A single click in the region of the blue area selected all of the sky.

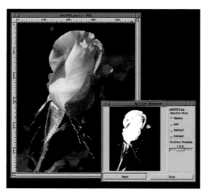

Similarly, a portion of the flower and stem were selected with a single click in this image. Note the grayscale preview of the selection. This, in itself, is an interesting image. Copying this selection to the default edit buffer, then pasting and using the desaturate option would produce a full size copy of the preview.

The grayscale version of the selection, pasted onto a white background. The effect looks much like a pencil drawing.

The preview window offers some interesting images using this form of selection. Saving the preview is possible by using the Save to Channel feature, which is discussed in a later section of this chapter. Once saved, the grayscale image can be copied and pasted to a new layer in the

regular image. Done skillfully, you can achieve effects like ghosts or
x-ray images using this technique.

Selection by color differs from Fuzzy selection in that the former will
choose all pixels that match the color and fuzzy threshold criteria, even
if those pixels are not adjacent. Fuzzy selection will select the pixels
that match the color and threshold criteria, but only if they are adjacent
to the initially selected pixel or pixels. You can therefore use the Fuzzy
selection to cut out regions of an image without affecting matching
regions in another part of the image. You would use the select by color
method to cut out all pixels matching the criteria, whether they are
adjacent to one another or not.

By default, there is no keyboard shortcut for accessing the selection by
color dialog window. See **Appendix B - Keyboard Shortcuts** for
information on how to install one of your own choosing.

Moving Selections

Any selection, once created and displaying the marching ants, can be
moved to a new location within the current layer. At the time the selection
is made, no matter which selection method is used, the selection can be
moved simply by placing the mouse inside the selection, holding down
the left mouse button, and dragging the selection to its new location.
Movement of this nature will cause the selection to become a floating
selection (see the next section). Moves of this nature will actually move
the region of the image bounded by the selection. To move the selection
path alone without changing the image, you need to use the ALT
keyboard modifier.

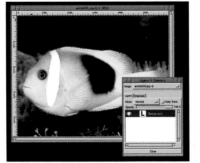

*Layers and Channels dialog before the
selection has been moved.*

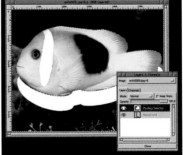

*After selection has been moved, the float-
ing layer is shown in the Layers and
Channels dialog.*

Modifiers

Selections can be moved without changing the image by using the ALT keyboard modifier. Press the ALT key down, then press and hold the left mouse button down and drag the selection outline around the image. Once the mouse button has been pressed, you can, if you choose, release the ALT key. The modifier stays in effect as long as the mouse button is held down.

Similarly, the selection can be moved using the arrow keys on the keyboard. Again, set the mode of the selection move by first pressing and holding the ALT key. Then move the selection outline by using any of the four arrow keys on the keyboard. Movement of this type is fincly granulated, meaning the movements will be small. If you want to increase the amount of the move and still use the arrow keys, just add the SHIFT key to the ALT key: SHIFT-ALT-arrow will move the selection outline in large increments.

The Move tool in the Toolbox cannot be used to move a selection. Its use is generally restricted to the movement of layers or the complete image.[4] If you change tools from the original selection tool you used to create the selection, you can click on one of the other tools and then place the cursor over the selected region and perform the move. Be sure that a selection tool is selected and that the cursor changes to the fluer before attempting the move. If you don't, you may lose your selection. If this happens, try using the venerable CTRL-z (undo) to bring back the selection. Then try the move again.

When you move a selection, you may find it useful to place a few guides first. Selections can also be snapped to the guides when you make them. We'll discuss this a little later in this chapter.

Floating Selections

Selections, once moved in any manner, become *floating layers* in the Layers and Channels dialog. A floating layer is similar to a normal layer except that it is limited in the ways it can be managed from the layers menu. You will need to make sure this floating layer is given a final disposition—either making it a new layer or anchoring it to the currently active layer—before continuing with your work. Floating

---

4. A notable exception to this is the use of the Move tool to position floating selections.

selections can also be made using the Image Window menu *Select->Float* option, available through the keyboard accelerator CTRL-SHIFT-l. This option can be used to float a selection in place, without moving it. This is often useful when you want to enhance one region of a layer and then recombine the enhancement with the original, using one of the many available layer modes.

After a selection has been moved, any further selections become selections inside selections. Sounds confusing, but try it and you'll see what I mean. What happens is that the new selection, which is outlined but does not have the marching ants effect (the floating selection keeps the marching ants to itself until it is anchored or made into a new layer), is intersected with the original floating selection, masking out anything outside of the newer selection. These new selections effectively become masks of the floating selection. You can create any number of these masks, adding and intersecting them in the usual manner of selections, before giving the floating selection its final disposition. However, the new selections don't take effect until the current floating selection has been anchored. The layer can be anchored either by using the layer menus or by clicking outside the selections.

Note that turning the floating selection into a new layer does not have the same effect. In this case, the masks are not applied and the new layer has the original, complete selection intact. The new selections remain and will now have the marching ants running about their edges.

Layers and Channels are discussed in the next chapter.

Modifying Selections

Once a selection has been made, it can be modified in a number of different ways. Of course, there are the previously discussed methods of adding, subtracting and intersecting one selection with another. Selections can also be feathered at the time of creation. Beyond these, there are a series of other modifications available from the Image Window menu's *Select* and *Edit* submenus.

Clearing and Filling Selections

Clearing a selection, available from the Image Window menus as *Edit->Clear* or from the keyboard as CTRL-k, will remove the selected region. The cleared area will be transparent if the active layer contains an alpha channel. If it doesn't, the cleared area takes on the background color. Filling a selection using *Edit->Fill* from the Image Window's menus or from the keyboard as CTRL-. (CTRL-period) will fill a selection to the background color.

Feathering, Antialiasing, and Merging

Any selection can be *feathered*. Feathering a selection means that the edge of the selection turns into a fading pattern, from current image to transparent. The feathering starts at the edge of the selection and continues out for the specified number of pixels. The Toolbox selection tools all have Tool Options to turn on feathering and to set the width of the feathered region. Selections can also be feathered by using the Image Window menu option *Select->Feather* (CTRL-SHIFT-f). Selections are not feathered by default, so you need to enable this feature manually if you want the feathering to occur.

Toolbox selections have an added feature: *antialiasing*. Antialiasing reduces the jagged appearance of the selection in some cases. The Tool Options dialog for the Toolbox selection tools provides a toggle button for enabling/disabling this feature, although antialiasing is already turned on by default.

The Fuzzy selection tool includes a *Sample Merged* option in the Tool Options dialog. This option allows the selection to be made based on the visible image, and not just the currently active layer. This is useful, since the Fuzzy selection works on a range of colors through a layer or image and not just on a user-outlined region.

Grow/Shrink

All selections can be grown or shrunk using the *Select->Grow* or *Select->Shrink* options, respectively. Both options, when selected, open a dialog window with a single text entry field. The field is used to specify the number of pixels to grow or shrink the current selection. The value for this field can be an integer or fractional value, such as 3 or 3.35. The options change the dimensions of the selection by the number of pixels specified in the dialog window.

Bordering

There may be times when you wish to select a *bordered region*, that is, an area that runs around all or part of the image with an equal width. An example might be to select the white edge of an old, scanned photograph. This can be accomplished using the *Select->Border* Image Window menu option. A dialog window opens, allowing you to specify the width of the border. The border will span the width specified centered along the original selection. This means that the initial selection should be made in the center of the region you wish to select, such as the center of the white edge in the photograph.

A scanned photo. We want to place a fuzzy white border around the photo.

First, we select a rectangular area around the edges of the photo using the keyboard shortcut CTRL-a.

Next, we create a 60 pixel border from the original selection.

Now we apply a square
gradient fill, using the default
foreground to background
settings and running from the
middle of the selection to the
outside edge.

The updated image, after the
border has been applied.

Sharpening

A selection can be made to have a hard edge, as opposed to the soft edge that comes with feathering, by using the *Select->Sharpen* menu option. The sharpened edge takes the boundary of the original selection, thereby removing any feathering that has been applied previously.

Snapping to Guides

One of the nicest features of the GIMP is the ability to snap selections to the Ruler Guides. The *View->Snap To Guides* Image Window menu option toggles the snap action on or off. By default, this feature is turned on. Snapping to the guides allows you to be a bit more accurate with your selections by setting the guides first, at the minimum and maximum pixels that will bound the selection region.

We would like to use guides to select a couple of the buildings in this image.

The two buildings have been selected by having the rectangular selection snap to the guides.

The selections with the guides removed.

Snapping to guides means that when you create a selection using a Rectangular, Elliptical or Free-hand selection, it is pulled to the guides—it gets snapped to the guide—when the selection is relatively close to a guide. For Rectangular selections, a side of the rectangle gets pulled to a guide. Any side can be snapped, and one or more or all sides can be snapped at a time. Elliptical selections snap X and Y minimums and maximums to guides. This means, for example, the highest point of the ellipse would snap to a guide. The guide would then be the tangent line to the ellipse at that point. Similarly, vertical guides would be tangent lines for the left-most and right-most points of the ellipse. Again, these points only snap to the guides if they move close enough to the guide. The Free-hand tool snaps to the guides as you approach them while creating the outline. Moving away from the guide stops the snap operation.

Unfortunately, there is no indication what the term "close" means in relation to snapping selections. Visually, you need to have the selection rather close to the guide, but the number of pixels (or inches or centimeters, depending on how the resolution is set in the `gimprc` file[5]) required to make the snap occur is not obvious. There is no way to specify what this measure should be, either. You simply need to experiment with the feature to get used to where snapping might occur. Then again, if you want snapping to occur, just start and/or end

---

5.   See **Appendix A - The gimprc File**.

your selection on the guides. If the snapping effect is annoying, and you don't want to remove or move the guides from their current positions, use the *View->Snap To Guides* menu option to turn off the feature.

Saving and Retrieving Selections

A selection is saved to a channel.

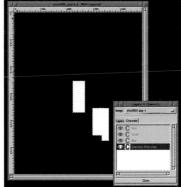

The layers visibility has been turned off and the channels turned on, showing the saved selection.

Selections can often be frustrating to deal with when they require extensive planning and precise placement, as with Bézier selections. When it is necessary to repeat selections or use similar ones, it would be helpful if you could simply save the selection and use it again later. Well, you can. The Image Window menu option *Select->Save to Channel* allows you to save a selection as a mask. It can be retrieved later using the Fuzzy selection or through the select *Select->By Color* menu option.

Saving the selection is simple enough. First, create the selection using one of the methods described in this chapter. Be sure the marching ants are displayed, signifying the selection is active. Next, choose the *Select->Save To Channel* menu option. This will create a new channel in the Channels window of the Layers and Channels dialog. The new channel will not be visible by default (the Eye icon will not be displayed next to it in the Channels window), but that doesn't matter. Once the channel has been created, it can be retrieved at any time. Be sure to name the selection so you can easily identify it later.

Named Buffers dialog

To retrieve a saved selection, go into the Channels window in the Layers and Channels dialog. Right click on the channel with the saved selection and select *Channel to Selection*.

More information on the use of Layers and Channels can be found in **Chapter 6 - Layers and Channels**.

Using Channels saves only the shape of a selection; it doesn't save the contents enclosed by it. Ordinarily, you would simply use *Edit->Copy* or *Edit->Cut* to save the contents of the selection. There are, however, a few other options. In the Image Window menu, under the Script-Fu submenu, you will find an option called *Selection*. This holds three options: save selection as a brush, save selection as a new image, and create a round selection. The last of these appears to simply round a rectangular selection or, if a rectangular selection does not exist, create a circular selection of a given radius. The first of the three options, save *To Brush*, will save the contents of a selection to a brush file in the user's .gimp/brushes directory. By default, the brush file name will be SlothBrush.gbr, but this can be changed in the dialog for this feature. Finally, the selection can be saved to a new image, using the save *To Image* option, which simply copies the selection to a new image window. If no selection is present, the entire current layer is copied to a new image window.

The contents of a selection can be saved in a number of ways. The *Edit* submenu in the Image Window menu offers several options for saving and retrieving image data from a selection. A selection can be cut from a layer or image using the *Edit->Cut* option. This will remove the pixels bounded by the selection (with appropriate feathering applied) to the default edit buffer. The *Edit->Copy* option works similarly by copying the bounded pixels to the default edit buffer. However, copying the selection does not remove the pixels from the layer or image.

Both *Cut* and *Copy* make use of the default edit buffer. This buffer is used by the *Edit->Paste* option to retrieve saved selections. An initial Cut or Copy operation will fill the default edit buffer, and any subsequent cuts or copies will overwrite that buffer. Alternatively, you can use *named buffers* to save selections. A named buffer is basically the same as the default buffer, except that you can have as many named buffers as you'd like. To use a named buffer, you would use either the *Edit->Cut Named* or *Edit->Copy Named* menu options. Retrieving the contents of the named buffer is done through the use of the *Edit->Paste Named* option.

Selections saved to the default edit buffer are usually retrieved with the *Edit->Paste* option. This option retrieves the saved selection as it looked originally. Another option, *Edit->Paste Into*, will paste the saved selection into a new selection. To use this, create an initial selection and copy it to the default edit buffer. Then create another selection. Choose the *Edit->Paste Into* option from the Image Window menu. The saved selection will be placed in the new selection with the new selection's outline becoming gray and unmoving. The pasted selection will hold the marching ants outline until it has been anchored to the new selection. You must anchor the pasted selection to return the marching ants to the new selection.

If the saved selection is not the same shape and size as the new selection, the new selection will be used as a mask for the paste operation. The pasted selection can be moved around the new selection, allowing you to position the former in the latter before anchoring it to the new selection. Once anchored, the marching ants return to the new selection and only that part of the pasted selection within the bounds of the new selection will be visible. Alternatively, you can create a new layer from the pasted selection. The new layer will also contain only that part of the pasted selection which falls within the bounds of the new selection; however, after creation, the new layer can be used just like any other layer.

Named buffers are pasted using a dialog window. The dialog contains a scrolled list of named buffers (the name is provided via another dialog when using the *Cut Named* or *Copy Named* options), a toggle button used to determine if the pasted selection should replace any existing selections, a Paste button, a Delete button, and a Cancel button. After selecting a named buffer from the list, click on the Paste button to have it pasted into the Image Window. If the *Replace Current Selection* toggle button is on (depressed), then any existing selections will be replaced by the pasted selection. If it is not, then the paste operation works like a *Paste Into* operation used with the default buffer. The Delete button in the dialog is used to delete a named buffer. The Cancel button closes the dialog without making any changes.

Finally, the *Edit->Copy Visible* menu option will copy the contents of the Image Window as they appear, even if there is more than one layer, to the default edit buffer. The other Copy and Cut operations only work on the currently active layer, so the results of an *Edit->Copy* and an *Edit->Copy Visible,* for example, can have quite different results.

All pasted selections cause a floating selection to be created. The floating selection will need to be either anchored (i.e., merged with the currently selected layer) or turned into a new layer before further processing of other layers can be done. See **Chapter 6 - Layers and Channels** for more on Layers.

The Undo (CTRL-z) and Redo (CTRL-r) functions do not affect the contents of either the default edit buffer or the named buffers.

Modifiers

Most of the save/retrieve operations for selections are available directly from the keyboard. The following table summarizes the default keyboard shortcuts. Note that the SHIFT key is used as a modifier to use named buffers for cut/copy/paste instead of the default edit buffer.

Save/Retrieve Operation	Shortcut
Cut	CTRL-x
Copy	CTRL-c
Paste	CTRL-v
Paste Into	No default
Cut Named	SHIFT-CTRL-x
Save Named	SHIFT-CTRL-c
Paste Named	SHIFT-CTRL-v
Copy Visible	No default

Stroking Selections

The GIMP does not have any built-in tools that would normally be considered line drawing tools. The Pencil, Brush, and Airbrush are close, but these are only good for freehand drawing techniques and do not lend themselves well to drawing distinct shapes. A plug-in called GFig became available late in the development cycle for the GIMP and is included in the 1.0 release. You can, of course, retrieve it from the GIMP Registry if it is not available with your version of the GIMP.

The Plug-In Registry is located at `http://registry.gimp.org/`.

Despite the lack of line drawing tools, it is possible to do some simple line drawing. Each of the Pencil, Paintbrush, and Airbrush tools can draw straight lines using keyboard modifiers (see **Chapter 8 - Drawing and Painting**). Beyond this, it is possible to draw lines around the border of a selection by using what is known as a *stroke path*. The stroke path takes the currently selected brush type and the current background color and traces a path around the outline of the selection. The brush dialog options, discussed in **Chapter 3 - GIMP Windows**, are used to determine which brush will be used and how it will be applied. Be certain to select the background color prior to using the *Edit->Stroke* menu option.

Stroked paths will follow the outline of the current selection, even if the current selection is not contiguous. This means if the selection you've made has a number of separate, closed regions, they will each be stroked using this feature. By default, the stroke function does not have a keyboard shortcut.

A stroked selection, using the stag brush.

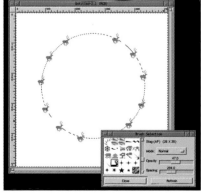

Same stroke, but with wider brush settings and lower opacity.

Moving On

Much of this chapter was about the use of Layers and Channels with selections. This is due to the fact that the use of selections is highly intertwined with the use of Layers and Channels—it is difficult to talk about one without discussing the other. Hopefully, you aren't too confused about this. If you are, then the next chapter, **Layers and Channels**, should help clear the air.

Tutorial

Selections are an important and frequently used part of the GIMP. Effective use of selections comes from a real understanding of how to use each type of selection, how to combine selections, and from just plain practice.

Let's take another look at the Bézier selection tool, which is arguably the toughest to master yet most versatile selection tool you will use. Before we start, be sure you have reset all your tools to their defaults. If you aren't sure if you have, simply exit and restart the GIMP. While you're learning the ins and outs, restarting is usually the simplest (if not the quickest) way to get back to a known starting point.

To start this tutorial, open a new 256x256 pixel Image Window with a white background. Pull two guides down from the top ruler and two guides from the left ruler. Space the guides so they form a rough square shape where they intersect.

Choose the Elliptical selection tool from the Toolbox. Now, starting at the upper left intersection of the guides, click and drag down to the lower right intersection. With all defaults turned on, you should find it fairly easy to know when you're on the intersection points because the selection will snap to the guides automatically. Your selection should now touch all four edges of the square formed by the intersecting guides.

Now choose the Bucket Fill tool. The default for this tool is to flood fill a region with the foreground color. In this case (with all defaults set), you should have a black foreground. With the Bucket Fill tool chosen, click inside the oval selection you just made. It should fill with a solid black color. Press CTRL-SHIFT-a to turn the current selection off.

It's time to try the Bézier tool. This is the most simple case for the Bézier selection—creating an oval selection (actually, making a square selection is even easier since you don't have to modify the control points at all for straight edged selections using the Bézier tool). We're simply going to practice moving the control points to create curves from the initial selection outline.

Click on the Bézier tool icon in the Toolbox. Now, click on or near the points on the black oval where it touches the guides in the Image Window. Start at the top of the oval, then to the right, bottom, and left sides. Click inside the first control point to finish this process. You should now have a diamond-shaped outline (not a selection yet!) with four control points. It might be a slightly skewed diamond or slightly mashed diamond. The beauty of the Bézier tool is that you can fix all this before creating the final selection!

Now click inside one of the control points, holding down the left mouse button and the CTRL key at the same time. Move the control point around a little to get the feel of how to adjust these points. Click on another control point and try again. If you click and drag, even just a little, without or before holding down the CTRL key, you will see the spline handles and won't be able to move the control point. This can get confusing, but just click on another control point to hide the splines and then try again.

After you've adjusted the control points so they are more properly aligned (at least to your own satisfaction), you are ready to adjust the curves between the control points. Choose one of the control points, click inside it and while holding the left mouse button down, drag the cursor. If you chose the top or bottom control points, drag left or right. If you chose the left or right points, drag up or down. For those not familiar with the term, this is "dragging at a tangent to the curve" of the black oval. Why do this? Because it makes seeing the splines and the adjusted curves easier to recognize. Remember: splines = handles. Get used to seeing them referred to either way.

When you drag, you may find that the curves have "looped" themselves. This happens when the splines are on the wrong sides of the control points. Just rotate them around to the opposite sides of the control points and you'll see what I mean. Play with this for a moment. It's important to understand how the dragging affects the curves between points.

At this stage, you are probably asking yourself "But how do I adjust only one curve and not both sides at the same time?" When you were dragging the mouse around just now, you had not selected one or the other spline specifically, so both splines were affected by the mouse movements. To change only one spline and leave the other in place, you must click on the end point of a spline and hold the SHIFT key down.

Hold down the SHIFT key, click on one spline's end box (while holding the left mouse button down) and drag it around a bit. Notice how the curve on one side of the control point moves while the other remains unchanged. Also notice the effect on the curve if you move in toward the control point or out away from the control point. Now try the other spline. Be sure to hold the SHIFT key down or you'll end up resetting the splines to their original positions, 180 degrees apart!

One last trick is to click in the control point with the CTRL key held down and with the splines displayed. If you do this, you can actually move the control point without turning off the splines. Once you've turned off the splines (by clicking on another control point), you can get them back by clicking on the first control point once again.

With all this practice, you can now try to create an oval selection of the black oval you created earlier. Go ahead, give it a try! After you've made the outline as best as you can, click inside the outline to activate the selection. The big test is to fill the selection with white (swap the default foreground/background colors and use the Bucket Fill again) and see if there are any remaining black edges. How did you do?

Just for fun

Instead of creating an exact oval outline and filling it with white, try creating an irregularly shaped outline over the black oval, turn it into a selection and fill it with another color. What do you think—instant logo? Maybe? Maybe not. But it shows that selections are not just for selecting existing regions. You can also use them to create new regions filled with colors and patterns!

Chapter 6 - Layers and Channels

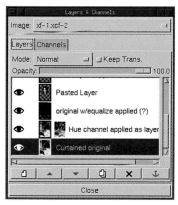

Layers and Channels dialog

The GIMP has been around for a number of years now, in what at times has seemed to be an interminable beta period. The inital release, 0.54, was based around using multiple Image Windows for a single project. These multiple windows were composited—mixed and blended—using a set of features known as Channel Operations, or more informally, *Channel Ops*. Channel Ops were quite popular. They were the basis of most major features in those early releases. The problem with using multiple windows for a single project was that it didn't take long before you had a few dozen windows opened. Soon, you could become lost trying to determine which image you wanted to use for a particular Channel Operation. Also, once you've performed a series of Channel Ops, it becomes difficult to remember, let alone reproduce, the sequence of steps you took to get a certain result.

Introduced during the lead in to the 1.0 release, *Layers* are the successor to using multiple windows for a single project. Layers allow you to have multiple images overlaid on top of each other, like a set of transparent acetate sheets. Unlike transparent sheets, layers allow you a wide range of methods for compositing the contents of each layer with the ones below it. The methods for compositing layers are known as *layer modes*. These are effectively the replacement for Channel Ops, although there are a few Channel Ops left that are accessible via the Image Window menu. Layers can be partially or fully transparent. They can be scaled, rotated, and moved. Their stacking order can be adjusted and each layer can have a mask applied, allowing only selected regions of the layer to be used in the final composite image.

Channels are a companion feature to Layers. A channel is basically a grayscale image, a mask, where higher levels of white indicate that more of the channel is to be used. There is a defined set of channels for

RGB, grayscale, and indexed images, but you can create any number of additional channels for your own use. Channels created by a user are often used as masks or to save selections or their boundaries.

Channels are used much like layers, except that channels can only be set on or off—they are not composited with layers using layer modes. Channels can be used to grab all pixels in an image with any level of red, green, or blue by using a specific channel. In this way, methods can be developed to selectively adjust color levels in an image, such as when removing a stain from a scanned version of an old photograph.

The Layers and Channels Dialog

Access to layer and channel functions is through the *Layers and Channels* dialog. This dialog is opened via the *Dialogs* submenu or from the *Layers->Layers and Channels* menu option, both found in the Image Window menu. In most cases, you will find it helpful to open this dialog soon after starting a project.

The Layers and Channels dialog consists of an options menu at the top and a notebook window with two tabs. A Close button runs along the bottom of the window, just below a set of Layer and Channel Function buttons. The options menu, labeled *Image*, is used to select the Image Window upon which you wish to work. Switching between Image Windows is fairly quick for those with few layers and small dimensions. If you are doing very large images and/or have a large number of layers in your Image Windows, you may find that switching can be a little slow, especially if you are limited in memory. More on this issue later, during the discussion on Layer Masks.

Layers Page

Layers page buttons

In the Layers and Channels dialog, the first tab in the notebook is the page for layers; the other is for channels. Click on either tab to switch pages. In the Layers page you will find a number of features, some of which are not visually apparent. The top of the page holds the Layers *Mode* options menu. Clicking on the menu will allow you to choose the method to use when compositing the current layer with layers below it.

Next to the layer modes menu is the Keep Transparency toggle. This button will be discussed a little later when we talk about using transparency in a layer. Below the menu and button is the transparency slider. This is used to adjust the overall transparency of the current layer, and will also be discussed a little later in the chapter.

Below these features you will find a scrolled window. This window is used to access each layer in the Image Window specified by the image options menu at the top of the dialog. By default, there should always be at least one layer shown, as long as you have at least one Image Window opened (if no Image Windows are open, then the scrolled window will be empty). Each layer is represented by a set of icons and text: an eye icon for layer visibility, the anchor icon, a thumbnail image, a mask thumbnail, and the layers name. A layer is *active*, or selected, when this set of icons and text have a blue background. To make a layer active, simply click once on the layer's name with the left mouse button.

The eye icon[1] is on for all layers by default. When displayed, the icon indicates that the current layer is being composited with all other visible layers to produce the image displayed in the Image Window. When the icon is absent, the layer is not composited with the other layers. To toggle the icon, just click on it with the left mouse button.

Next to the eye icon is the anchor icon. This icon is off by default. When enabled, the icon displays as the familiar move icon—the fluer. We'll discuss anchoring operations later in this chapter.

After the anchor icon comes the layer *thumbnail*. A thumbnail, in general, is simply a smaller version of a full-size image. In this case, the thumbnail is a smaller version of the contents of a layer. Thumbnails in the Layers page can be set to three different sizes. The default is to use small thumbnails, but medium and large sizes are also available. Using thumbnails requires quite a bit of extra memory. If your layers are large and you have many of them, you may want to consider turning off the thumbnails. Changing the size of the thumbnails or disabling them completely can be done via the Display page in the Preferences dialog. If the thumbnail setting is set to *None,* then the image thumbnail displays a white square with the letter "L" displayed.

Next to the image thumbnail is a thumbnail for the layers mask. A mask is a grayscale image used to determine what part of the layer's image will be used in compositing. White areas are used, black areas are not, and gray areas are used as levels of transparency for the layer's image. The display and/or size of the mask thumbnail is controlled by the same

---

1. To users in the United States, this might look a little like a flattened version of the CBS logo.

setting as the image thumbnail in the Display page of the Preferences dialog. Like the image thumbnail, the mask thumbnail displays a square with the letter "M" when the thumbnails are turned off in the Preferences dialog.

Edit Layer Attributes dialog

On the right side of the layer's entry in the scrolled window is the layer's name. When you open a new image, there will be one layer—the background layer. If you double click on the name with the left mouse button, you get a small dialog window which you can use to update the name. This is the *Edit Layer Attributes* dialog; however, with the 1.0 release, the name is the only editable attribute that can be modified using this window.

Channels Page

Channels page buttons

The Channels page in the Layers and Channels dialog is similar to the Layers page, except that there are no modes or transparency settings for channels. The scrolled window shows each of the available channels in the current image. Channels are not specific to individual layers—they exist as components of the overall image. However, you can use any or all of the channels to affect the status of the currently active layer. This is done by making individual channels active or inactive by clicking on the channel name before you make changes to the image.

Edit Channel Attributes dialog

Channels page dialog

114

Like the Layers page, the entries in the Channels page consist of a number of features. The eye icon represents the visibility of the channel, just like in the Layers page. There is a grayscale thumbnail for the channels which shows that portion of the current layer to which the current channel is related. Like their layer thumbnail counterparts, the channel thumbnails will display a white square with a "C" when the thumbnails are turned off in the Preferences dialog.

Channels come in two forms: the reserved color channels and channel masks. The reserved color channels are named *Red*, *Green*, and *Blue* for RGB images, *Indexed* for indexed images and *Gray* for grayscale images. These channels cannot be deleted or modified directly. They are used to select a particular component of each pixel of the image for modification—a way of selectively addressing the color components of all the pixels at a time. The other form of channel is channel masks. These are similar to layer masks, but are not tied to individual layers. They also have a color component that layer masks do not.

Each channel has a name. The names for the reserved color channels cannot be changed. Other channels, such as those created by saving selections to channels, can be named in the same manner as layers are named. The dialog that opens when you click on a channel mask is the *Edit Channel Attributes* dialog. It contains a field for setting the channel's name, a fill opacity slider, a color selection panel and the OK/Close buttons. Changing the name simply requires typing a new name and clicking on the OK button. The opacity slider determines how much the channel will affect the current layer. Lower values make the channel more transparent; higher values make it more opaque. When fully opaque, the channel's levels of white will completely determine how much of the layer is visible. With lower levels of opacity, more of the original image shows through the channels mask. The effect is that the darker areas of the channel will darken the original image. Lighter areas of the channel will cause the original image to be changed very little or not at all.

The *Color Selection* panel in the Edit Channel Attributes dialog is used to select the color of the mask that the channel will use as a blend with the original image. Clicking on the panel will open the Color Selection dialog (see **Chapter 7 - Colors and Text**) which can be used to select a color for the mask. By default, the channel color is black (except for the named color channels—they have a specific color that is not modifiable). That means where the grayscale thumbnail is black, the image will be black. Where the thumbnail is white, the image will be its original color. If the color panel is changed to blue, then the image will be blue where the thumbnail is black.

Gray regions of the thumbnail composite the original image color with the channel's blend color. This may seem a little confusing at first, but play with it a little while and the effect becomes more obvious.

Note that only non-reserved channels can have their opacity or blend color changed. You cannot edit these attributes for the reserved color channels (red, green, blue, indexed, and gray). Also, the Edit Channel Attributes dialog does not preview the changes you make in the Image Window. You must click on the OK button for the changes to become visible. The Undo and Redo features do not manage changes to Channels, so be sure you know the current channel attribute settings before you change them so that you can change them back manually if needed.

Each entry in the scrolled window of the Channels page represents a different channel. For RGB images there are three default channels, one each for red, green, and blue. By default, all three of these channels are active—they all have the blue background. If you make one of these inactive (by clicking the left mouse button on the channel name) then any changes you make to the current layer will affect only the other two channels in that layer. When you click on a mask channel to make it active, all of the reserved channels will become gray—you cannot select a particular color channel on which to apply changes via a mask channel. In other words, changes to mask channels affect all the reserved color channels the same way.

   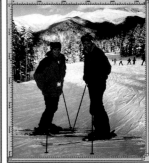

Figure A. An original scan is too dark. We need to adjust it a little.

Figure B. With all three color channels active, the brightness and contrast are adjusted to higher levels using the Image->Colors->Brightness and Contrast dialog. Both slider settings are set to the value 49. This helps with the original darkness, but now the colors are washed out.

Figure C. Reverting to the original again, we adjust only the blue color channel this time. Both brightness and contrast values are set to 49, but again, only for the blue channel. This looks very blue compared to the original, but the colors stand out more.

Figure D. Now we can adjust the image brightness and contrast for the image in Figure C. This time we set the brightness to 49 but the contrast we raise to 62. The image now has slightly more vibrant blues than the original adjustment in Figure B and the colors are no longer washed out.

Using the channel mask opacity and color panel—original image before editing.

The sky has been selected and the channel mask color panel has been set to blue. The opacity of the mask is set to 50%.

Same image, but the opacity setting has been moved to 99%. Note that the maximum level for the opacity setting in this dialog is 99%.

The channel mask used in these examples. The selection of the sky was made using a combination of the Select by Color and Free-hand selection tools.

The Layers Menu

Both layers and channels come with menus that are accessible by holding down the right mouse button over the layer or channel name. The Layers menu consists of fifteen options. The following table summarizes each of the options.

Layers Menu Option	Shortcut	Description
New Layer	CTRL-n	Creates a new layer above currently selected layer.
Raise Layer	CTRL-f	Raises the currently selected layer one level in stack.
Lower Layer	CTRL-b	Lowers the currently selected layer one level in stack.
Duplicate Layer	CTRL-c	Creates an exact duplicate of the currently selected layer.
Delete Layer	CTRL-x	Deletes all traces of the currently selected layer from stack.
Scale Layer	CTRL-s	Enlarges or shrinks a layer.
Resize Layer	CTRL-r	Extends or clips the borders of a layer, without affecting the layer contents.
Add Layer Mask	none	Enables a layer mask, which turns on the mask thumbnail for the layer.
Apply Layer Mask	none	Applies the current layer's mask to the layer's image or discards the mask, at the user's discretion.
Anchor Layer	CTRL-h	Composites a floating layer with the layer that was currently selected prior to the creation of the floating layer.
Merge Visible Layers	CTRL-m	Composites the currently visible layers.
Flatten Image	none	Creates one layer, composited from all the others plus all channels.
Alpha To Selection	none	Creates a selection from all opaque and semitransparent parts of a layer.
Mask To Selection	none	Creates a selection in the shape of the current layers mask, if it has one.
Add Alpha Channel	none	Creates an alpha channel for layers which don't contain them.

Not all options are available for all layers. Only layers that do not have alpha channels will have access to the *Add Alpha Channel* option, for example. Similarly, only floating layers will have access to the *Anchor Layer* option. There are other similar situations. If an option is not available, it will be grayed out.

Some of the Layers menu options are also available via the buttons along the bottom of the Layers and Channels dialog. These buttons, from left to right, provide the ability to add a new layer, raise, lower, duplicate or delete the current layer, or anchor a new layer, respectively. There is no difference between using these buttons or their equivalent Layers menu options, except it is a little more obvious how to access the functions provided by the buttons (simply because they are already visible).

Layer Ordering

Layers are displayed in the scrolled window in their stacking order. The first layer is the one on the top, the last layer is the one at the bottom. In the Image Window the image is displayed by compositing the layers starting with the bottom layer and moving up the stacking order. As you see, the order of the layers is important. Moving a layer up or down the stack is done using the Layers menu. The *Raise Layer* option will move the current layer up one level in the stack. The *Lower Layer* option moves it down one level. Keep in mind that the Layers menu operations start on the layer from which the menu is opened. This should be obvious, since when you click on the layer's name to open the menu, that layer becomes the active layer.

If a layer does not have an alpha channel, it cannot be raised above a layer that does have one. In most cases this only happens if you try to raise the background layer or lower a layer below the background layer. You can fix this problem simply by adding an alpha channel to the layer by using the *Add Alpha Channel* option.

Duplicating a layer copies the entire layer, opaque and transparent pixels alike, to a new layer. The new layer inherits the same name as the original with the word copy appended to it. The duplicate will always be added as a new layer directly above the original in the layer stack.

Scaling and Resizing

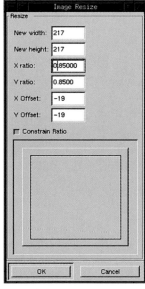

Scale dialog

Layers can have any dimensions, not just the dimensions of the visible Image Window. This means that a layer can be wider or taller than the Image Window. It can also be thinner and shorter. Anything outside the layer boundaries is considered transparent if it falls within the boundaries of the Image Window, is ignored if it is outside. The layer's size can be adjusted in two different ways: by scaling the layer or by resizing it.

Selecting the *Scale Layer* option in the Layers Menu opens a dialog that allows you to specify the new dimensions for the layer. The dimensions can be specified either in units of width and height or by specifying a change in width and height ratios. An X ratio of 1.5, for example, would increase the layer's size by 1.5 times its current width. The width/height units or ratios can be constrained as well. The *Constrain Ratio* toggle is used to force recalculation of the dimension not specifically set. Using the previous example, with the Constrain Ratio toggle set, the Y ratio would change to 1.5 also. By default, the Constrain Ratio is already turned on.

Scaling a layer causes the GIMP to recompute the layer's contents to stretch or shrink it to fit the new size. This changes the actual contents of the layer. Alternatively, the layer can be resized using the *Resize Layer* menu option. This option also has its own dialog window. Like the Scale Layer dialog, the Resize Layer dialog allows you to specify either unit or ratio dimensions. Additionally, you can specify X and Y offsets. Resizing the layer is like placing a window over the layer and moving it around—what you can see through the window is the region that the new layer will contain after the resize operation. To show this, the dialog has a window pane beneath the Constrain Ratio toggle. The window shows the relationship between the current layer and the way the layer will look after the resize operation. If the new size is larger than the current size, the window shows the original as a raised area. The smaller the raised area, the larger the new size in comparison. If the new size is smaller than the original, the window shows the new size as a box outline inside the raised area. The smaller the outline, the smaller the new size in comparison.

Resize dialog

Saving Layers - Flattening and Merging

When you are working with the GIMP you use layers to more easily modify selected portions of the composite image. The layers are images in their own right, however. When you save images, you need to determine if you will be saving the image as it is displayed in the Image Window, if you want to save the layer information, or if you want to save an individual layer.

Saving the image with layer information intact requires that you save the image using the XCF[2] file format. This is the GIMP native file format. All information, including layers, channels and guides, is saved to a file. Because the amount of information saved can be quite large, the file size will generally be considerably larger than a JPEG-, TIFF-, or GIF- formatted file of the same dimensions.

A layered image that is to have two of its layers merged.

None of the other file formats supported by the GIMP will support saving the layer information intact. If you save the image to TIFF, for example, only the currently active layer will go in the TIFF file. The same is true for any other format you use beside XCF. This can be useful if you simply want to save a single layer to an image file of its own. For example, you may want to save the layers of an image as a series of JPEG-formatted files. These could then be combined at some point in the future using external tools to create an MPEG animation.[3]

Layers to be merged are visible—their eye icon is displayed.

But then, what do you do when you are ready to save the file as it appears in the Image Window? At that point, you need to flatten the image using the *Flatten Image* option in the Layers menu. This will combine all of the layers in the image into a single layer. This layer will have the same dimensions as the Image Window. If the background layer—the bottom layer in the stack—included any transparent regions, then the flattened image will also include transparent regions. Layer transparency is discussed later in this chapter.

Flattening an image will composite all the layers in the image that are marked as visible in the Layers and Channels dialog. Those layers that are not visible are discarded. Often, you will find it useful to combine only a select group of layers, leaving all others in place and untouched. In this case, you will want to use the *Merge Visible Layers* option. This option combines all layers that are marked visible into a single layer,

---

2. See **Chapter 2 - GIMP Basics**.
3. The 1.0 version of the GIMP does not support creation of MPEG files directly. You would have to use the JPEG files with some other tool, such as `mpeg_encode`, to create the MPEG animation.

but leaves the layers that are not visible in place. The composited new layer inherits the name and position of the lowest visible layer in the stack.

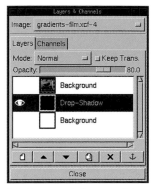

The Layers and Channels dialog after merging has taken place. Note that the merged layer inherited the lowest visible layer's position in the stack and its name.

A merged layer gets its dimensions through the Layers Merge dialog. This dialog opens when *Merge Visible Layers* is chosen from the Layers menu. There are three possible dispositions for the merged layer: expand as necessary, clipped to image, and clipped to bottom layer. The first of these will cause the merged layer to inherit the largest dimensions among all the layers used to create the composite. The second option, clipped to image, will force the merged layer to be no wider or taller than the Image Window display dimensions. Clipping the merged layer to the bottom layer will force the merged layer to fit the dimensions of the last layer in the stack of visible layers. In other words, the merged layer will have the same dimensions as the lowest visible layer. The first and last options differ from flattening in that the merged layer can still be larger or smaller than the Image Window display dimensions. The second option can be smaller than the image displayed, but never larger.

The Channels Menu

Like the Layers page, the Channels page also offers a Channels menu, which is accessible by clicking the right mouse button over the channel name. Unlike the Layers menu, however, the Channels menu offers only six options. These six options, similar to their Layers menu counterparts, are described in the following table.

Channels Menu Option	Shortcut	Description
New Channel	CTRL-n	Creates a new channel above currently selected layer.
Raise Channel	CTRL-f	Raises the currently selected channel one level in stack.
Lower Channel	CTRL-b	Lowers the currently selected channel one level in stack.
Duplicate Channel	CTRL-c	Creates an exact duplicate of the currently selected channel.
Delete Channel	CTRL-x	Deletes all traces of the currently selected channel from stack.
Channel to Selection	CTRL-s	Creates a selection from the channel.

All of these options work just like their layer counterparts. The *Channel to Selection* option works like the layer's *Alpha to Selection*, where the opaque and semitransparent regions of the channel are converted into a selection.

Creating a new channel will open the New Channel dialog, which is exactly the same as the Edit Channel Attributes dialog in look and function.

The currently active channels have the now familiar blue background. However, since there are two forms of channels, the grayed out options in the Channel menu differ depending on which channel types are active. If the reserved color channels are active, then only the New and Duplicate options are available. In reality, only the New option really does anything: it will create a new channel mask. Clicking on a channel mask will gray out the reserved color channels and give you access to all the options in the Channels menu. Clicking on the channel mask again will switch the active channels back to the reserved color channels.

Using Layer Modes

These mode examples are used to show how modes work when combined with an original image. The examples start with a background layer of a veined Pink Marble, add a slightly smaller layer of Topographics Oceans,[4] and adjust contrast and brightness of both layers to bring out color variations. These two patterns were chosen not because they look good together, but because their color differences show the effects of all modes fairly well.

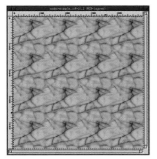
Background veined Pink Marble layer

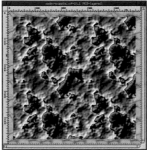
Topographic layer on top of background in normal mode

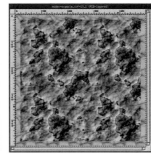
Dissolve

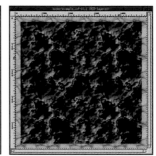
Multiply

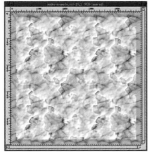
Screen

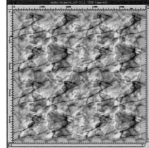
Overlay

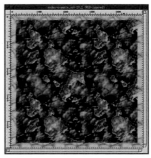
Difference

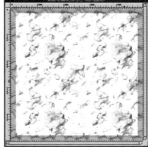
Addition

---

4.   Both the Pink Marble and Topographic Oceans are patterns available in the default distribution of the GIMP.

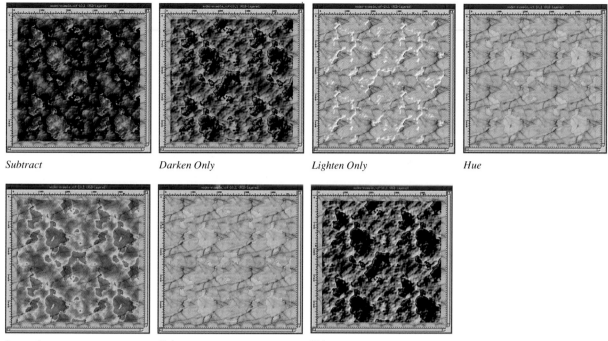

Subtract   *Darken Only*   *Lighten Only*   *Hue*

Saturation   *Color*   *Value*

Any layer can be composited in one of 14 ways with the layers below it in the stack. The methods of compositing are called Layer Modes and are accessed from the *Mode* options menu in the Layers page of the Layers and Channels dialog. Although this menu is specific to the Layers page, the use of these 14 composite modes can be found in numerous places in the GIMP: gradients, brushes, and bucket fills for example. It is highly recommended that you learn how each of these modes works, since odds are that you will be making use of them often. The following table summarizes the different layer modes.

Layer Mode	Description
Normal	The fully opaque pixels in the current layer replace the corresponding pixels of any layers beneath it. Transparent and semitransparent pixels are composited with the underlying pixels on a percentage basis.
Dissolve	Used in conjunction with transparency slider to produce grainy effects.
Multiply	Multiplies current layer with lower layers and divides by 255. Tends to darken the visible image.
Screen	Brightens images, bringing out highlights.
Overlay	Brings out the color intensities of the image.
Difference	Subtracts lower layers from the current layer and takes the absolute value of the result. This has a tendency to create somewhat psychedelic colors in the resulting image.
Addition	The color of a pixel in the current layer is added to the color of the composited pixel of all underlying layers to give the visible pixel. The maximum value for the addition is 255, which is the color white.
Subtract	Subtracts lower layers from the current layer, clamping the result to black if necessary. This will dramatically darken images. It can also be used to create ghosted effects where one image has been removed from another.
Darken Only	If the lower layer color component is darker than the current layer, uses the lower layer's component. If not, uses the current layer's. Works on each channel individually for all pixels in the current layer.
Lighten Only	Same as Darken Only, but the choice is made by which layer component is lighter.
Hue	Takes the hue content of the lower layers and replaces it with the hue content of the current layer. Useful for shifting the color in an image without affecting its brightness.
Saturation	Same as Hue, except the saturation content is used. This will wash the colors out of an image, desaturating it.
Color	A combination of Hue and Saturation modes, this leaves only the lightness from the lower layer pixels.
Value	Same as Hue, except that the value content is used.

In *Normal* mode, if a pixel is semitransparent then the resulting pixel color is taken by calculating the current layer's pixel value times the opacity and combining it with the lower layer's pixel value times the transparency of the current layer. Keep in mind that the transparency of the current layer is one minus the opacity of the current layer.

Dissolve works by taking a random number and comparing it to the current transparency level. If the random number is greater than the transparency, then the pixel is fully transparent. If not, then it is either fully opaque or, if it already contained some transparency, retains its current transparency. This produces a grainy effect on the image. The lower the opacity setting, the higher the number of transparent regions in the current layer and the more grainy the image will appear.

Multiplying a layer with the layers below it is like stacking two acetate sheets and shining a light through them. Where the colors of both sheets are dark, the resulting image is dark because less light gets through. White parts in the current layer have no effect on the resulting image— they are neutral in a multiply operation. The transparency of the resulting image is either the minimum transparency (highest opacity) between the current and lower layers, or simply the transparency of the lower layers (if the current layer does not have an alpha channel). If neither has any transparency, nor will the resulting image.

The *Screen* mode works by combining the brightness of the current layer with the layers below it. Screening a layer causes the current layer to act somewhat like a mask, but instead of indicating which areas are visible, it decides which areas to brighten. The current layer's whitest areas cause the most brightening. The darkest areas cause the least amount of change to the visible pixels.

An *Overlay* is actually a combination of a Screen and a Multiply of the current layer with the underlying pixels. The effect is that the current layer causes the underlying pixel's color intensities to become stronger. Reds get redder, blues get bluer, yellows get—well, yellower. Whereas white is neutral in Multiply and black is neutral in Screen mode, 50% gray is neutral in Overlay mode. This makes the Overlay mode good for use with the emboss filter to create the illusion of three dimensions in the image.

Addition adds the pixel colors to calculate the resulting color, with a maximum value of 255 (white). This decreases the overall color intensity of the composited layers.

Difference and *Subtract* are almost exactly the same—the lower layer's pixel values are subtracted from the current layer's pixels. In Subtract mode, if the result is a negative value it is set to zero (black). You may hear this referred to as clamping the value to 0. In Difference mode, if the result is negative then the sign is removed from the result so that the resulting pixel is something other than black.

Darken Only, *Lighten Only*, *Hue*, *Saturation*, *Color*, and *Value* modes all work on each of the individual channels of the pixels. Keep in mind that all layers in an image must be of the same image type (RGB, grayscale, or indexed) although they may or may not each have an alpha channel. The Hue, Saturation, and Value modes first convert the RGB value of a pixel into HSV color space to determine which parts of the pixels to use.

Using Layer Masks

Layer Masks dialog

Some of the most useful features of layers are *masks*. These are grayscale images used to determine which parts of the layer are visible and which are not. In the mask, white pixels mean that the corresponding pixel in the layer is visible. Black areas in the mask hide the corresponding pixels in the layer. The gray areas of the mask make the corresponding pixels in the layer semitransparent. This transparency is combined with whatever transparency the pixel originally had. You can use layer masks to clean up the edges of a selection, making it appropriate for a matte[5] operation. You can also use layer masks to fade one layer into another by using a gradient. Masks and gradients provide some powerful effects in the compositing of layers.

---

5. A matte is where one image is superimposed on another, making it look like the former was originally part of the latter. Matte images are commonly used as special effects in movies.

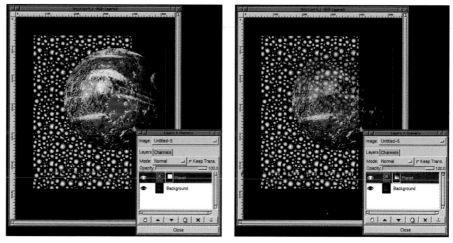

Original image with a fully white layer mask.

Default gradient applied from upper right to lower middle of the layer mask.

Layers and Channels dialog with medium sized thumbnails showing the gradient as it was applied to the layer mask.

To create a layer mask, select the *Add Layer Mask* option from the Layers menu. This will open a small dialog titled Add Mask Options. Three toggle buttons in the dialog allow you to specify how the mask will be created. The first toggle, *White*, will create a fully white mask. This mask will not affect the visible image when it is created. The second toggle, *Black*, will create a fully black mask. This has the effect of hiding the current layer from the composite image displayed in the Image Window. The last toggle, *Layer's Alpha Channel*, will create a mask that contains black in all transparent regions of the layer and gray to white everywhere else (depending on whether the pixels in the layer have any transparency in them). Effectively, this creates a grayscale version of the transparency levels in the layer. Once created, this mask will have no visible effect on the image displayed in the Image Window.

After creating the mask, you'll need to edit it. To do so, first click on the mask's thumbnail in the Layers and Channels dialog. This will activate the mask for that layer (you can see this by the white box drawn around the thumbnail). Any edits you make will show up in the mask thumbnail (if the thumbnails are turned on in the Preferences dialog). Drawing or painting in the mask with any color except black will cause black or gray regions to become white, which will allow more of the layer to become visible. Erasing the mask will turn the mask black in

129

those regions, and the visible parts of the layer will decrease. This will also happen if you paint or draw with black ink.[6]

After you have completed your edits on the mask, you may wish to perform more edits on the layer itself. To make the layer image active, click on the image's thumbnail. The thumbnail will be outlined by a white box to show it has been activated.

Alpha Channels for Layers

Like the red, green, and blue channels, which each determine the amount of a particular color in each pixel, the *Alpha* channel describes the amount of transparency for each pixel. Most layers are created with alpha channels, but not all. Adding an alpha channel is often necessary for the background layer that is created when a new Image Window is opened. To add the channel, simply choose the *Add Alpha Channel* option from the Layers menu.

When you are working with layer masks, you are really working with the alpha channel of the layer image. You do this by specifying how much of the image will be opaque and how much will be transparent once the mask is applied to the image. By default, the effect of the mask is immediately visible if the layer is visible. However, the layer image itself is not modified until the layer mask is actually applied to it.

Applying and Discarding Masks

Until the layer mask is applied to the layer image, the GIMP has to compute the transparency of the image based on the composition of the layer image and its mask. If you apply the layer mask to the layer image, you reduce some of that computational overhead.

To apply a layer mask to the layer image, you use the *Apply Layer Mask* option in the Layers menu. A dialog window opens that allows you to specify whether you truly want to apply the layer or discard it. You may find your work with the mask has not turned out as you expected and you want to start over. In that case, it will be necessary to use the *Discard* option of the dialog. Other times, you may find you aren't quite done with the mask, but you need to apply some filter to the layer image and the filter won't work on layers with masks. In that case, you will

6. Selecting colors for paint and draw operations is discussed in the next chapter, **Chapter 7 - Colors and Text**.

want to discard the mask, apply the filter, and then recreate the mask. After you've used the GIMP for awhile, remembering the filters which do not work with layers that contain masks will be second nature to you, and mixing their use with masks will seem less intrusive.

Masks can also be made into selections. The *Mask to Selection* option in the Layers menu will create a selection around all non-black pixels in the mask. This selection can be used just like any other selection, including saving it to a channel.

The Layers menu options *Mask to Selection* and *Apply Layer Mask* are available only if the layer already has a mask. The former will create a selection based on the mask which you can then use on the mask, the current layer image, or another layer (once a selection has been created on one layer, you can change layers and use it on another!).

Selections can be made on any one layer image or layer mask and used on another layer image or mask simply by clicking on a different layer thumbnail. Selections are discussed in **Chapter 5 - Selections**.

Enabling and Disabling the Layer Mask and the Layer Image

While working on a layer mask, you may find it useful to see the mask in its full glory in the Image Window. The mask will become visible when you hold down the ALT key and click on the mask thumbnail. When you do this, the border around the mask will turn green and the Image Window will display the grayscale mask. You can zoom in and make modifications using any of the drawing and painting tools. Keep in mind that any drawing or painting in the window will always be black, gray or white, no matter what color the foreground color window is in the Toolbox. The Eraser tool will always use the grayscale version of the background color with the mask pixels. If the background is a dark color, then light pixels in the mask get darker and dark pixels are unchanged. If the background color is light, then dark pixels in the mask get light and light pixels are unchanged. When you are done working on the mask, use the ALT-click combination again to toggle the mask's visibility.

Alternatively, you can view a layer without its mask (if it has one) by pressing the CTRL key and clicking the left mouse button over the mask thumbnail. To show that the mask is turned off, the mask thumbnail border turns purple.

Note that if the layer image is active, not the layer mask, then the CTRL and ALT modifiers have no effect. You can click on the thumbnails a few times to see the border bounce back and forth. Although not always obvious, after a time you should be able to recognize at first glance which thumbnail is bordered.

Layer Visibility and Transparency

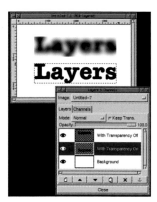

A layer is visible when the eye icon for that layer in the Layers and Channels dialog is visible. When a layer is visible, it means that the layer is used by the GIMP when it computes the composite image you see in the Image Window. If the layer is not visible, it is not included in the composite. By default, new layers are set to visible when created. Channels, on the other hand, are created invisible. If you want to use them in the composite image, you have to manually click their eye icon.

The first text layer has a Gaussian Blur of 25 pixels applied to it, but with the Keep Transparency toggle on the effect is unnoticable.

The eye icon is an all-or-nothing choice. It determines whether the layer (and its mask, if it has one, or a channel) is used in the composite image. The layer can also have multiple forms of transparency. The entire layer can be made fully or partially transparent using the *Opacity* slider in the Layers page of the Layers and Channels dialog. Moving the slider to the left will decrease the layer's opacity, thereby increasing its transparency. The amount of transparency defined by the slider is applied equally to all pixels in the layer.

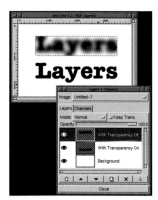

Each pixel in an image can also have its own amount of transparency. Feathered selections cause pixels in the feathered region to become increasingly transparent, starting with no transparency on the inside of the selection and moving to fully transparent at the outer edge. This form of transparency is referred to as the *alpha channel* for the layer. It can be adjusted to higher levels of transparency through the use of layer masks. Once a mask is applied to a layer image, however, the transparency level of the alpha channel cannot be reduced without combining it with another layer.

Another layer has the toggle turned off. The blurring is obvious here. Note that the blur process did not bleed outside the edges of the text layer!

The amount of transparency applied to any given pixel is based on the value of its alpha channel and the Opacity slider setting. These two values are combined, up to a maximum setting which makes the pixel fully transparent. If the layer also includes a layer mask, then the transparency of the pixel is computed by applying the layer mask to the pixel's alpha channel and then adding in the Opacity slider value. If the layer mask is turned off (CTRL-click), then the mask is not used in the computations.

Transparency can be used to form boundaries around images. The *Alpha to Selection* option in the Layers menu will create a selection of all pixels whose opacity value is greater than zero—that is, any pixels that are not fully transparent. Similarly, if the *Keep Transparency* toggle is turned on, then filter effects such as blur will stop when they get to the fully transparent pixels. Turning the toggle off will allow the effects to "bleed" into the transparent regions if necessary. By default, the Keep Transparency toggle is on for new layers.

Layer Anchoring and Aligning

Align Layers dialog

There will be many occasions where a particular layer will not be positioned exactly as you'd like. Suppose you had a SuperNova design on one layer and it needed to be aligned underneath some text. Using the Move tool, you can move the nova layer to its appropriate position. Place the mouse over the image, press and hold the left mouse button and drag the mouse until the layer is properly positioned. There is a catch here, however—the Move tool will move the layer whose pixel is currently displayed beneath the mouse cursor! That pixel may or may not be in the current layer. When the mouse is over a visible portion of the currently active layer, the mouse cursor will change to the fluer symbol. This is how you can tell when a click-drag operation will move the current layer: if the mouse cursor is the pointing finger symbol, you are not over a visible part of the current layer. Performing a click-drag operation in this case will cause the active layer to change to whichever layer contains the visible pixel under the mouse. You can tell this happens by noting the change in the Layers and Channels dialog and by noting the layer boundary change (if the layers are of different sizes and/ or in different positions).

A text effect is created with a default Script-Fu logo script and a SuperNova filter is applied to the background layer. The nova is misaligned, however.

The nova has been moved to sit behind some of the lettering using the Move tool.

This feature of layer moving can be annoying if you have a very large image with lots of layers and limited memory. Once a move has been initiated—even if you haven't moved the layer—the GIMP will recalculate the composite image as soon as the mouse button is released. If the wrong layer has been moved, you will have to undo the move operation and then try again. This can take quite some time on large images. To avoid this problem, hold down the SHIFT key with the left mouse button click to force the move to apply to the current layer, even if the mouse is not over a visible pixel for that layer.

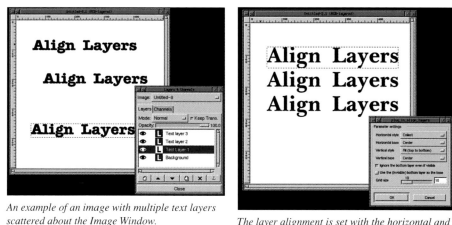

An example of an image with multiple text layers scattered about the Image Window.

The layer alignment is set with the horizontal and vertical bases centered and the vertical style top to bottom.

The alignment was changed to use a left edge for horizontal base and the bottom edge for vertical base. The horizontal style of snap to grid affected this alignment more than anything else—can you tell why?

What do you do if you wish to move more than one layer at a time? Click on the anchor icon. When displayed, the icon looks like the Move tool icon in the toolbox. This anchors the layer to all other anchored layers and the active layer. When you perform the click-drag operation to move the active layer, the anchored layers will move with it. While you move the multiple layers, an outline which encompasses all the layers involved will move around the Image Window. When you release the mouse button, the layers are repositioned and the composite image is recalculated.

With anchored layers, the mouse cursor will change to the fluer if it is over a visible pixel that belongs to any of the anchored layers, but only if the current layer is anchored too. In this case, the move operation will move all the anchored layers and the current layer. If the current layer is not anchored, then the mouse cursor will be the fluer as long as it is over a visible pixel in the current layer. If it moves over a pixel that belongs to another layer, the cursor changes to the pointing finger. If the layer that pixel belongs to is anchored, then the a click-drag operation will move all the anchored layers (plus change the currently active layer to the one to which the pixel belongs). Finally, if the current layer is not anchored but other layers are anchored, and you use the SHIFT-click-drag operation, then the anchored layers and the current layer will move in unison.

Although this may sound confusing, it really is not. Try the different combinations a few times, using an image with the default background and a couple of text layers. And if all else fails, just be sure to anchor the currently active layer before trying to move multiple layers at one time.

The anchor icon allows alignment of layers to be maintained during a move operation. Another feature of layer alignment comes from the Align Layers dialog. This dialog offers a number of different methods for aligning two or more visible layers.

The Align Layers dialog is not available from the Layers menu as you might expect. It is available only from the Image Window's menu under the *Layers* option: *Layers->Align Visible Layers*. Once the dialog has opened, you will find four options menus—two for horizontal settings and two for vertical settings. The horizontal and vertical styles define the method of alignment. The base options define where to align. The following tables summarize the options for both horizontal and vertical settings.

Base options	Meaning
Horizontal: Left Edge	Horizontal alignment is done using layer's left edges.
Horizontal: Center	Horizontal alignment is done using layer's centers.
Horizontal: Right Edge	Horizontal alignment is done using layer's right edges.
Vertical: Top Edge	Vertical alignment is done using layer's top edges.
Vertical: Center	Vertical alignment is done using layer's centers.
Vertical: Bottom Edge	Vertical alignment is done using layer's bottom edges.

Style	Meaning
None	No change to horizontal or vertical position.
Collect	Snaps lower layers to top layer positions, using the set base options.
Fill left to right/top to bottom	Aligns edges with top layer on left/top and bottom on right/bottom.
Fill right to left/bottom to top	Aligns edges with top layer on right/bottom and bottom on left/top.
Snap to grid	Snaps selected edges to nearest corner of invisible grid system.

The number of combinations possible with these options is quite large but don't let that deter you from using them. It takes only a little practice to realize, for example, that setting both the horizontal and vertical base options to center will make the layers stack up like a deck of cards (albeit with different sized cards).

Also, keep in mind that this dialog works only on visible layers. Be certain you've turned off the visibility of any layers you do not want aligned prior to using this feature.

Floating Layers

In the last chapter, we discussed how selections could be cut and pasted in Image Windows. A pasted selection becomes a *Floating Layer* in the Layers and Channels dialog. A selection can also create a floating layer using the *Float* option from the Image Window menu's *Selection* submenu.

A floating layer is a special form of layer that requires a final disposition be applied before work on other layers can continue. When a floating layer is created, it is placed at the top of the stack of layers in the Layers page of the dialog using a special icon. All other layers become grayed out (insensitive to user input). The floating layer's icon is a picture of

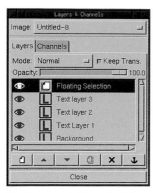

The Layers and Channels dialog with a floating layer

one piece of paper, or clear acetate sheet, over another. A floating layer will have one of two eventual dispositions: it can be anchored to the layer that was active before the floating layer was created, or it can be turned into a new layer at the top of the stack. If it is anchored using the Layers menu *Anchor Layer* option, it is immediately composited with the active layer. The composite is just between the floating layer and the active layer—no other layers are composited at this point—and the result is that it replaces the contents of the active layer. Note that the *Anchor Layer* option is available only to floating layers. All other layers have this option grayed out.

Floating layers cannot be duplicated, nor can their position be changed in the stack. They can be resized or scaled and selections can be made in them. All filters work on floating layers just as they do on normal layers. All color and transform tools also work the same in both types of layers. The Opacity slider and Keep Transparency toggle can be set on the floating layer before it is anchored or turned into a new layer. In the former case, the transparency is composited just like the color channels of the layer, and the toggle will inherit the position of the active layer's setting. The active layer will keep the Opacity slider setting it originally had prior to compositing with the floating layer.

A floating layer is created when all other layers become grayed out. When this happens, the floating layer becomes a temporary active layer and inherits the blue background. Because of this, you can't tell which layer was selected before the floating layer was created. If you think you may want to anchor the floating layer, you will want to keep track of which layer is active before the floating layer is created. If you find you've forgotten, just hit CTRL-z to undo the float operation. When you find out which layer is active, you can hit CTRL-r to redo the float operation.

Editing Channels

Up to this point in the chapter we've talked mostly about layers. Part of the reason for this is that there are far more options for layers than for channels. Still, a few things should be noted about working with channels. Most important is what sort of editing operations can be done in channels.

Color Channel Edits

If you create a selection in a particular color channel and copy it to the default (or a named) buffer, the data stored in the buffer includes all the color channels. In other words, you can't make a selection in just the red channel and save that to a buffer. You can use a selection to provide a boundary for painting operations in channels, however. The drawing, painting and eraser tools can all be used in individual color channels. Using the Eraser tool on a color channel has the effect of removing that color from the pixels over which the eraser is used. For example, selecting the red channel from the Channels page of the Layers and Channels dialog and then erasing a section of the current layer will cause the red portion of all pixels in that region to be removed (depending on the brush type, its composite mode and opacity level). The green and blue channels of the pixels are unchanged. Erasing, along with using the painting and drawing tools within the color channels, can be used to remove stains from photographs, change the color of highlights, or simply change the overall tint of an image.

Use of the color channels for editing is a somewhat advanced topic and a bit beyond the scope of this text. If you really need to edit the color channels individually, including making cut-and-paste operations, you can first decompose the image. The *Image->Channel Ops->Decompose* menu option in the Image Windows menu will create three new Image Windows that are grayscale versions of the original. Each window uses the grayscale image to specify the levels of a particular color channel. You can edit these new windows just as you do any other Image Window. When you are done editing them, you can combine them back into the original image, plus edits, by using the *Image->Channel Ops->Compose* menu option. The new composite image will have a single layer.

A couple of key points about the use of compose and decompose: first, decompose works only on RGB or RGBA images. Images with an alpha channel will still have only three new grayscale windows opened—no window is opened for the alpha channel. Decompose does not work for indexed or grayscale images. Next, decomposition will work on the active layer in an image. If there is only one layer, that layer is used. Similarly, if you compose the three grayscale images, you need to be sure they are flattened first. Composition does not work at all on images with more than one layer. If you specify an image with more than one layer in the Compose dialog, the process will not be carried out. Finally, the three grayscale windows will inherit the name of the original image, plus a suffix that names the channel from which that window was created.

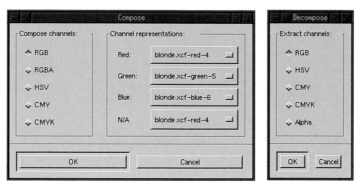

Compose dialog   *Decompose dialog*

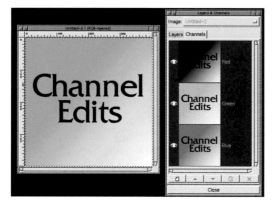

Channel editing—green gradient applied on background layer behind some text.

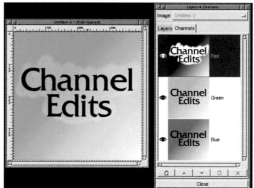

Red channel only is selected and the Eraser tool is used. The result is that the blue and green channels are left in place—leaving an orangeish region. Notice how the erased region shows up only in the red channel's thumbnail.

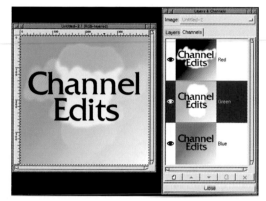

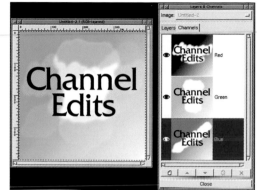

The green channel is selected next and the process repeated.

Finally, the blue channel is selected and erased. Why does some of the erased region now show up as white, while other regions show up as blue or pink?

Channel Mask Edits

Channel masks can be edited just like their layer masks' counterparts. You simply select the channel mask by clicking on it to make it active and then perform your edits. Unlike their color channel cousins, channel masks can be cut and pasted using selections. The paste operation will create a new layer, however, not a new channel mask. To make a new channel mask from an existing one, make the new layer and then, using the same selection, save the new layer to a selection using the *Selection->Save to Channel* menu option from the Image Window menu.

One last thing: edits performed on channels using the drawing and paint tools apply only to the current layer. Be certain the correct layer is selected before choosing the channel to edit.

Static vs. Animated Images

One aspect of layers that might be overlooked is their use for animations. Animations are really nothing more than a series of static images strung together to play at a certain frame rate (number of images per second or per minute). Layers are perfectly suited for creating a series of images.

To create an animation with layers, there are a couple of methods you can use. The first is to save each layer to an independent image file. For example, you click on the background layer (the first frame of the animation) and choose *File->Save As* to save the layer as a JPEG image. Then click on the next higher layer in the stack and do the same thing. After all the layers have been saved, you can combine the JPEG images into an MPEG movie using mpeg_encode.[7] This method works if you want to create an animation using any image file format other than GIF, assuming you have a tool which can later combine those files into an animation. GIF has its own method—and this is built directly into the GIMP.

Save as GIF dialog

To save a set of layers as a GIF animation, you must first convert the image from RGB or grayscale into an indexed image (if it's not already in that format). Then simply specify a .gif extension on the file name in the Save Image dialog (*File->Save as* from the menus). Leave the Determine File Type options menu set to *By Extension*. By default, the animation will loop but you can turn this off using the Loop toggle button

---

7. mpeg_encode is a tool for creating MPEG-formatted animations. The source and precompiled binaries for some UNIX platforms are available at ftp://mm-ftp.cs.berkeley.edu/pub/multimedia/mpeg/encode/.

in the Save Image dialog. Also, you can specify how layers are used in the animation—either as individual frames, or by having each layer composited with the underlying layers first and then saved as a frame.

Saving layers with the GIF Plug-In can produce an animation for you, but it may not be the most efficient GIF animation you could produce. Other tools, such as MultiGIF, may produce a smaller GIF file which would be preferable for use on web pages. The AnimOptimize Plug-In produces what are probably the smallest possible GIF animations for a given set of frames. Still, it is nice to know that you can at least quickly test the animation simply by saving it as a GIF and then loading the file into a browser that supports animated GIF images.

Moving On

This chapter focused on the use of Layers and Channels, a topic that you will find yourself referring back to repeatedly during your travels with the GIMP. We've already discussed selections and the basic tool sets of the GIMP in previous chapters, so now we're ready to talk about the use of color and text in your images. Many of your images will contain at least some text—a visible signature if nothing else. The use of color, hue, tint, brightness and shading, of course, is fundamental to all images.

Tutorial

Are you a Layers and Channels expert yet? No? Well, maybe you just need a little practice. Let's run through a few simple features of both.

First, create a new image window. Next, open the Layers and Channels dialog using the Image Window menu. When the dialog opens, you'll see a single layer. Create a new layer by right clicking on the background name. That will open the Layers menu. Select *New Layer*. When the layer has been created, it will have the generic name "New Layer". You can change this in the New Layer dialog or you can double click on the name to open the Edit Layer Attributes dialog. Change the name to "tutorial".

Now try duplicating the layer. Open the Layers menu again, and find the right menu option. What's the name of the new layer? Select the duplicated layer by clicking on it. Now use the down arrow button along the bottom of the Layers and Channels dialog to move this layer down one spot. Now try to do it again. Oops! It won't go any further. Why? Because the background layer—the layer at the bottom of the current layer stack—does not have an alpha channel, so it cannot be raised above another layer. Use the Layers menu to add an alpha channel to the background layer, then raise the background layer so it becomes the middle layer in this three layer stack.

So far so good, right? Managing layers is pretty easy once you get the hang of it. Now, let's take a look at the difference between resizing and scaling of layers. Open one of the images from the CD. Any one will do for this tutorial. Change the Layers and Channels dialog to this new image using the Image menu at the top of the dialog. Open the Layers menu and duplicate the background layer. Now select *Resize Layer* from the same menu. In the dialog that opens, try a few different sizes using both absolute X and Y values and X and Y ratios. Notice how the small display at the bottom of the dialog changes as you make your changes. Try changing the X offset to see how the display at the bottom of the dialog is affected.

Now, set the X and Y ratios to .5 and click on the OK button. What happened in the Image Window? It now has a dotted yellow box inside it. Click on the eye icon for the background layer. You can now see that the resize operation changed the duplicate layer to the new size. What would happen if you resized this to be just a bit bigger, but still smaller than the original background layer?

Okay, now try scaling that duplicate layer, the one you just resized. Make the scale ratio 1.25 for both X and Y. What happened now? Is this the same as if you had resized it to make it larger? Nope. It's different, try it!

Now add a white mask to an image layer. First, open an existing image (remember, there are plenty of images on the CD). Now duplicate the background layer. Select the background layer (not the copy you just made). Add an alpha channel to the background layer. You can do this by selecting the very last option in the Layers menu (right click on the "background" name to open the menu). Remember: nothing visible happens after you add the alpha channel.

Now type CTRL-a to select the entire background layer. The marching ants will dutifully run around the edges of the Image Window. Type CTRL-x. This will delete the contents of the background layer. Nothing visible happens, however, because the background copy covers the background completely. How can we see the change to the real background, then? The easiest way is to click on the eye icon for the background copy layer. That turns off the visibility of the background copy and you should see, as long as you haven't changed the defaults in the Preferences dialog, the gray and black checks which represent the alpha channel of the background layer.

Turn the eye icon back on by clicking where the icon should be (even though you can't see it right now). The icon will be redisplayed when the layer is made visible again. Click on the background copy name to select that layer. Add a layer mask to it from the Layers menu. The mask will be active by default. Click on the mask and the image thumbnail next to it once or twice to see how they look when each is active. Be sure the mask is active when you're done.

Now click on the Blend tool in the Toolbox—remember which one that is? In the Image Window, click and hold the left mouse button, drag from the top left to the bottom right of the image window and release the button. You've just created a simple gradient using the default colors (black and white) in the layer mask. What happened is that where the mask is black, the current layer is transparent; where it is white the current layer is visible. You can copy a selection from a layer and paste it into a mask, even if it's not black and white. The GIMP will know what to do with a color image copied into a mask—convert it to a grayscale image!

Try inverting the mask: *Image->Colors->Invert* from the Image Window menu. The effect of the mask can be seen a little more clearly when you do this. You can also try the Brightness/Contrast adjustments (*Image->Colors->Brightness-Contrast*) to see the effect a little more dramatically.

Chapter 7 - Colors and Text

Whether you use the GIMP for day-to-day production work or to create a digital Mona Lisa, you will find both color and text to be your most constant companions. Color can be adjusted globally through the use of brightness, contrast, hue, saturation and lightness settings, as well as used for drawing and painting. These latter two aspects of color, drawing and painting, are covered in the next chapter. This chapter looks at how colors can be adjusted in their own channels and varied between color spaces.

In **Chapter 2 - GIMP Basics**, the variety of color spaces that exist in the computer graphics world were described. The GIMP works only in RGB color space, but can make adjustments to the HSL and HSV components of those colors. It can also adjust colors between RGB and their complimentary colors, cyan, magenta and yellow. It can convert an image to the CMYK color space for printing to certain printers, but does not allow editing directly in this color space in the 1.0 release. Sampling of color values within images can be used to create selections. Variation of colors in one or all color channels can be adjusted so that the range of values fits a specific distribution curve. Such adjustments can be used to enhance edges and simulate three-dimensional effects, for example.

The GIMP supports only three types of images:[1] RGB, grayscale and indexed palette images. In most cases outside of animations and web page graphics, you will find yourself working with RGB images. Animations may be worked on in either RGB or indexed color palettes, depending mostly on whether you are creating the animation directly

---

1. Remember that image types are different from color spaces. See **Chapter 2 - GIMP Basics** for details.

in the GIMP or touching up an existing set of animation frames. Web pages are often worked on directly as indexed color palettes due to the nature of web browsers and their need to support low-end displays.

Beyond color, you will often need to add text to your graphics. Text support in the GIMP is actually fairly basic. Text can be specified on a single line using any font already supported by the X server. True Type fonts are not directly supported in the 1.0 release. The text can be any size and can be positioned just as any other selection might be. The true worth of using text comes not from the basic text support, but from what is done with the text after it has been turned into its own layer.

Compose/Decompose

In **Chapter 6 - Layers and Channels** we discussed the use of channels, how they are accessed and what they can be used for. One thing you can do with channels is to create separate grayscale images from each of the color channels in an RGB image. You can then edit each new image separately, recombining them into a new RGB image when you have finished. This gives you the ability to edit individual channels just as you would any other grayscale image.

Original image to be decomposed

Decompose dialog

Red channel   Green channel

Blue channel

The first step in this process is to create the individual grayscale images from the original RGB image. To do this, select the *Image->Channel Ops->Decompose* option from the Image Window menu of the original RGB image. The Decompose dialog allows you to select one of five methods of decomposing the image. The default of RGB will cause three new image windows to be created, each with a single layer and each with a grayscale version of one of the color channels of the original. The name for each new image window, as shown in the Layers and Channels dialog, will be the same as the original image with the channel color appended. For example, an image titled `bird.jpg` that was decomposed would create `bird-green.jpg`, `bird-blue.jpg` and `bird-green.jpg`.[2]

---

2. The GIMP also numbers each new image window sequentially, so the name of each window also includes the image window number.

Hue channel   Saturation channel

Value channel

Similarly, the HSV and CMY options in the Decompose dialog will also open three new windows. The contents of the windows will vary depending on the colors and intensities of the original image, of course. The CMYK option will open four windows. Although you might expect the CMY and CMYK images to be very similar, they may actually vary quite a bit depending on the amount of black contained in the original image. The last option, Alpha, will create a new window only if an alpha channel is present in the original image.

Decomposing works on the current layer, or the entire image if it contains only a single layer. Be certain that the layer you want decomposed is first selected in the Layers and Channels dialog. This dialog is discussed at length in **Chapter 6 - Layers and Channels**.

Once the image has been decomposed, you are free to work on the new images just as you would any other image. Keep in mind that the new windows are grayscale images, and not all features of the GIMP are available for use on them. If there is a feature you want to use that works only on an RGB image, you can first convert the image to RGB using the *Image->RGB* option in the Image Window menu. However, you must convert it back to grayscale (*Image->Grayscale*) prior to composing.

Compose dialog

The decomposed parts of the original image can be put back together, forming a new RGB image, after editing has been completed. This process is called compositing. To accomplish this task, you select the *Image->Channel Ops->Compose* option from the Image Window menu. In the dialog window that opens, you will need to specify which grayscale image is to be used for which channel. There are all sorts of variations you can use here. For example, try decomposing an image first into its HSV components, followed by a second decomposition into its RGB components, and then composite them using the RGB option in the Composite dialog. You can mix and match which of the decomposed windows you use for the red, green, and blue channels, as long as the image is a grayscale image. You might, for example, composite the red, hue, and saturation grayscale images. The Compose dialog's options menu allows you to select only image windows that display grayscale images. Any other open image windows that are not grayscale will not show up in this menu.

Here is another possible option—using a grayscale version of another image as one component of the new composite. Take an image and convert it to grayscale. Next, decompose another image into its red, green and blue components. Then composite the red and blue components, using the first image as the green component. You've created a green ghost in the new image! If the secondary image is not the same size as the other components, the composite will fail; however, you can either resize the smaller component or simply cut and paste into one or more of the other channels. Then flatten that channel prior to compositing. As you see, you can do most of the same operations on the grayscale component images as you can on any other image.

Decomposing an image is a good way to find out how the colors in an image are balanced. If you've scanned a photo that seems too dark, you can decompose the image to visually inspect the various component parts of the image. Perhaps there is too much red—the grayscale image of the red channel will be relatively white compared to the other grayscale images. If an image is dull, it may show up as a dark saturation channel. Each of these can be adjusted manually using the brightness and contrast controls in the GIMP prior to compositing the component parts.

Brightness/Contrast

Roosevelt Memorial—before contrast and brightness adjustments.

One of the most common production tasks you may encounter with day-to-day use of the GIMP is enhancing the color quality of a scanned photo. Adjusting a scanned image's color quality through a series of brightness and contrast adjustments on one or more color channels will often be your starting point when creating your digital works of art.

Brightness/Contrast adjusted.

The Brightness-Contrast dialog (*Image->Colors->Brightness-Contrast*) has two sliders ranging from -128 to +128 each. Initially these are set at 0, with the slider tab in the middle of the slider. Moving the slider to the right increases the value; to the left decreases it. You can also type a value in the text field next to each slider. The slider position is updated as you type in the value. If you type in a value that is beyond the valid range for the sliders, the slider is set to the maximum or minimum value.

A *Preview* toggle is also provided in this dialog. When it is depressed, the image being adjusted will be updated as you move the sliders. This can be problematic on very large images, so getting into the habit of turning off the preview first is highly recommended. After the adjustments have been made, click on the preview toggle to view the changes. Previews update the visible image, but are not permanent. The settings you've selected are not actually applied to the image until you click on the OK button in the dialog. If you click Cancel, the changes (even if previewed) will be lost and the image will be returned to its original settings.

Auto-Stretch Contrast applied to original.   *Auto-Stretch HSV applied to original.*

Using the Brightness-Contrast dialog allows manual adjustment of an image. There are two options in the Image Window menu that allow automatic adjustments: *Image->Colors->Auto-Stretch Contrast* and *Image->Colors->Auto-Stretch HSV*. The first of these takes the minimum and maximum values for each color channel and uses them to stretch the range of values to run between 0 and 255. The effect can cause the loss of hues in the image but works well on images which are already close to being fully color corrected. The second, Auto-Stretch HSV, works just like the first, but in the HSV color space. Unlike the Auto-Stretch Contrast, the Auto-Stretch HSV will preserve hues.

Curves and Levels

The Brightness-Contrast dialog and the Autostretch Contrast feature both work on all channels at the same time. The Autostretch HSV works only in HSV space, but operates on all three of those channels at the same time. What if you need to adjust only one channel at a time? What if the image is nearly correct, but you want to bring out the mid-level blues? In this case, you will want to make use of the Curves dialog (*Image->Colors->Curves*).

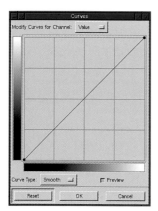

Curves dialog

The *Curves* dialog uses a graph with a curve, by default a linearly increasing curve or straight line, running from the lower left to upper right and representing the range of colors in the image. You adjust the brightness of the colors by making changes to the line. At either end of the initial curve you will find two filled circles, referred to as grab points. These initial points represent the darkest and brightest pixels in the image. The rest of the curve represents all the other pixels that fall between the two end points. To adjust the brightness of a range of color, you click above or below the line to create a new grab point. You can then drag the grab point around the grid area to adjust the curve.

Below and to the left of the grid area in the dialog are gradient representations of the range of pixel values for the curve. The gradient to the left represents how light pixels will be. The gradient below the grid shows the range of pixels, from darkest on the left to brightest on the right. When an upward adjustment is made on the left side of the curve, darker pixels will become brighter. Similarly, downward adjustments on the right side of the curve make brighter pixels darker. These changes can be visually examined on the lower gradient, which is divided into an upper and lower half. The upper half visually shows the variations in brightness between grab points.

Above the grid area is an options menu labeled *Modify Curves for Channel*. This menu is initially set to *Value*, which means that changes to the curve affect all three color channels. The Curves dialog works only on the red, green, and blue channels of an image. It does not directly manipulate hue or saturation. If the Channel Options menu is set to Red, then changes to the curve will affect only the red channel of the image. You can make changes to all three channels plus the Value curve at the same time by using the Curves dialog. Keep in mind that the curve represents only the existing range of color values. It cannot stretch that range in the way that, for example, Auto-Stretch Contrast does.

Below the grid is another options menu, labeled *Curve Type*, containing two options: *Smooth* and *Free*. By default, this menu is set to Smooth so you can create grab points and drag them around the grid. This process will automatically generate a smooth curve between grid points. Changing the Curve Type menu to Free will allow you to draw the curve in a hand-drawn mode, similar to the way a Free-hand selection is made.

When set to the Smooth mode of operation, the cursor will become a cross hair while over the grid area of the dialog in a location where, when the mouse button is clicked, a new grab point will be created. If the mouse is within a given distance of an existing grab point, the cursor becomes a fluer symbol. Clicking at this point will snap the nearest grab point to the location of the mouse cursor and update the curve. In Free mode, the cursor is always a pencil when it is over the grid area of the dialog.

Like many other dialogs, the Curves dialog includes a Preview toggle button. By default, this toggle is turned on, which means that changes to the curve force immediate recalculation of the Image Window contents. You may find it useful to turn this off before making changes to large images. Whether you turn the toggle on or off, the changes to the Curves dialog are not permanently applied to the image until the OK button is clicked. Remember: you can always undo this operation using the Undo keyboard shortcut CTRL-z.

A few key features of the dialog:

- Grab points can be removed by dragging them away from the curve to the left or right. When the drag operation moves a grab point past its nearest neighbor, the point being dragged will be removed. The curve will be redrawn to fit between the neighbors to either side of the old point. If the Preview toggle is depressed, then the Image Window will be updated accordingly.

- Changes made while in Smooth mode remain in effect if you change to Free mode, and vice versa. Changing from Free mode to Smooth mode can produce a very large number of grab points. Don't be suprised if this happens. You can always remove any excess points.

- It doesn't matter which mouse button you use to create and drag grab points.

- If you are experimenting with the curve and want to return to the original linear setting, you can use the *Reset* button. However, once a curve is applied to an image by clicking on the OK button, the next time you use the Curves dialog the curve will be linear—the changes you made earlier will not be reflected in subsequent invocations of the Curves dialog.

The Curves dialog is used to make changes which can range from minor to dramatic. Whereas the Brightness-Contrast dialog is like a dimmer switch on a ceiling light, the Curves dialog is like track lighting with dimmer switches for each light and interchangeable color filters over the lights. Another tool, the *Levels* dialog, can be used to make minor changes on a global scale, as if using a single dimmer switch on track lighting.

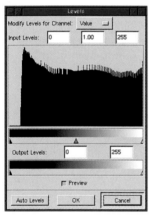

Levels dialog

The Levels dialog (*Image->Colors->Levels*) contains a histogram display which shows the distribution of color brightness in the image. Input and output levels can be adjusted using either text input fields or range slider indicators. The input range defines the tonal range of the image. If the histogram does not extend to both ends of the display, then the full tonal range of colors is not being used—in other words, the black pixels are not as black as they could be and/or the whites are not completely white. Adjusting the input range slider indicators (the small triangles beneath the gradient bar under the histogram) stretches the tonal range. The two indicators on the ends are the minimum and maximum values and the indicator in the middle is the midpoint of all pixels. Moving the middle indicator to the right darkens an image, because you're telling the GIMP to spread distribution of dark pixels and shrink distribution of light pixels. On the other hand, moving the middle indicator to the left will lighten the image. Moving the indicator at either end of the range adjusts the minimum and maximum values that the range will cover. Changes to the tonal range of the histogram are actually contrast adjustments in the image.

Beneath the input ranges is a gradient slider bar for the output range, with two indicators, a minimum and a maximum. Adjustments to the output slider change the lightness of the image—moving the maximum indicator to the left, towards the minimum, darkens the image. Moving the minimum indicator to the right washes out the image. Although the movements of the output slider might seem to cause effects opposite to those of the input slider, you have to consider what each slider is really doing. The input slider is stretching the brightness for a range of pixels. The output slider is shrinking the distribution of lightness for all pixels.

Like the Curves dialog, the Levels dialog allows changes to be made to all three color channels at the same time or to each channel independently. The options menu at the top of the dialog, labeled *Modify Levels for Channel,* is used to select the channels on which to operate. Also, the Levels dialog permits you to preview changes using the Preview toggle. Again, it is recommended that for large images you turn this off while making initial settings. Finally, changes made with the Levels dialog are not actually applied to the image until the OK button is pressed, even if the preview button is selected.

One of the most common uses for the Levels dialog is to automatically stretch the tonal range of an image. The *Auto Levels* button in the dialog will perform this function. This has the effect of reducing excessive red, green or blue tints in an image and is often used after other adjustments have been made. The primary difference between the Curves and Levels dialogs is that the Curves dialog allows finer control over the range of color levels. Whereas Brightness-Contrast and Curves are for image overhauls, the Levels dialog Auto Levels feature is used for fine-tuning.

The Histogram Dialog

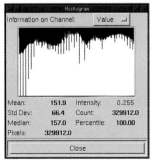

Histogram dialog

Another significant dialog is the *Histogram* dialog. This is a near duplicate of the Levels dialog, except that the Histogram dialog is informational only—you don't use it to make actual changes to the image. The dialog is accessed from the Image Window menu's *Image->Histogram* option. The statistical information provided may be of use with sophisticated image processing techniques, but is not likely to be used by graphic artists in their day-to-day work.

Image Correction Example

At this point you have enough information to follow a real example. Let's look at a few variations of a color-corrected image and how we can make those corrections. The first thing we need is a scanned photograph—say a photo of one of the world's favorite vacation destinations. The first image is a scanned photo of a street in the United Kingdom section of EPCOT in Disney World Florida. The original image is fairly crisp, but could use a little touching up.

A street in the United Kingdom section of EPCOT at Disney World Florida.

The first step is to check the image's color distribution using the Levels dialog. The next figure shows the histogram for the original image's overall brightness distribution. The distribution runs to the minimum and maximum, and a quick check of the three color channels shows similar distributions. Still, it won't hurt to apply the Auto Levels to the image to see what happens. The result can be seen in the next image. Although not drastically changed, the yellowish tint has been removed, and the colors appear more crisp. Unfortunately, the image is still too dark in some spots.

The histogram for the original image.

Auto Levels applied.

Image is brightened and contrast increased.

Final, color-adjusted image. Auto Levels operation was reapplied and the minimum and midpoint indicators adjusted to bring out the contrast

Opening the Brightness-Contrast dialog, we set the slider values to 44 and 54, respectively. This makes, as the third example shows, more dramatic color changes over the whole image and brightens the image overall. We now open the Levels dialog again and reapply the Auto Levels function. The results are a brighter, more vibrant image (not pictured), but still not quite as vibrant as we want. Adjusting the minimum range indicator to line up with the low end of the histogram and then moving the midpoint indicator to the right just a bit, now we have the image we want!

Using Thresholds to Create Pencil Drawings

Similar to Levels and Histograms is the *Threshold* dialog (*Image->Colors->Threshold*). This dialog contains a histogram which shows the range of brightness in the image—to the left are darker pixels, to the right are lighter ones. Unlike the other two dialogs, this one allows you to select the range of values you want by highlighting them directly in the histogram. When the dialog opens, a default range of pixels is selected and the image changes to black and white. The pixels represented by the selected range become white, while those outside that range become black. The effect is somewhat like a drawing made with a pencil or ink pen.

The original image's histogram as seen in the Threshold dialog, with the default range selected.

The Dallas skyline.

The so-called penciled image—after the threshold settings have been applied.

Hue, Saturation, and Lightness

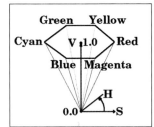

HSV diagram

Color spaces come in many flavors. One of these is the HSV color space, which describes an image in terms of hue, saturation and value. These have a mapping to the red, green and blue with which you are now quite familiar, but the mapping is not exactly simple. In order to explain the use of the HSL and Color Balance dialogs, it is important to discuss briefly how RGB and CMY relate to HSV.[3]

If you think of the colors red, yellow, green, cyan, blue and magenta as being the vertices of a hexagon (six-sided figure), you can begin to visualize how they relate to hue, saturation and value (we'll talk about lightness in a moment). Imagine this hexagon on top of a six-sided cone, with the point of the cone some distance below the hexagon. The

---

3. HSV and HSL are very similar and are covered in brief later in this chapter. However, an in-depth discussion of their differences is beyond the scope of this text.

distance between the hexagon and the tip of the cone is the scale for value, and runs from 0 to 1. The higher the value, the brighter the color (it's actually an inverse measure of the amount of gray in the color). Now, a line drawn from the center of the hexagon to the edge of the hexagon represents the saturation. The further out along the saturation line, the more pure the colors become. If you were at V=1, S=0 you would have a pure white. Moving out along S toward the red vertex you get increasing amounts of red color. To get the hue, you simply move around the edge of the hexagon, starting at the red vertex. A hue of 0 is red, and a hue of 180 is cyan. The HSV diagram shows this mapping visually.

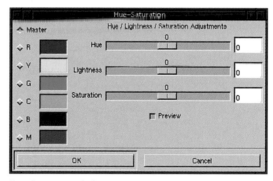

Hue-Saturation dialog

The GIMP provides a means of adjusting the hue, saturation and lightness of an image and/or its independent RGB color channels and selections. The Hue-Saturation dialog consists of three sliders and three text fields. As with many of the GIMP windows, you can adjust the HSL values either by using the sliders or by typing in the text fields. Changes entered directly in the text fields will cause immediate updates to the sliders. Along the left side of the dialog is a series of colored blocks and toggle buttons. Each toggle/block pair represents one vertex, or more precisely, one hue in the HSV hexagon. At the upper left corner of the dialog is a toggle labeled *Master*. When selected, this toggle causes changes to the sliders to affect all colors in the image at the same time. Selecting the other toggles causes the effects to change only the associated hues.

Updates to the hue slider will rotate the current hue (or all the hues if the Master toggle is set) between -180 and +180 degrees from its current value. Think of this in relation to the hexagonal cone discussed earlier. If the hue is blue, rotating the hue +120 degrees around the hexagon will give you red. Rotating -60 degrees from cyan gives you green. Increasing the saturation slider will increase the purity of the hues, whereas decreasing the saturation will wash out the color toward a shade of gray.

Now we'll talk about the lightness slider. This gives you a greater range for the brightness of the colors. In the HSV model, the value ranges from 0 to 1, with 1 lying in the plane of the hexagon. In the HSL model, the lightness runs along the same center line as the value does in HSV, but crosses the plane of the hexagon at 0.5 instead of at 1.0. Whereas in the HSV color model a setting of S=1, V=1 would give a maximally saturated hue, in the HSL model a setting of S=1, L=0.5 does the same. Going higher with the lightness setting (i.e. moving the slider to the right) will begin to oversaturate the colors, washing them out somewhat. A maximal setting for lightness, however, will not turn the color completely white. This can be done only if the saturation is set to 0, which means moving the saturation slider to the left.

All of this technical explanation is useful only if you want to know how to move specifically from one color to another or one brightness level to another. Most often, especially if you use the GIMP to simply unleash your creative side, you will find that using the Hue-Saturation dialog is a trial and error proposition. Again, as with other dialogs discussed in this chapter, the Preview toggle should probably be turned off for large images prior to making changes to the dialog.

Color Balance

The colors in an image are displayed in levels of red, green and blue. It is possible to adjust the amount of each of these between their pure colors and their complementary colors: cyan, magenta, and yellow, respectively. Foley, et al.,[4] describe complementary colors this way:

Complementary colors are those that can be mixed to produce white light.

Color Balance dialog

This is an understandable statement, but hard to associate with the format of the *Color Balance* dialog. This dialog, accessed through *Image->Colors->Color Balance*, is used to adjust between complementary colors. Looking at the dialog, you find a row of text boxes across the top (labeled with Color Levels) and a set of three sliders below. The text boxes correspond left to right with the sliders, top to bottom. Beneath the sliders are the now-familiar Preview toggle, and a Preserve Luminosity toggle. Below these are a set of radio buttons—only one of these at a time can be set.

When using this dialog, you should think of the HSV hexagon. The first

---

4. *Computer Graphics: Principles and Practice*, 2nd Ed.; Foley, van Dam, Feiner, Hughes; Addison-Wesley Publishing Company, p. 582.

slider lists cyan on the left and red on the right. On the HSV diagram, these two colors are 180 degrees apart in hue. Similarly, the second slider's magenta and green values are also 180 degrees apart, as are yellow and blue. So, moving a slider in one direction adjusts a color toward the hue on that end of the slider.

An additional feature of this dialog is the set of radio buttons at the bottom: *Shadows*, *Midtones*, and *Highlights*. Selecting one of these determines which pixels are to be affected by the color adjustments made with the sliders. Shadows are pixels with low amounts of a given color. Remember: pixels are made up of three values ranging from 0 to 255 for each of red, green, and blue components. Midtones are pixels with middle ranges of the specified color, and highlights have high values. When adjusting the sliders, the changes are global, that is, they affect the entire selection, layer or image as long as the pixels fall within the range of the selected radio button.

Finally, the *Preserve Luminosity* toggle can be used to ensure that changes to the hues will not affect the overall brightness of the image. By default, this toggle is turned off, which means it's possible that updates will cause a perceived change in brightness in the Image Window. The toggle button can be switched on or off to compare the differences immediately, as long as the Preview toggle is turned on.

Desaturate, Equalize, Invert, Posterize, Normalize

A number of features found under the *Image->Colors* menu have either no dialog or a very limited interface. Each of these does a very specific task and requires only minimal effort to understand how to use it.

The first tool is called *Desaturate*. It simply converts an RGB or indexed color image to a grayscale image of the same format. This means the image is still an RGB or indexed color image; it just happens to be filled with varying shades of gray pixels. How does this work? Remember the HSV hexagon? Well, each pixel's color is completely desaturated. That means the colors are removed, leaving only a grayscale value. Using the previous HSV diagram, each pixel in the image would now lie somewhere on the value line which runs through the center of the hexagon.

You might think that once an image has been desaturated you can get the original colors back by using the Hue-Saturation dialog and setting the Saturation slider all the way to the right. But that doesn't work. Once the image is desaturated, the hue angle is lost (remember, the hue is represented by the line which is some angle away from the line out to red on the hexagon). Setting the Saturation slider to +100 simply causes a red tinted image to be created from the desaturated one.

The Desaturate option has no dialog. Similarly, the *Equalize* option is not accessed through a dialog. Equalize is often used to correct an under- or over-exposed image. The correction is somewhat similar to the Auto Levels adjustment, but has a harsher result. Equalize takes the darkest pixels and makes them black, the lightest pixels and makes them white, and stretches the histogram (and thus the remaining pixels) to fit that range. For images with high contrast regions, this adjustment can cause a serious loss of detail. In general, use of the Equalize option is best for images which need only minor adjustments.

Normalize is a variation of Equalize and Auto Levels. The difference is that the image's contrast is stretched. The technical differences between these three options is hardly worth mentioning. Suffice it to say that you may want to experiment with the Equalize, Normalize, and Auto Levels options to see which provides a better improvement to an image's quality.

Another option without a dialog window is the *Invert* menu option. This feature takes the color values of an image and inverts them, that is, subtracts them from 100. This would be the same as placing a white layer beneath the image and setting the layer mode for the image (not the white layer) to Subtract. The resulting image is a color negative of the original. Other than that, the usefulness of this feature depends upon the user's creativity and imagination.

The Dallas skyline, original photo with Posterize set to three color levels.

Finally, one of the more unusual color options is *Posterize*. This option uses a dialog that allows the specification of the number of levels to use for the posterization process. The level is used in a computation based on the maximum range of values (1 to 256) divided by the number of levels. These new values are saved in an array. The image is then processed top to bottom, using each pixel's current color as an index into the new array of colors. The new color is then used to create the posterized image. The effect is to offer less detail in the image in exchange for higher color contrast and more extravagant colors.

Indexed Color vs. RGB/Grayscale

Most features discussed so far in this chapter do not work with indexed color images. This will become obvious if you try to use a feature on an indexed color image because the menu options will be grayed out, preventing their selection. If you need to work on color corrections using any of these tools, you should consider converting an indexed color image to either RGB or grayscale first.

Color Selection Dialog and the Color Picker Tool

As we've seen in this chapter, color manipulation with the GIMP can be done using a variety of tools. All of these tools allow you to modify ranges of colors and hues, brightness or contrast, and various other pixel characteristics. But what about selecting a specific color? How is that done?

In a previous chapter we discussed the Color Picker tool, available from the Toolbox. By placing the cursor over a pixel in the image, an existing color can be selected for the foreground color. But can we pick a color that doesn't already exist in the image? Certainly. The *Color Selection* dialog allows for an arbitrary selection of colors.

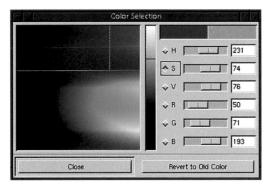

Color Selection dialog

To open the Color Selection dialog, click on either the foreground or background color box in the Toolbox. Remember that the box you choose must already be selected. You can tell if it is selected because it will appear depressed into the toolbox. The dialog consists of a color box on the left, a vertical gradient bar next to that, and a set of sliders on the right. The sliders represent the hue, saturation, value, red, green, and blue levels of the currently selected color. You can use the sliders or their associated text fields to manually specify values. Alternatively, you can click and drag in the color box and the gradient bar. When you click in the color box, horizontal and vertical lines appear at the cursor location. By default, moving the mouse up and down changes the saturation level, and to the right and left changes the value. Clicking in the gradient bar places a horizontal bar at the cursor. Dragging up and down in this bar changes the hue setting. Changes to the hue, saturation and value settings also have an effect on the red, green, and blue values. In essence, you can learn a little about how HSL maps to RGB by experimenting briefly with this dialog.

Above the sliders in the dialog is a rectangular box that is divided into two halves. The right half shows the color that was set when the dialog was opened, and the left half shows the currently selected color. Next to the sliders are toggle buttons. By default, the hue toggle is turned on and the color box shows the range of colors that exist for the current hue level. Selecting a different toggle will change the way dragging in the color box and gradient bar affects the current color. The selected toggle is associated with the gradient bar. Selecting the saturation slider's toggle means that dragging up and down in the gradient bar will change the saturation level, while the horizontal bar in the color box will change the value and the vertical bar will change the hue. Similarly, the value toggle will cause the gradient bar to allow modifications to the value setting.

After experimenting a little with these options, you will find that there are quite a few variations available for choosing a specific color. With practice, you will be able to easily select the exact color you need using the Color Selection dialog.

Text Tool Dialog

One tool that makes use of the current foreground color is the Text tool. In **Chapter 4 - The Toolbox** we discussed how to place text into an image:

1. Click on the Text tool icon in the toolbox.

2. Type the text you want in the Text tool dialog.

3. Select the font and font characteristics you need.

4. Click on the OK button in the dialog.

Text tool dialog

The text is displayed in the image window as a floating layer with the marching ants outline.

In essence, this is a simple process, and quite possibly one you will use often. But we haven't discussed the other features of this dialog. The fonts available with the Text tool are those registered with the X server. The number of fonts varies from system to system,[5] so the number of fonts displayed in the Text tool dialog will vary as well. If you have a few hundred fonts installed, choosing an appropriate font can be a daunting task.

Fonts on UNIX systems are made up of a number of characteristics: the font family, the foundry name, weight, slant, width, encoding and so forth. In order to choose a specific font, you need to make a choice for each characteristic. Along the left side of the dialog is a scrolled list of all the font families on your system. A set of option menus on the right allow you to set font characteristics. The option menus are, in order:

1. **Foundry** - The foundry is the name of the originator, i.e., the company or group that created the font family. Examples include Adobe and Bitstream.

2. **Weight** - The weight defines the darkness of the text, similar to the way an old manual typewriter might give darker or lighter text depending on how hard you pressed the keys.

3. **Slant** - Italic, oblique, and Roman (i.e., regular, unslanted text).

4. **Set width** - Multiple widths are often provided for proportional (varying width) fonts. Variations can include condensed, semi-condensed, and extended and are based on the Foundry type. This menu, however, supports only regular and semi-condensed formats. Many of the freely available and shareware fonts that support other widths are distributed as separate fonts, with different font names such as *alliance* (the regular font) and *allianceextended* (the extended-width version of the same font).

5. **Spacing** - Most fonts you will use for your images will be proportional fonts, specified by the "p" option in this menu. Other types you may encounter include monospace ("m", i.e., fixed-width fonts), and character cell ("c").

5. See **Appendix C - Adding Fonts to Your System** for details on how to add fonts to your system.

6. **Registry** - This menu represents the character set of the font. The default set of fonts available with any X Windows installation includes fonts belonging to what are known as the ISO Latin-1 character set. These fonts are represented by the ISO 8859 registry. Other registries are often used for languages other than the Western European languages supported by the ISO 8859 specification.

7. **Encoding** - For most Western European language fonts you will find this menu will have only one option available (not grayed out), generally the "1" option. Encoding is used by languages that use something other than 8 bits per character in their font definitions, such as the Japanese character sets of hirigana, katakana and kanji.

The availability of the options in each menu depends on whether the currently selected font family actually supports those features. In the case of many freely available and shareware fonts, many of these features are not supported. Commercial fonts are more likely to support a greater variety of these options. Asian fonts may support variations for Registry and Encoding that most North American and European users will never see. You can browse the font families to see which ones include which features, but that can be a time-consuming experiment. Currently, the Text tool dialog does not allow you to narrow down the list of font families by specifying other characteristics first. All of the option menu settings are based on selection of a font family.

Font characteristics do not need to be specified for a font family—you can use the default settings, represented by an asterisk. When you use the defaults, the GIMP will ask the X server to choose the first font which matches the characteristics you have specified. At a minimum, you must select a font family from the scrolled list of font names. If you choose one font family, then select some non-default font characteristics and then choose another font family, the dialog will automatically reset any characteristic to its default if the current setting is not supported by the new font family.

Fonts can be set to any size using the text field and unit specification option at the top of the dialog. Just type in the size of the font and hit ENTER. The text you typed in the text field at the bottom of the dialog will automatically be updated to reflect the new size. The size can be specified in either pixels or points. Fonts are based on rules of typography that have been around for many years. Printers have used a standard measurement of 1/72 of an inch to represent one point in a typeface. Specifying points instead of pixels will change the size of the displayed text depending on the resolution for which the font was originally designed and the resolution at which the X server is running on your monitor. Unfortunately, there is no way to determine this directly from the Text tool dialog, so your choice of points vs. pixels will probably depend on whether you really need to use points and whether you truly understand how points and pixels are used to calculate the true size of the text for a given font. Such discussion, however, is beyond the scope of this book. In general, you will find little noticeable difference between the two.

Below the set of font characteristic option menus is a text box labeled *Border*. The border setting adjusts the size of the floating layer in which text is created. The border is the space around the text between the text and the edges of the layer. To add space around text, which can also be done with Resize Layer after the text has been created, just enter the number of pixels to use as the border width. The default value of 0 means that the extreme edges of the text will sit on the borders of the layer. You may want to specify a non-zero border if you plan on blurring the text. Don't forget to turn off the Keep Transparency toggle before blurring the text!

Examples of Effects Using Text

Now that we know how to create text, it would help to know what we can do with that text. A few examples are in order. We'll create a simple drop shadow and show you how to create three-dimensional text using the standard set of Script-Fu Logo scripts. Creating these effects will take a little knowledge of plug-in filters, a set of features in the GIMP that will not be covered in detail until later in this book.

Drop Shadows

A drop shadow is nothing more than a shadow layer placed behind and/or under another layer. Drop shadows are often associated with text, but can be created for any shape or object. We'll create a drop shadow for some text first, then use one of the stock Script-Fu scripts to automatically generate one.

Open a new Image Window using the default foreground and background colors. Select the Text tool and click in the Image Window. Enter some text and select a font family and size, then click on the OK button in the dialog. Make the floating layer that is created a new layer. You should now have some black text over a white background in an image that contains two layers.

Now, using the Layers menu, duplicate the text layer. Set the Keep Transparency toggle to off. We intend to rescale this layer to add some space around the text. Use the Layers menu *Resize Layer* option to add 30 pixels to the border of the layer.

Now go into a new area—the *Filters* submenu of the Image Window menu. Under the Filters submenu are a variety of options, nearly all with their own menus. Select the *Blur* option, then the *Gaussian Blur (IIR)* option. This opens a small dialog prompting for the radius of the blur and toggles for selecting the direction of the blur. Leave the two toggle buttons enabled (we want to blur both horizontally and vertically) and the blur radius set to 5. Using a larger radius would cause the drop shadow to appear too soft around the edges. When you click on the OK button, a progress dialog opens to show the status of the blur calculations. When this dialog closes, the text in the duplicate layer should appear blurred.

The next step is to offset the duplicate layer from the original text layer. Select the Move tool from the Toolbox. Grab the duplicate layer and move it to the right and down, so the two layers appear offset. The further the offset, the more height the real text layer will appear to have. However, with the blur radius set to 5, the shadow will have a soft but relatively well-defined edge. Such shadows are more common when an object is close to the surface upon which they are casting a shadow.

Finally, the shadow layer needs to be moved below the original text. Use the *Lower Layer* option from the Layers menu on the shadow. Now, you should have a simple drop shadow. The shadow layer may appear too dark at this point, so adjusting the opacity level might increase the visual effect. Not very flashy, but you can see that simple effects are easy to do with the GIMP. More importantly, complex effects are often based on simple ones, so exercises such as this are building blocks for further experimentation.

Script-Fu Drop Shadow

This operation is much more simple when using a Script-Fu script. If you recall from earlier chapters, Script-Fu is a scripting interface based on the Scheme interpreted language. Script-Fu scripts are text files that are fed to the built-in Scheme interpreter in the GIMP. These scripts have access to any image processing, layer handling, or other feature set within the GIMP that is registered with the GIMP Procedural Database (also referred to as the PDB).

Under the Image Window menu is an option for accessing the Script-Fu filters. Under this submenu you will find a variety of scripts that come with the standard GIMP distribution. One of the categories under the Script-Fu submenu is *Shadow*. This is a submenu with (currently) two script options: *Drop-Shadow* and *Perspective*. We'll use the former for this experiment.

Drop shadow created using Script-Fu

Once again, create a new Image Window with the default background and foreground colors. Add some text, just as before. With the text layer selected, choose *Script-Fu->Shadow->Drop-Shadow* from the Image Window menu. This is an instant drop shadow. Over time, you will find that creating drop shadows with the Script-Fu script is certainly more convenient than creating them manually.

The other Script-Fu Shadow script, Perspective, creates a shadow that extends from the bottom of the original text layer, giving the impression that the text is sitting upright on a flat surface. Both scripts provide dialogs for modifying the overall effect of the shadow.

Script-Fu Logos

You may have noticed that the Xtns menu in the Toolbox holds a Script-Fu option, just like in the Image Window Filters menu. These are not the same menus: the Xtns version holds scripts that work by creating new Image Windows and that are not associated with any existing Image Windows. The scripts accessed from the Image Window menu operate on that Image Window or one of its layers.

Under the *Xtns->Script-Fu* menu are numerous options. The one covered here is the *Logos* submenu. Here you will find 21 separate canned logo generation scripts. Each script creates a different style of logo, and each offers you the opportunity to specify text, colors, background images, and any number of other configurable options. Creating a logo with these scripts simply requires selecting the appropriate menu option, filling in the associated dialog and clicking on the OK button. The GIMP does the rest. The following images show the logos you can create and the dialog settings used for each.

Script-Fu Logos are a cool and quick way to add pizazz to your artwork. You may find yourself using Script-Fu Logos a lot!

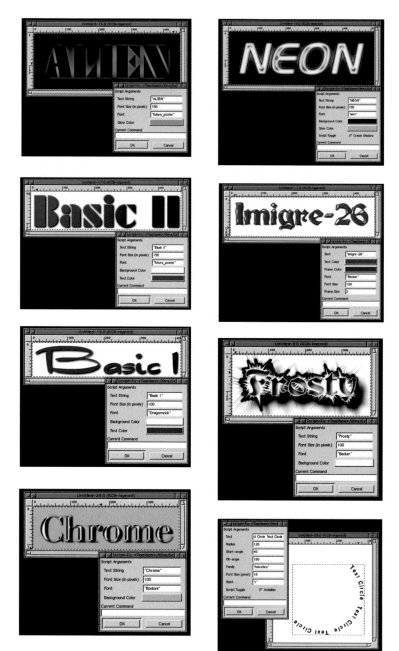

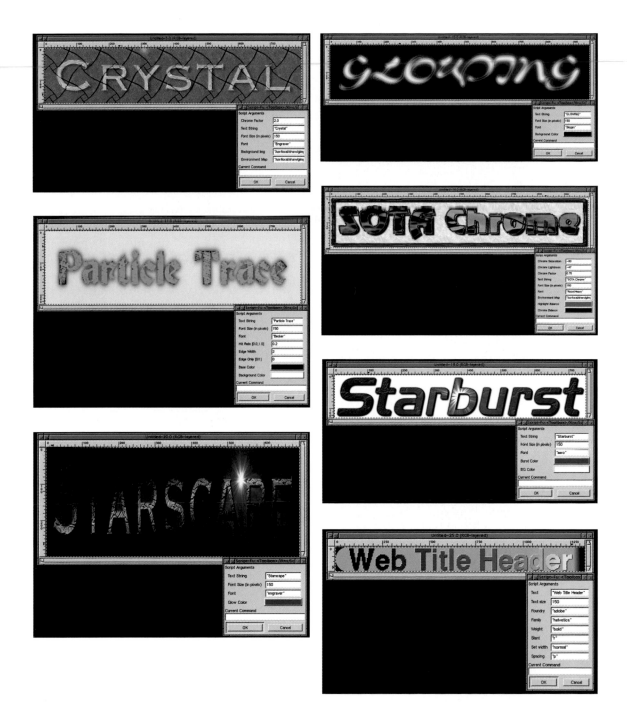

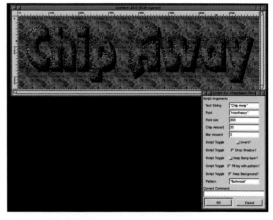

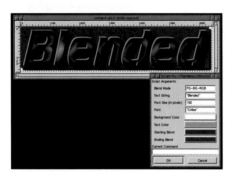

Moving On

All of the tools in the *Image->Color* submenu can operate on selections, entire layers or images. Most do not work on indexed color images. In this chapter we discussed the basics of using each of the color tools and showed how some of them can be used to color correct scanned photos. A number of the tools are variations on adjusting the histogram of an image and provide nearly identical effects. Practice and experimentation will be your best methods for learning which tool best fits which image.

Color adjustment tools like those discussed in this chapter work over a range of pixels. The GIMP can be used for more than just color correcting existing images. A limited set of drawing and painting features exist, such as the Pencil and Bucket Fill tools in the Toolbox. Before we can discuss these tools in depth we need to understand the use of brushes, palettes and patterns. Drawing tools make use of each of these, so you should understand how to set them before moving on.

Tutorial

Colors and text are important elements of any graphic design work. Let's use a simple example to take another look at some of the color features available.

First, open a new Image Window with a white background. It can be a generic 256x256 window. Create a selection using any shape you desire. The more irregularly shaped the better, however. Feather the selection, perhaps by about 5 pixels or so, just to create a soft edge. Now use the Blend tool, with the default settings and the default foreground/background colors, to create a gradient from the upper left of the selection to the bottom right. Press CTRL-SHIFT-a to turn off the selection.

Now find out what happens to this soft-edged gradient when you apply a few of the color manipulation filters to it. We'll try the Brightness-Contrast filter first. Set the contrast high, to over 75, for example. The blend becomes generally darker and the edges become more distinct. The blend also shortens—the length of the blend becomes shorter because the lighter pixels got whiter and the darker pixels got darker. Choose Cancel in the Brightness-Contrast dialog so that the changes are not implemented and we can examine the effects of another manipulation.

Now try the Levels dialog. Move the middle slider tab below the histogram to the right, then to the left. The gradient is affected, but nothing really happens to the white background. Try moving the left indicator to the right, then move the middle indicator a bit more. Moving the left indicator darkened the gradient, and subsequent moves of the middle indicator caused greater variations than when the left indicator was in its original far left position.

Cancel those changes. Let's try Posterize. This creates an interesting effect with this simple gradient. The higher the levels are set, the more banding you get through the gradient. It almost appears, depending on your gradient, like a piece of paper that's been folded and then unfolded. Quite an unexpected effect, given the simple nature of this color filter! Cancel the changes again.

Finally, take a look at the Threshold filter. This time, you get to see how the Threshold tool really works, because you can see the selected portion of the gradient turn white when you select a portion of the histogram. It becomes obvious, then, that darker pixels are selected with the left side of the histogram and lighter pixels towards the right.

These are simple examples, meant to walk you through the easiest use of these tools. Still, they do let you see the most basic effects of these tools. These changes can have very significant effects upon color photographs.

Chapter 8 - Drawing and Painting

Although not originally part of the design criteria for the GIMP, several ways to draw and paint have been developed. Tools include a variety of brush types (Pencil, Airbrush, etc.), brush shapes and sizes (from the Brushes dialog), patterns and line/fill types. A recent addition to this set of tools is the GFig Plug-In, which allows you to design and draw primitive shapes.

This chapter introduces you to the basic configurable items for drawing and painting, such as brush types, shapes and pattern types, followed by the tools which make use of these configurations. A comparison of the results of using different brush types is also given. A discussion on using brushes to draw primitive shapes is followed by descriptions of color palettes and the Cloning and Convolver tools. Finally, the use of the GFig Plug-In is covered in brief.

Brushes

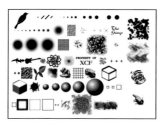

Sample of brushes included with standard distribution

An important part of using the GIMP is understanding how to use brushes. All drawing tools in the GIMP use the currently selected brush. A number of brushes are included in the standard distribution, and you can also create your own using the .gbr file format.

The Brush Selection Dialog

To select one of the installed brushes, choose the *Brushes* option from the *Dialogs* submenu in the Image Window menu to open the *Brush Selection* dialog. This dialog contains a scrolled display of the available brushes, a brush mode options menu, an opacity slider, and a spacing slider.

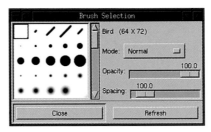

Brush Selection dialog

First, select a brush. Each icon in the scrolled window is a different brush. Since this scrolled window fits all the brushes into equally sized boxes, some of the brushes are not fully displayed. Click on the first brush shape—the one that looks like a blank square. The brush shape is expanded in a pop up box so you can see the complete image. In this case, the brush shape is really the picture of a bird! You wouldn't have guessed that from looking at the brush shape in the scrolled window. Notice that you need to hold down the left mouse button to see this pop-up window of the brush. When you let go, you see the brush icon's outline is now black, showing that the brush has been selected. Also, the name of the currently selected brush and its square dimensions are displayed above the mode options menu. All brushes are actually square. However, if the drawing tool which is using the brush supports transparency, then the white area of the brush image won't draw anything; where the image is gray or black the brush tool leaves a mark. We'll talk more about this when we discuss the specific drawing tools available in the GIMP.

Brush strokes can be applied to any layer using any one of fifteen different brush modes. The modes act exactly like their layer mode cousins,[1] except that with brush modes you get an additional mode called *behind*. The behind mode works by drawing only in transparent regions of a layer, effectively placing the drawn portions behind the contents of the current layer but above any lower layers.

---

1. See **Chapter 6 - Layers and Channels** for more information on layer modes.

The *Opacity* slider affects the opacity of the brush in general. Remember we talked briefly about the use of brushes with tools that make use of transparency? In this case, the Opacity slider affects how much of the original brush will be transparent; that is, how transparent the originally black and gray areas should be. This opacity level will be applied to the brush when the brush is applied to the layer. The layer's opacity is combined with this, so if you have a layer that is 50% opaque and use a brush that is 50% opaque, the brush's marks will end up being 25% opaque when applied—halfway visible on a halfway transparent layer.

The *Spacing* slider affects how often the brush is applied as you move the cursor around the Image Window. Lower settings apply the brush stroke more often, higher values less often. This has nothing to do with how fast you move the mouse—think of the spacing as a timer that determines how often to allow ink to flow out of the nib of a calligraphy pen or how often a rubber stamp is applied, no matter what rate the paper underneath or the stamp arm might be moved. For continuous tone lines, you will want to set the slider to a very low setting. Note that the slider has a poor level of granularity when you move it—dragging the slider makes fairly large jumps in the displayed spacing value. You can get around this, as you can with all sliders in the GIMP, by clicking on the slider to select it and then using the left and right arrow keys on the keyboard. The arrow keys will move the slider in single-unit increments and decrements.

All of the drawing tools use the current foreground color to do the drawing. If the brush type is not a solid pattern, the darker areas of the brush come out in the foreground color and the lighter areas of the brush come out transparent (with pixels in underlying layers showing through the area the brush doesn't cover). This behavior can be modified using the Mode and Opacity settings on the Brush Selection dialog.

Pencil, Paintbrush, and Airbrush

As with any artistic tool set, drawing in the GIMP starts with a Pencil. This basic brush works much like an ordinary sharpened pencil: the edges of the lines you draw are sharp and clean. In this case, however, the Pencil applies the shape of the selected brush using hard, distinct outlines. The Paintbrush tool, on the other hand, gives a soft edge to the selected brush. How do these differ? Again, we go back to the discussion on using transparency with brushes. Where the brush image is white, the Paintbrush treats the region as transparent; where it is black, the brush image is fully opaque. Where the brush image is gray, however, you have different levels of opacity. This is what causes the soft edges with the Paintbrush. With the Pencil, on the other hand, there are no levels of opacity—the pixels of a brush image are either fully opaque or fully transparent. If there is any level of gray in the pixel, then the Pencil treats that pixel as fully opaque. This is what produces the hard edges in the brush strokes from the Pencil tool.

Comparison of Pencil vs. Paintbrush.

This difference between the Pencil and the Paintbrush is best shown with a few examples. The first figure shows two different brushes applied with a Pencil and a Paintbrush. The first brush, the bird brush, has two obvious areas of gray—the eye and the wing. Using the Paintbrush these distinctions are visible, but with the Pencil, the bird is a solid block. Also, the edge of the bird is more jagged with the Pencil. The Paintbrush creates a soft edge.

The next example shows the "Yeah You!" brush, a hand with a pointing index finger. When using this with the Paintbrush, the details of the hand are obvious: the fingers, and the hole through which the hand has been poked. With the Pencil the outline is rough, the details have been lost and the three-dimensional effect of the hand coming through the page is gone.

The Airbrush works in a manner similar to the Paintbrush when it comes to soft edges and brush types. With the Airbrush, however, the overall transparency of a single brush stroke starts at a very high level. In other words, the Airbrush acts like a paintbrush that has a very slow but steady amount of ink being applied through the tip of the brush. The longer you hold the mouse in place with the left button pressed, the more ink is applied.

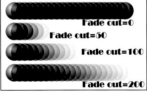

Examples of Paintbrush strokes using differing levels of the Fade Out slider.

Both the Airbrush and the Paintbrush have configurable features in their respective Tool Options dialogs. The Paintbrush offers a slider that allows you to specify the rate at which the brush will run out of paint. Imagine this as being what happens as you dip a brush in paint and begin to apply it to the canvas. Eventually, the stroke begins to fade as the brush runs out of paint. The Fade Out slider for the Paintbrush tool determines how quickly a single brush stroke runs out of paint. Higher values mean the stroke takes longer to fade out. Lower values mean you "return for more paint" sooner. When you set the value to zero, however, it will never fade out. You don't actually have to do anything to get more paint other than let go of the mouse button and then press it again to start another paint stroke. When drawing with any of the drawing tools, including the Paintbrush, a stroke is a continuous movement from the time you press and hold the left mouse button until you release it.

The Airbrush Tool Options dialog has two settings: *Rate* and *Pressure*. The first of these determines how quickly paint will be blown from the brush's tip—actually, it determines how quickly another brush stroke is applied. Higher values mean a higher paint flow rate, which means brush strokes are applied more quickly. This rate of application is distinct from the spacing that is specified in the Brush Selection dialog. To understand this, think of the Airbrush as a real airbrush connected via two hoses, one to a paint supply, the other to an air pump. The spacing would be a valve on the paint supply that cycles rhythmically, allowing paint to flow only every so often. It doesn't determine how much paint flows, it simply opens and closes on schedule. The rate setting is more like the air pump. It hums rhythmically, too, at the rate you specify in the dialog. The air pump determines when paint is actually blown onto the canvas. The higher the rate setting, the more often the air pump pumps. If the spacing valve is off and the air pump pumps, nothing shows up on the canvas. Similarly, if the paint is flowing but the air pump is not pumping, you still get nothing on the canvas. Only when the paint is flowing and the air pump is pumping do you get a brush stroke. You can see this by setting a high spacing rate and drawing across a large blank window. As you drag the brush across the window, you get multiple brush strokes applied in small groups— one, then a bunch of blank space, then two quick strokes, then more blank space, then two more quick strokes, and so forth. Increasing the Rate setting for the Airbrush will cause more paint to get through more often, spreading out the clumps of strokes and increasing the total number of strokes applied in the same space. However, the darkness of each stroke remains the same. That gets changed by adjusting the Pressure slider.

The Pressure slider for the Airbrush would be more like the nozzle on a real airbrush. Every time the spacing valve was turned on, allowing paint to flow, the rate nozzle would determine how much paint could actually get through the brush and onto the canvas. Higher pressure settings mean more paint flows out the tip of the Airbrush each time the air pump (the Rate setting) pumped. Confused? Don't be—it is actually fairly easy to figure out how each slider affects the Airbrush just by playing with them for a little while. Experiment on a new, blank window. Use CTRL-z to clear the last set of brush strokes, if you want.

Creating New Brushes

The GIMP comes with a fairly large set of brushes, but you are certainly not limited to this stock set. If you need a specialized brush, you can create one of your own. The GIMP uses brush image files that use the .gbr extension. In order to create a brush, you can follow these steps:

1. Create a selection of any shape.

2. Save it to the default edit buffer using *Edit->Copy.*

3. Create a new window with a white background, just big enough for the selection you just saved.

4. Paste the copy buffer into the new window and anchor the new layer to the background layer.

5. Convert the new window to grayscale using *Image->Grayscale.*

6. Save the new window as a .gbr file, preferably in the $HOME/.gimp/brushes directory, since this is where the GIMP looks by default for your brushes. A dialog is presented so that you can name the brush as it will appear in the Brush Selection dialog and the initial Spacing parameter for it.

At this point, you have a new brush. All that's left is to tell the GIMP to update the brush dialog. You do this simply by clicking the Refresh button in the Brush Selection dialog. The brushes are sorted alphabetically, and depending on how many brushes you have installed previously, you may need to do a little searching in the scrolled list to find a brush you have created.

An alternative, and probably the preferred, method of creating a brush is to use the Script-Fu *Selection->To Brush* option. This will automatically create a brush out of the current selection. In order to use this tool, you will need to create a selection first. Once the *Selection->To Brush* option is chosen, you will be prompted for the name of the brush (the Description), the file name for the brush (without the .gbr extension), and the default Spacing to use for the brush. The script will automatically update the Brush Selection dialog for you, so you shouldn't need to use the Refresh button.

A few tips about creating brushes. A brush is a grayscale image, so creating a brush with a white background and a gray-to-black image will produce the usual brush stroke effects described earlier in this chapter. Inverting the image will produce more unusual effects—the image area will become blank or transparent where the brush stroke is applied.

Also, for relatively small brushes—no more than 32x32 pixels in size—you may find it easier to create a large image first, then scale it down just before saving it to the brush file. Of course, you don't need to scale the brush down. There is no limit to the size of a brush, so creating a very large brush is possible, if not completely practical.

Eraser

Eraser used on layer without an alpha channel

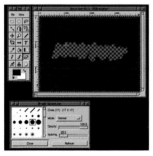

Eraser used on layer with an alpha channel

The Eraser tool does just the opposite of the Pencil tool, in that the shape of the brush is used to remove the underlying pixels. Note that this does not mean the new color for the pixels is the background color. Instead, the pixels become transparent—unless the layer you are working on does not have an alpha channel. In that case, the background color is used and the Eraser acts just like the Paintbrush (except it uses the background instead of the foreground color).

Selections in floating layers can be modified using the Eraser. If you erase an area of the selection that is transparent, then the selection will reshape itself to the nearest non-transparent regions. The selection won't reshape if the pixels have not been completely erased, so you may need to erase the same region twice just to make sure you get all the pixels. Keep in mind that this feature works only for floating selections. If you make a selection in a normal layer, you can either choose *Select->Float* to create a floating layer or use *Edit->Copy* and *Edit->Paste* to create a new floating layer.

You can use this technique to add highlights to a layer by using the *Alpha To Selection* option in the Layers menu, copying the selection to the default edit buffer, pasting it back in as a floating layer and removing all but the parts of the selection you wish to use as highlights. Convert the floating selection to a new layer and change the layer mode to Screen, Addition, or Overlay. Voilà! Highlights!

Drawing Primitive Shapes

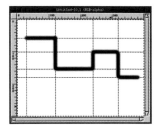

Drawing lines using guides

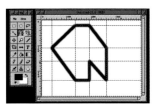

Drawing lines using Bézier selections

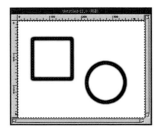

Drawing lines using rectangular and elliptical selections and Edit->Stroke

Now that you are familiar with the basic drawing tools, you can learn how to use them to create a few basic shapes. Start with a straight line. It is quite simple to draw a line using the Pencil or Paintbrush, but chances are that even the steadiest hand can't draw a straight, clean diagonal line. The GIMP makes this fairly easy by allowing you to specify the end points of the line. First, choose your brush and drawing tool: Pencil, Paintbrush or Airbrush. Next, click in an Image Window once to specify the start of the line. You'll get a single brush stroke at the point of the click. Now move the mouse to where the end of the line will be. Do not hold down the mouse button. Now, press and hold the SHIFT key, and then click left mouse button again. The GIMP draws the line in the current foreground color from the start point to the end point using the selected brush. Now try clicking somewhere else using the SHIFT key again. The end point of the last line is used as the starting point of a new line. Each subsequent click with the SHIFT key held down will continue to draw straight lines from the end point of the last line to the new spot.

This is a nifty trick, and is especially useful when used with Image Window guides. Drag a few guides down from both the top and side of the window. Now draw straight lines between intersecting points of the guides. Using a little math and the rulers, you can draw fairly accurate outlines this way.

Guides can also be used with another drawing method—stroking. A *stroke* is a line drawn around the edge of a selection using the currently selected brush and the Paintbrush tool. To use this method, first create a selection of any shape. Next, select your brush type and foreground color. Finally, select *Edit->Stroke* from the Image Window menu. The outline of the selection is turned into a drawn figure. You don't need to specify the use of the Paintbrush; the GIMP automatically uses this tool for the stroke operation.

Guides can be used here by using Rectangular and Elliptical selections and the Snap To Guides feature (*View->Snap To Guides*) in order to get more exact shapes. You can use the keyboard modifiers to create exact circles or boxes and to add and subtract selected regions before performing the stroke operation. Quite complex outlines can be created in this way.

As you can see, although some basic tools are provided, drawing using the base GIMP features is somewhat limited. The ability to create distinct shapes is primarily based upon your creative talent in making selections and using guides. However, a recent addition to the GIMP's stock set of plug-ins has added greater flexibility to your basic drawing tools. *GFig* is a handy tool that allows you to create, position, and modify various primitive shapes such as boxes, ellipses, ordinary curves and even Bézier curves. GFig will be covered at the end of this chapter.

Color Palettes

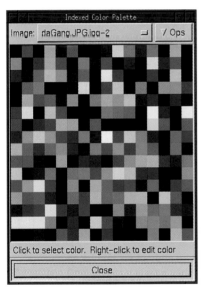

Indexed Color Palette

Another tool used for painting is the Bucket Fill tool. Unlike the Paintbrush or Airbrush, the Bucket Fill tool does not use brushes. Instead, it makes use of foreground colors and patterns. Before we get to patterns, we need to take a deeper look at handling colors.

One of the most common problems encountered while creating images is getting exactly the right colors. Many times, the color you want is buried in another image and you have to go searching through old files to find it. Or perhaps, in the case of creating images for web pages, you want to use one of the colors defined in the Netscape colormap. How can you accurately pick one of these colors? How can you make access to that color easier for future reference?

The answer is the color palette. A palette is just like the one a painter uses: it is a convenient place for holding a defined set of frequently used colors. In the GIMP, there are two kinds of palettes: the Indexed Color Palette, and the more general Color Palette. The former is used with indexed color images while the latter is used with RGB images.

When an indexed color image is created, it has, at most, 256 distinct colors. If you open the Indexed Color Palette dialog, *Dialogs->Indexed Palette*, you will see the defined set of color entries. If the image has fewer than 256 colors, then not all of the palette will be filled—the empty part of the palette will be gray. You cannot add colors to this palette, but you can edit the existing colors. Clicking the right mouse button on any of the indexed color palette entries will open the Color Selection dialog. Choose the new color and click OK. The palette and the Image Window are updated immediately.

Along with the set of index entries, the Indexed Color Palette dialog has two options menus. The first, labeled *Ops*, currently has only one option: Close. The other options menu is labeled *Image*. If you open the Indexed Color Palette from an RGB Image Window, and there are no other Indexed Color images open, the palette will be empty and the menus and buttons, except for the Close button, will be grayed out. In other words, you can open the dialog but you cannot use it for that (or any) RGB image. However, if another open Image Window contains an indexed image, then the dialog will show that window. When more than one indexed image exists, the Indexed Color Palette dialog's Image menu allows you to choose which indexed image's palette you wish to use. Choosing an image from the Image options menu means you will be working directly with that image. You cannot choose one image to get its palette, and then apply its changes directly to another window. In order to transfer a color from one palette to another, you must go through the foreground color.

Left click on the palette entry that has the color you want in the first image. That will save the color to the foreground box in the Toolbox. Then select the other image you want to update. Right click on the palette entry you want to change. The Color Selection dialog will open. Here comes the tricky part: click on the foreground color box in the Toolbox—another Color Selection dialog opens, but this one shows the current foreground color settings. Adjust the first Color Selection dialog's sliders (or just type the values in the associated text fields) to match the second dialog, and click on OK in the first dialog. You have now updated the indexed palette with the new color. Be sure to close the foreground color's Color Selection dialog when you've finished.

When converting an image from RGB to Indexed (*Image->Indexed*), a dialog is presented for selecting the method of conversion. The Indexed Color Conversion dialog contains four toggles: Generate optimal palette, Use WWW-optimized palette, Use custom palette, and Use black/white (1-bit) palette. The optimal palette will generate an image that is most likely very close to the original. The "# of colors" text box can be used to limit the number of colors to be used in the palette. By default, all 256 entries will be used.

The original RGB image, before converting to Indexed.

Same image, converted to Indexed, along with the Indexed Color Palette for this image.

A WWW-optimized palette is one that uses the colors from the Netscape colormap, that is, the set of colors known to exist in Netscape, so that images will be guaranteed to get the colors they need when loaded into a Web surfer's Netscape browser. For some images, indexing using the Netscape palette may improve the way it's displayed on the Web. However, it isn't appropriate for all situations.

Using a custom palette allows you to change the set of colors to be used when the conversion is done. A number of predefined palettes are available for the GIMP. If you run a web site that needs a generic color scheme, you might consider picking one of the predefined color palettes and converting all your images to the palette before saving the images.

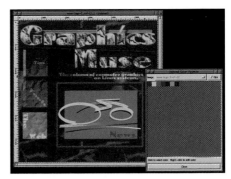

Original image converted using the Warm Color Palette.

Effect of editing one palette entry, changing it to a shade of blue.

When converting from RGB to Indexed Color, the number of colors in the original image is reduced to fit the number of colors in the indexed palette. For the optimal palette that would be 256 colors, but if you use a custom palette, the number of colors can be quite small. To make sure the conversion makes the best possible use of the limited set of colors in the indexed palette, you should use the Floyd-Steinberg dithering option. This toggle will cause the conversion process to attempt to pick the best color from the indexed palette to match the existing color in the RGB image. By default, this toggle is turned on, so you shouldn't need to change it. There will be cases, of course, when the dithering does not produce the conversion you were hoping for, and you may want to turn this option off. These cases are likely to be the exception and not the rule.

General Color Palette

The other palette dialog in the GIMP is called simply the Color Palette. This dialog, accessed from the *Dialogs->Palette* menu option, is very similar to the Indexed Color Palette dialog. It has a scrolled window of palette entries (the Indexed Color Palette's window does not scroll) and an Ops menu. In this dialog, however, the Ops dialog is used to create new palettes and delete existing ones. Unlike the Indexed Color Palette, the Color Palette dialog is used more to manage palettes than to directly modify colors within an existing image. The *Ops->New* option will create a new, blank (the scrolled window is black) palette. To add an entry to the palette, click on the New button at the bottom of the dialog. An entry is created using the current foreground color. The Edit button next to the New button will open the Color Selection dialog to allow you to change the currently selected palette entry. The Delete button will remove the current entry from the window. Once you've completed work on a new palette and its entries, you can use the *Ops->Refresh Palettes* menu option to save the palette to disk.

When you convert an RGB image to an Indexed image, you have the option of choosing an existing color palette to use for the conversion. These palettes are listed in the other options menu (which is labeled with the currently selected palette, if any) at the top the of Color Palette dialog. Selecting a palette from this menu will cause the scrolled window of color entries to be filled with that palette's colors. If you left click on a color entry, its name shows up in the text box that lies between the palette entries below and the menus above. The color for the entry you just selected also becomes the foreground color. You can change the symbolic name of the palette entry in this way; however, the use of color names is fairly limited in this version of the GIMP. You can then change the color for this entry by using the Edit button at the bottom of the dialog. However, unlike the Indexed Color Palette, these changes do not directly affect any of the open Image Windows. Again, this dialog is for managing palettes in general.

If the Indexed Color Palette is used to change the colors of an Indexed image by directly manipulating the index entries, for what would you use the more general Color Palette dialog? As mentioned previously, this is where you store frequently used colors. Suppose you want to create a color scheme for an image with multiple buttons. You experiment awhile and find a nice shade of green that works well for the buttons, given the colors in the rest of the image. You also find that the border of the buttons is another shade of green, the text in the buttons is still another shade and a horizontal stripe through the text is yet another. What's worse, the horizontal stripe is actually a blended layer on top of the text layer that is overlaid on the button. You could use the Color Picker to grab the colors for the buttons, but that's convenient only if you are working in the current image. Suppose the same colors are needed for a series of images. With the Color Picker, you would always need to keep the original image open. With the Color Palette, you simply stash the button colors in a palette and jump directly to the color you want each time you need it. The colors are easier to access, quicker to identify, and the palette dialogs require less memory to use—a key issue if the original image is very large.

So, with all this information, you might wonder how you can create a palette from an existing image. The simplest way to do this, in fact the only really reasonable way, is to convert the image from RGB to Indexed (if necessary) and then use the *Image->Save Palette* Image Window menu option. This option will open up the *Export GIMP Palette* dialog, which is a variation of the traditional file selection window used in the *File->Open* menu option in the Toolbox. You specify the name of the palette file, and click OK to save the palette. The palette will be saved to your $HOME/.gimp/palettes directory by default, although you can specify another location using the Export GIMP Palette dialog. Once the palette is saved, you need to use the *Ops->Refresh* option in the Color Palette dialog to add the new palette to the menu of available palettes. At this point, the palette would also show up in the Indexed Color Conversion dialog's Custom Palette menu.

Why doesn't the Color Palette show an RGB image's set of colors? Simple answer: there would be too many entries—up to 16 million. How would you adequately display and access each one? For this same reason, you cannot save an RGB image's palette. You must first convert it to an Indexed image before you can save it to a new palette.

All palette files use the same file format. Each is a text file containing a value triplet and a color name. The value triplet is a set of three numbers ranging from 0 to 255 representing, respectively, the red, green, and blue content of that color. If you are handy with a text editor and feel you could more easily create a new palette by hand, feel free to edit an existing palette. You might, for example, simply copy an existing palette to a new palette file and edit the new one. Remember to use the *Ops->Refresh* option in the Color Palette dialog when you've finished with your changes.

Patterns and Bucket Fills

Pattern Selection dialog

So, now you know how to deal with palettes. It may seem like a lot of work just to be able to set the foreground color. But setting the foreground color may be the most commonly used function in the GIMP. One tool which can make use of the foreground color to fill a large region is the Bucket Fill Tool.

As discussed in **Chapter 4 - The Toolbox,** *Bucket Fill* is used to do what is known as a *flood fill*—filling a given region with a specific color or pattern. The Tool Options dialog for this tool contains sliders for setting the opacity and threshold for bucket fills. It also allows the fills to be blended using the same types of modes provided by the Brush Selection dialog discussed earlier in this chapter. A Sample Merged toggle is also available, allowing the fill to be done by blending with the visually displayed color instead of only with the colors that actually exist in the current layer.

Along with these options are two toggle buttons for selecting either a Color Fill or a Pattern Fill. The *Color Fill* uses the foreground color to do its painting. The *Pattern Fill* uses the currently selected pattern, as defined by the *Pattern Selection* dialog. To open this dialog, select the *Dialogs->Patterns* option from the Image Window menu.

The Pattern Selection dialog consists of a scrolled set of squares, each a sample of a different pattern. Although the squares in the scrolled window are the same size, the patterns can actually be any size. If you left click on one of the squares, a pop-up window opens to show the full-size pattern. Also, once you've clicked on the square, that pattern becomes selected. A black outline is drawn around the square, although with some patterns this outline is a bit hard to see. The name and dimensions (using whatever units of size are specified in the `gimprc` file) of the selected pattern are printed along the top of the Pattern Selection dialog.

Creating New Patterns

As with palettes and brushes, the GIMP provides a means of creating your own patterns. The process is a little less automated with patterns, but requires only a few basic steps:

1. Select a region of an existing image to use for the pattern.

2. Copy this to a new Image Window.

3. Resize the new window to the size of the pattern. Don't use the Scale option—that will scale the pattern as well. What you want to do in this step is simply crop the Image Window down so that the pattern fills the entire window and the window is no bigger than the pattern you wish to save.[2]

4. Save the image as a pattern file using the .pat file extension. When you specify a .pat extension and click OK, you will be prompted for a description of the pattern. This description will be displayed across the top of the Pattern Selection dialog when the new pattern is selected in that dialog.

The trick is to first make a decent selection of the pattern. You will generally want a square selection, unless you are willing to fill in blank areas in the new Image Window with a solid color later. You can also create a very large pattern in a large Image Window, then scale it down to a more reasonable size to save as the pattern. If you do this, it should be the last step you perform and should not be done instead of the Resize step described above. After creating the new pattern, you need to use the Refresh button in the Pattern Selection dialog to gain access to the new pattern.

Keep in mind that patterns are full-color images, not grayscale images like brushes. You should remember this when creating your own patterns. Also, you may want to consider creating an image for use as a full-color pattern, as well as a grayscale version for use as a brush. In this way, you can use the brush with the Eraser (or one of the other drawing tools) to "stamp out" parts of a bucket fill that used the pattern. Conversely, you can use the Clone tool to paint patterns into an image.

---

2. You can use the Crop tool if you like. This is discussed along with other Transform tools in **Chapter 9 - Using Transforms**.

Cloning

The *Clone* tool is used to copy pixels from one location, the source, to another, the destination. This process makes use of the currently selected brush from the Brush Selection dialog. The Clone tool offers a Tool Options dialog with three toggles. The first two, Image Source and Pattern Source, are mutually exclusive and determine where the source pixels will be taken from. If the *Image Source* toggle is selected, then the user can select a location within the current layer from which to clone. To do this, you first click, with the CTRL key held down, on the spot which you wish to use as the source. When you do this, a cross hair cursor is displayed to show where the clone source has been marked. Release the CTRL key and mouse button and move to the spot where you wish to begin cloning. As you move the mouse around the window with the left mouse button held down, the distance and angle between the source point and the destination point stays constant. That is, as you move up and to the left of the destination, you are cloning from up and to the left of the source. Note that cloning in this way works only with the source on the current layer. If the current layer is transparent at the source (even if lower layers are not), then nothing changes at the destination.

The *Pattern Source* toggle causes the Clone tool to work similarly, except it takes the currently selected pattern from the Pattern Selection dialog as the source image. There are two modes to using this option: aligned and unaligned. The *Aligned* toggle, when turned on (which is the default), will tile the pattern over the size of the layer. If you use this method over a blank white window it appears as if you are erasing the white layer to see the pattern underneath! In essence, however, it is the other way around—you are combining the pattern over the layer. When the Aligned toggle is turned off (unaligned mode), each use of the Clone tool will result in a distinct tile orientation, unlikely to integrate with previous applications. Keep in mind that whatever blend mode is configured in the Brush Selection dialog will be in effect during the cloning process, no matter which method (image or pattern) is used.

Cloning can be an under-utilized gem for new users. One of the most common uses of the Clone tool is to hide scratches in scanned photographs. By taking a nearby part of the image and patching over the scratch, you can quickly clean up old and damaged photographs. The effectiveness of this process, which is referred to as "retouching", depends on the quality of the scan and the size of the scratch, as well as your ability to find clone sources that closely resemble the color and texture of the scratched area. When using the Clone tool for this sort of clean-up operation, it would be best to experiment with different brushes to find the one that best suits the scratches in question. The Clone tool operates like the Paintbrush, so using a soft edged brush such as one of the Circle Fuzzy brushes is recommended.

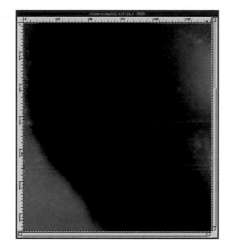

Closeup of some of the damaged image, which is very pitted and scratched.

Same region after cloning operation has been completed. The Circle Fuzzy (03) brush was used to perform most of the cloning.

Blur and Sharpen with the Convolver

Although the Clone tool can offer you the ability to clean up scratches and imperfections, you may find that on closer inspection the patches are not quite as clean as you'd like. One way to clean them up even further is with the Convolver tool's blur option.

The *Convolver* takes the current brush settings and mixes nearby pixels according to predefined matrices. The matrices determine which nearby pixels to mix and how much to mix them. The *Pressure* slider in the Convolver's Tool Options dialog can be used to increase or decrease the effect. Higher values cause a greater effect, lower values diminish it. This is similar to the way the Pressure slider on the Airbrush works.

Convolver's Tool Options dialog also allows two modes of operation: Blur and Sharpen. The *Blur* option can be used to mix the previously discussed Clone operations. It can also be used to remove some of the graininess of a scanned image by reducing the range of variation in

193

colors of nearby pixels. The *Sharpen* mode does the opposite—it increases the graininess, which in turn brings out the details within the region of the brush shape.

To use the Convolver, simply click on some part of the image while holding down the left mouse button and begin dragging, just like you do with the Paintbrush. The blurring or sharpening happens almost immediately, although with some brushes, the calculations can take a moment to complete on slower machines. You may want to use this tool slowly until you get used to how long the updates take to become apparent. If the effect is not visible, try zooming in on the region to be blurred or sharpened and then applying the Convolver.

Cloned image blurred using the Convolver to smooth the shading.

The Convolver, because it works with brushes, acts like a variation on the previously discussed drawing tools. Although it doesn't draw or paint with the foreground color or with patterns, it can process regions linearly between two click points. Like the Paintbrush or Pencil, just click once to set the starting point, then click with the SHIFT key held down to cause the Convolver to blur or sharpen following the straight line between the two end points.

The GFig Plug-In

We've covered colors and painting, brushes and patterns, pencils, paintbrushes and erasers. With all these tools you find after much experimenting that drawing in the GIMP is, in many ways, a hit-or-miss operation. You want a little more control, something that allows more precise alignment, more accurate curves and lines, and something that doesn't require repeated use of CTRL-z to undo operations that just don't look right. You need the GFig Plug-In.

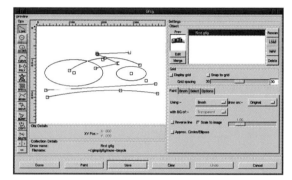

GFig Plug-In interface

GFig, a plug-in from Andy Thomas, allows you to do all these things and more. This plug-in is accessible from the *Filters->Render->GFig* Image Window menu option. When selected, a window opens with a large number of options. The interface is a little confusing at first, but it doesn't take long to become familiar with it. Basically, the window is divided into two halves—the left side is where you make your drawing edits, and the right side is where you manage options for rendering (or applying) the drawing to your image. GFig is a vector drawing tool, meaning that instead of drawing by hand, as with a pencil, you specify points between which lines and arcs are to be drawn. The collection of points and their connecting lines and/or arcs is called *objects*. Editing is done by moving object points either individually, which will change the shape of the object, or collectively, which moves the entire object.

On the left side of the GFig interface is a column of buttons labeled *Ops*. These are the set of drawing tools and the tools used for editing objects. An object is one of the primitive shapes: line, circle, ellipse, curve, polygons, three pointed stars, spirals, and Bézier curves. Each of these has a button in the Ops column. When you click on one of the buttons, you can then place points in the drawing window just to the right of the Ops buttons. The drawing window has rulers like the image

Sample GFig image

Sample GFig image

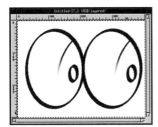

Sample GFig image

windows, but these do not have guides in them. Instead, you can use GFig's built-in grid. We'll talk about turning on the grid and setting the spacing of grid lines when we talk about the right side of the GFig interface.

To create one of the primitive shapes, you have to place the points for that shape in the drawing area. For lines, this means clicking once to set the starting point and then dragging the mouse, left button down, to the end point. The procedure is the same for circles, except the first point is the center of the circle and the distance to the endpoint is the radius. For ellipses, the endpoint determines the width and height of the ellipse. This is similar to the circle, except the ellipse can be flattened top to bottom or squeezed left and right by dragging the end point around the drawing window. The polygon, star, and spiral objects all operate by specifying the center point and dragging an end point to create the primitive shape. When you let go of the mouse button, the object is created. Two objects, the curve and the Bézier curve, require you to specify individual points to define the object. The regular curve requires that you click in three different spots. The first and last clicks specify the end points of the curve, and the middle click is the point through which the curve must run. The Bézier curve requires three or more clicks. The first and last also specify end points, and any in between specify control points that adjust the curve of the line. The Bézier object also requires that the last click be performed with the SHIFT key pressed in order to anchor that last point and end the curve.

Once you've created your objects, you can edit them by choosing one of the editing Ops buttons: Move, Mvpnt (single point move), Copy, or Delete. The *Move* button allows you to click on one of the control points, represented by small squares, of any object to move it around the drawing window. The *Mvpnt* button lets you move individual control points. This has the effect of changing the shape of the object based on the object type. The *Copy* button allows you to click on a control point and drag, left mouse button down. When you do this, a copy of the object on whose control point you clicked is created. With the *Delete* button, clicking on a control point will delete the object associated with that control point.

Below the Ops buttons are three smaller buttons: <, >, and =. The first two, the < (less than) and > (greater than) buttons, allow you to cycle through the objects in the drawing window. When you click on one of these buttons, all of the objects disappear except one. This allows you to single out a particular object when you have a large number of objects in the drawing area and the control points become difficult to isolate. The = (equal sign) button redisplays all objects and their control points in the drawing window.

An important thing to note about GFig and its drawing window: the drawing window will be created in the dimensions of the currently active layer of the image from which GFig was invoked. If you are working on a very large image, you should consider creating a blank layer that is significantly smaller in which to render the drawing, so that the drawing window in GFig will be of a reasonable size. By default, GFig will render the drawing—that is, actually draw the shapes—in the active layer. This can be changed to make GFig create a new layer of the same size in which the drawing will be done by selecting the *New* option in the *Draw On* menu in the right side of the GFig interface.

The right side of the GFig interface is broken into three parts: an object manager with a preview window and Rescan/Load/New/Delete buttons, a grid settings box, and a set of notebook pages with tabs labeled Paint, Brush, Select, and Options. The object manager allows you to save the current drawing window to a file, load an existing GFig file, or start a new GFig file. The Save button is actually at the bottom of the Gfig interface's window. Next to the Rescan/Load/New/Delete buttons is a list of GFig object files, if any, from which you can load. These files are saved in the user's $HOME/.gimp/gfig directory by default. You can specify another directory when you save a new file, but you will need to add that directory to the GFig directory configuration in the gimprc configuration file in order for it to show up in the list of available GFig files. The GFig line in the gimprc[3] file should look something like this:

```
# gfig pattern directory
(gfig-path "${gimp_dir}/gfig")
```

The first entry after gfig-path is the default directory, which for most users will be $HOME/.gimp/gfig. If you want to add another directory after that, just add a colon followed by the quoted path:

```
(gfig-path "${gimp_dir}/gfig":"/usr/local/gfig")
```

Below the object management buttons are the toggles and a slider for managing the built-in grid for the drawing window. The grid is off by default. To turn it on, click on the *Display grid* toggle. The grid will be drawn in the drawing window on the left side of the interface. Next to the Display grid toggle is the *Snap to grid* toggle. When this is turned on (it's off by default), the object centers and control points in the drawing window gravitate toward grid line intersections. Below this toggle is the

---

3. See **Appendix A - The gimprc File** for details on the format of the default gimprc file.

Grid spacing slider. The spacing is in whatever units are currently configured in the gimprc (pixels, inches or centimeters). Higher settings spread the grid lines out, smaller values squeeze them in. The grid lines are used for alignment purposes only. When rendered, the drawing will not include the grid lines. They are simply used to aid alignment operations.

The set of four notebook tabs below the grid management slider controls how the drawing will be rendered. The first tab, *Paint*, defines how the objects will be used: as the outline for brush strokes, as the outline for a new selection without actually drawing, or as an outline for a new selection that gets flood filled around the selection border. The *Draw On* menu offers you the choice of rendering the drawing (or selection) on the current layer, a new layer or multiple layers. The latter option will create a new layer for each object in the drawing window. If you choose to create new layers, the background can be set to *Transparent*, *Background*, *White*, or *Copy the current layer*, using the last of the options menus in the Paint page. A more esoteric option, the *Reverse line* toggle, can be set to cause the rendering to draw from end points to start points (for lines and curves) or counterclockwise (for closed objects like circles and stars). By default, GFig will render from start points to end points (for lines and curves) and clockwise (for closed objects). The *Scale to image* toggle allows you to scale the relative size of the objects. With the toggle turned on, the scale is 1:1. When you turn it off, you can adjust the slider next to it to increase or decrease the relative size of the objects. These changes are reflected immediately in the drawing window.

GFig Brush page

The next page in the notebook is the *Brush* page. This page allows you to select a brush type in the scrolled window. If the options menu is set to *Brush* (which is the same as Paintbrush), *Airbrush*, or *Pencil*, the foreground color is used for the rendering. If the menu is set to *Pattern*, the currently active pattern is used instead. Both the Brush and Airbrush options in the menu permit setting slider values, similar to the settings of their Toolbox cousins' Tool Options dialog.

GFig Select page

Following the Brush page is the *Select* page. None of the features in this page will be accessible unless either *Selection* or *Selection+Fill* is chosen from the Paint page's *Using* menu. The options on this page are just like their Toolbox selection cousins: Antialiasing, Feather, and Feather Radius. A *Selection type* menu allows you to specify how to combine objects as selections, the way you normally would using keyboard modifiers with the Toolbox selection tools. Below these options are menus for specifying how to fill selections and what to fill them with.

GFig Options page

The last page in the notebook is the *Options* page. These are general rendering options and options for the drawing area and interface. The grid menus really belong with the other grid options, and may change locations in the interface by the time this text reaches the shelves. Most features of GFig provide *tool tips*, those small yellow windows that pop up when the mouse is placed over a button, slider, or some other window component. You can turn these off if they become annoying by using the tool tips toggle on this page.

Finally, the buttons in the bottom row in the GFig interface have various uses. The Save button has already been mentioned. The Clear and Undo buttons deal with the drawing window. *Clear* removes all objects. The number of levels of *Undo* can be set with a slider in the Options page of the notebook. The *Paint* button is the one to use when you're ready to render the drawing into your image. When you click it, each object becomes a selection and is either stroked or filled as defined by the many settings available in GFig. The Paint button will not close the GFig interface. The *Cancel* and *Done* buttons will do that. Both do the same thing. Cancel does not, however, undo any changes that Paint may have done.

Rendering is done by first creating selections that match the outlines of the primitive shapes in the drawing window. Each selection is rendered one at a time. This means that in the Image Window you will be able to undo a certain number of the renderings using CTRL-z. Be careful with this, however. If you create a large number of objects but have the default setting of five levels of Undo set, then you may not be able to undo all the renderings that GFig has done. Your best bet is to always render to a new layer so that if things don't come out just right, you can simply delete that layer. When you use the *New Layer* option with GFig, the layer will be labeled "GFig 0".

GFig is still in early development. The interface may be tidied up just to make it feel less crowded and more intuitive, and there are a few more features that should be implemented, but overall this is the best plug-in available for use directly in the GIMP for detailed drawing and painting. Expect to see more improvements in GFig in the near future.

Moving On

Most chapters thus far have been relatively long-winded—there has been quite a bit of information to cover! The next two chapters offer a little respite. The first covers various methods of transforming the dimensions and orientation of images and layers. The following chapter covers the topic of gradients and how to create, use and edit them.

Following these next two chapters will be the final chapter in the first part of this book, **Chapter 11 - Scanning, Printing, and Print Media**. Finally, **Part 2** covers the vast set of plug-in filters available in the standard GIMP distribution.

Tutorial

In previous chapters you learned how to create selections and layers. In this chapter, you learned techniques for drawing and using the Bucket Fill tool to add solid and patterned fills to selections. Let's combine these to create a simple effect: a television-like frame with three buttons and a squiggly video display.

The first thing you'll make is the frame, then the buttons. This may actually be the hardest part of the whole tutorial. We'll use a set of selections, one box and three circles, along with the *Edit->Stroke* menu option to draw the outlines of our TV screen and some controls to one side. First, be sure the foreground and background colors are reset to their defaults. Next, open a new Image Window using the default 256x256 dimensions and the default background color (which should be white if you've reset the colors correctly). This will make a fairly small TV screen, but it is only an example.

In the Image Window, create a square selection that covers most of the left and middle of the window, leaving the right side open for the buttons. Next, add three circular selections. Remember: hold down the SHIFT key to add to a selection, and keep it down to draw a perfect circle. You can align the circles by placing one vertical guide near the square selection, and three horizontal guides that start at the top of the square and space evenly down the height of the square. Use the intersection of the horizontal guides and the vertical guide as your starting point for creating the circles. If you hold down the SHIFT key while you create the selections, you'll get three fairly consistent circles (there are tricks for making them exactly the same—think about how you might do it using *Selection to Channel*). After you've made the selections, you can remove the guides or simply turn off their visibility using the *View->Toggle Guides* menu option.

Although it might not seem obvious, we're going to need these selections again later. Save the selections to a channel. When you do this, the active layer becomes inactive (you should have only one layer at this point). Check the Layers and Channels dialog and click on the background layer to make it active again. We don't really need to name the new channel we just created, although we could. Also, remove the square selection—hold down the CTRL key before clicking the mouse, then release the CTRL key. Remember how to remove selections? When you finish you should have only the three circular selections. Save those to a channel, too. Then get rid of all the selections with SHIFT-CTRL-a.

At this point, you should have the square screen and three round selections for the buttons. Choose the *Edit->Stroke* option from the Image Window menu. Remember to select a reasonably sized brush. If the stroked outline is too thick (you don't want it very thick, or very thin for that matter, for what we'll be doing with it next), just use CTRL-z to undo the stroke operation, then pick a better brush. A soft edged brush will work better than a hard edged one. Try the Circle Fuzzy that is 11x11.

Next, we'll make use of a filter for the first time. We're going to use the *Emboss* filter, which falls under the *Filters->Distorts* submenu. When you select this option, a dialog opens. If the Emboss option is not accessible (grayed out), then you don't have the background layer selected in the Layers and Channels dialog. The Emboss dialog is a fairly straightforward filter to use. First, select the Emboss option (as opposed to the Bumpmap option). Next, set the Azimuth to 35, the Elevation to 23 and the Depth to 9. You can use other values, but these will assure that your image is comparable to the one I created with the steps in this tutorial.

The *Azimuth* is simply the direction of the lighting on the embossed image. If you move the slider from the far left to the far right, you can watch the preview window as the light on the image moves around the raised area. The *Elevation* is a sort of contrast adjustment. The higher the contrast, the greater the three-dimensional effect shows up. In our case the value of 23 gives us a fairly obvious raised area. With other images, the value may not have the same effect. It is very dependent on the colors in the image. Finally, the *Depth* just adds a sort of shine to the image. Lower values dull the image; higher values make it shine more.

Again, the level to which you have to raise this value before the shine is obvious changes from image to image.

So now you have the three-dimensional effect for the TV screen and the buttons. Next, we'll fill in the region around the screen and buttons with a wood grain finish. This choice brings to mind a very early model television, compared to modern ones with plastic casings. Use the Fuzzy selection tool and click anywhere outside the square raised area. That should select all of the gray area around the screen and buttons. Now click on the Bucket Fill tool. Be sure its Tool Options dialog is set to fill using a pattern and not a solid color. Open the Patterns dialog and choose one of the wood grain patterns. I chose Parque #3. Click inside the selected region to fill it with the pattern.

Turn off the current selection and reselect the area inside the square raised area using the Fuzzy selection tool again. This is where we'll put our TV picture. After you select the Bucket Fill tool again, choose another pattern, say the Flat Earth pattern, and click inside the new selection. For added effect, open the Video dialog by choosing *Filters->Misc->Video*. You can choose any effect you want from the dialog that pops up. I think the Staggered pattern type looks most realistic for this image, but you can try any of the options that you like.

We're almost done. We just need to do something interesting with the buttons. Go over to the Channels page in the Layers and Channels dialog and click on the channel with the three white buttons. Click on the channel name with the left mouse button to get the Channels menu, and select *Channel to Selection*. Go back to the Layers page and click on the background layer again to make it active. The selection will cover part of the raised area, so shrink it a little using *Select->Shrink*. Set the amount to 5. That should select just the inside region of the buttons.

If all went well, your image should look something like this.

Once again, choose a new pattern. Click inside one of the button selections. And that's it. It doesn't look exactly like a TV, but you see how easy it is to create simple effects. You can experiment to find a way to make the buttons more like dials, with text inside them instead of a pattern. You can play with the colors in the screen or run it through a few more filters to get some really strange effects. The point is, none of this is very difficult to get started on. Expertise comes from practice and experimentation, so don't be intimidated by the options in the GIMP; explore and play with them.

Chapter 9 - Using Transforms

Images and their individual layers can be rotated and resized in a number of different ways with the GIMP. These modifications are referred to in the graphics world as *transforms*. This chapter looks at all the basic transform tools.

Cropping

The first type of transform is a *crop*. Cropping is a simple process where the original image is clipped, like you would cut a photograph with a pair of scissors to fit in a frame. The excess pieces of the image are thrown away. With the GIMP, however, the crop can be done only along the horizontal and vertical edges. You can't make a diagonal or round crop of an image. Of course, with the GIMP you can usually recover the cutout pieces of a cropped image, depending on how many levels of undo are set.

Autocrop

The simplest crop is performed using the Autocrop Plug-In, *Image->Transforms->Autocrop*. This plug-in will examine the image for what it believes is the background color for the sampled image. To do this, the plug-in first examines the image as it is displayed in the Image Window, disregarding layer information. It examines the corners of the image to find four, three, or two colors that match. If it finds such a match, then that color is used as the background color. If no match is found, then an average of the four corners is taken and that color is used as the background color for the image. The background color is then used as a source against which all other pixels are compared, starting at the outside edges and working in toward the center of the image.

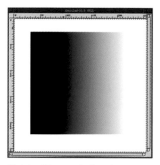 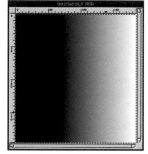

Original image, before Autocrop has been applied.

After Autocrop has been applied. The white border has been removed.

The vertical and horizontal edges of the cropped image will be those columns and rows which contain at least one pixel that does not match the background color. Autocrop then passes the new dimensions for the image to the GIMP's built-in crop tool for final cropping and redisplaying of the Image Window.

Autocrop works on any image type (RGB, indexed color or grayscale). Since there is no chance of an image without at least two corners having the same color being cropped, use of Autocrop is generally limited to images with solid borders.

Zealous Crop

Another form of crop is the *Zealous Crop, Image->Transforms-> Zealous Crop*. This plug-in works very much like the Autocrop Plug-In, except that the comparisons for each row and column are not made against the corners of the image. They are made against the first pixel in each row or column, depending on which direction is currently being examined. A normal gradient applied over the entire background of a new Image Window with a small white circle cutout would get cropped to the minimum/maximum points of the circle along the axis upon which the gradient was applied. This is counter to the Autocrop Plug-In, which would not perform any cropping at all.

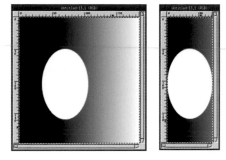

Original image, before Zealous Crop has been applied.

After Zealous Crop has been applied. The width has been modified because the columns on the outside of the image had matching pixels from top to bottom. But the height hasn't changed, because none of the rows had matching pixels from left to right.

Like Autocrop, Zealous Crop works on any image type. Zealous Crop will crop more images than Autocrop might, but only when either a solid border is present or a smooth gradient is applied exactly horizontally or vertically in the image.

Crop Tool

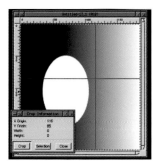

Crop Information dialog

If the automatic nature of Autocrop and Zealous Crop is not for you, there are other ways to crop an image down in size. The Toolbox offers the *Crop* tool, the small knife-like icon on the right side of the third row of buttons. This tool is more like an adjustable rectangular template that can be placed over an image. The template can be resized and moved prior to performing the crop operation.

Clicking once on the Crop tool icon will enable the Crop tool. This tool has no Tool Options dialog, but it does have its own special dialog, the *Crop Information* dialog, for specifying dimensions and the method for selecting a crop outline. To open the Crop Information dialog, you click once in the Image Window you wish to crop. The dialog shows the current dimensions of the crop region. If you click and drag in the Image Window, you can manually create the rectangular region to which the crop will be applied.

Using the Crop tool effectively can take a little practice. There are a number of tricks to using it. First, the initial mouse click will specify an anchor location for the crop outline. The outline is made up of four lines, one each extending from one edge of the Image Window to one corner of the outline. Each corner also has a small box drawn from the edges of the outline in toward the center of the outline.

The first time you do this, you can click and drag in any direction away from the anchor point and the outline will be drawn accordingly. However, once you let go of the mouse button, the direction of the outline with respect to the anchor point becomes fixed. If you click and drag again, the outline follows the mouse but it will not allow you to go through one of the lines (horizontal or vertical) running through the anchor point—the anchor point moves when you try to do this! At first this might be frustrating. You can move the anchor point in one direction only, but you can't move it back. The trick here is the setting of the anchor points. If you click and hold the mouse button down for a second (as opposed to clicking and dragging immediately) the anchor point will jump to the location of the cursor, with a cross hair marking that spot. At this point, you can drag in any direction, just like you did the very first time you specified an anchor point. Again, once you let go, the direction of the drag becomes fixed with respect to the new anchor.

When you drag the mouse around the Image Window, the outline for the crop moves with you. Once you release the mouse button, the outline stays put, but you may need to alter its size or placement. If you click outside the outline, the outline is once again modifiable. If, however, you click inside the crop outline, the crop operation is performed. Don't despair! As long as you have one or more levels of undo configured, you can get the old image back using CTRL-z. Of course, once you've placed the outline the way you want it, go ahead and click inside the outline.

Another trick is using the squares that sit on each corner of the crop outline. If you click and drag immediately from one of these points, the outline can be resized. The corner across the diagonal from the anchor point (always the upper left or lower right corner, depending on the direction of the outline from the anchor point) simply moves the edges of the outline. The other three corners will cause the box to snap to them—adjusting it either horizontally or vertically, or (in the case of the anchor point) in both directions. This only happens, however, if you click and drag immediately.

If you click and hold the mouse button for a second in one of the corners not on the diagonal from the anchor point, then you can move the outline without changing its size. The way to tell what you can do at any point within the Image Window while using the Crop tool is to look at the cursor shape. The table on the next page shows the meaning of the various cursor shapes when used in conjunction with the Crop tool.

Cursor Shape	Crop Tool Function
Fluer (i.e., the Move tool icon)	Allows you to move the crop outline without changing its size.
Arrow pointing into a corner	Allows changes to the size of the crop outline only.
Cross hair	Allows either changing crop outline size (via immediate click/drag) or resetting of the anchor point (via click and hold).
Box	Inside the crop outline. Clicking here will cause the crop operation to be performed.

The Crop Information dialog contains a button for setting the initial crop outline to encompass the current selection. To use this feature, first create a selection within the Image Window. The shape of the selection doesn't matter—it can be rectangular, circular or any other shape. Once the selection has been completed, select the Crop tool and click once in the Image Window. Now click on the Selection button of the Crop Information dialog. The crop outline will now enclose the entire selected region in a rectangular box. As mentioned earlier, the crop outline will always be rectangular, so the cropping doesn't necessarily follow the selection outline (unless it happens to be rectangular).

Scaling vs. Resizing with Layers and Images

All of the crop tools discussed up to this point operate on the entire Image Window. They do not deal with cropping of individual layers. Cropping also assumes you want to cut your image down in size, either in height, width, or both directions at the same time. What do you do if you want to enlarge the image? Or change the dimensions of individual layers? What if you want to make a layer larger without changing the size of the contents of that layer? In these cases, you need to make use of either the Scaling or Resizing tool.

There are two sets of scaling and resizing tools in the GIMP: one set for the image as a whole, and one set for dealing with layers. The former are accessed from the *Image->Scale* and *Image->Resize* options of the Image Window menu. The latter are available from the Layers and Channels dialog.

The Image Scale dialog. The Scale Layer dialog is exactly the same.

The Image Resize dialog. Like the Scale dialogs, the Layers version of this is the exactly the same.

Scaling an image or layer changes its dimensions. The GIMP stretches the pixels to fit the new dimensions. *Resizing* changes the dimensions but does not change the existing pixels. Transparent pixels are added around the edges to fill in the extra space created by the resize operation. If a resize operation is done on an image or layer that does not have a transparent channel, the transparent channel is automatically added.

Scaling and Resizing Dialogs

The dialogs for scaling both images and layers are the same, but with different titles. The same is true of the Image Resize and Resize Layer dialogs.

The Image Scale and Scale Layer dialogs are opened via the *Image->Scale* Image Window menu option and the *Scale Layer* Layers menu option[1] respectively, and provide the ability to set either specific width and height values, or proportional changes using the X and Y ratio text input fields. A toggle button, which is turned on by default, constrains the ratio of width to height. This means that if you change the width of the image, for example, the height will change to keep the proportions of the image the same. This applies to all the fields, so changes to the New width text field with the Constrain Ratio toggle set will cause updates to all four fields in this dialog. With the toggle turned off, you can change width and height independently. Note that changes to the width text field cause updates to the X ratio text field, and vice versa, even if the Constrain Ratio toggle is not set. The same is true for the height and Y ratio text fields.

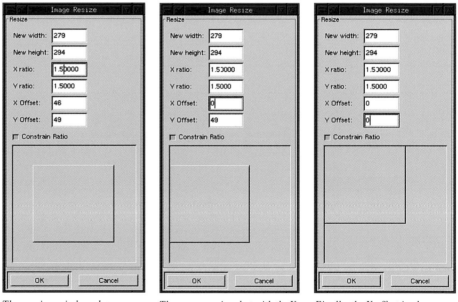

The preview window shows a raised section for the original window and a depressed region where the new pixels will be added. The preview here shows a 1.5 times increase in the original.

The same preview, but with the X offset changed to 0.

Finally, the Y offset is also changed to 0. The original image will now be positioned in the upper left region of the resized image with the rest of the image becoming transparent.

---

1. Right click on a layer in the Layers and Channels dialog to view all of the Layers menu options.

The Image Resize and Resize Layer dialogs offer similar fields, plus a few extras. Since a resize adds pixels around the edges of the original image (when resized to a larger size), these dialogs have offset text fields to specify where pixels will be added. To see how these work, you can specify a new size and see the new dimensions displayed visually in the preview window below the text fields. If you specify a new width that is 1.5 times the original, the preview shows the original as a raised region and the new area as a depressed region. The offsets are automatically adjusted to set the original into the center of the new image. Changing the offsets to 0 will move the original to the upper left corner of the new image, causing all new pixels to be added to the right and bottom sides of the image. In this way, you can use the Offset fields to position the original image however you wish in the resized version.

If resizing makes the image smaller, the effect is the same as cropping the image. The preview window displays this a little differently. The raised region is the original image and a black box is drawn inside this to show the region which will be left after the cropping is completed. The black box is always centered in the preview, and changing the offsets will move the raised region around.

Transform Tool

Transform Tool Options

Another tool available from the Toolbox is the Transform tool, which is actually a set of four different types of transforms: Rotation, Scaling, Shearing, and Perspective. *Scaling* works like the scale dialogs, but is more interactive. By clicking on a layer (the Transform tool works only on individual layers) or selection you create a bounding box. Clicking in the box and dragging up, down, left or right will scale the box and its contents. Scaling a selection automatically floats the selection. When you click in the layer, either in the bounding box or outside of it, the closest edges of the bounding box will be moved when you drag. Keep in mind that scaling in this manner can cause the contents of the bounding box to become jagged. The *Smoothing* toggle will reduce this effect to some extent, but some images—especially those with text—are prone to distortion when scaled repeatedly.

Shearing is used to slant the layer or selection. As mentioned in **Chapter 4 - The Toolbox**, the effect is like pushing an empty cardboard box to one side. *Perspective* causes a layer to appear to be angled away from the viewer. This is done by adjusting the corners of the bounding box independently of one another.

Rotations are unique among these transforms in that the bounding box's shape is not changed, it is simply rotated around its center. The rotation can cause the size of the layer to change in order to fit the rotated section. This means that a rotation will never cause part of the bounded region to be clipped to the layer's current size. Rotations using the Transform tool can be arbitrary angles. In order to increase the level of granularity (i.e., decrease the amount of change in rotation angle as you move the mouse), you need to move the mouse further away from the center of the bounding box, although there is a practical limit to how small the change in rotation angle will get. If you hold down the CTRL key, the rotation of the selection will snap to exact 15 degree angles, which makes it easy to create (for example) an exact 45 degree rotation.

The Transform tool can work on any layer, including floating layers. If you make a selection in a floating layer and try to perform a transform on it, the original floating selection is automatically anchored to the previous active layer, and a new floating selection is created.

Image and Layer Rotations

Rotate dialog

The Transform tool's rotation function allows manual rotation of a selection or layer. You can also use one of the rotation transforms available from the *Image->Transforms* submenu in the Image Window menu.

There are three types of rotations available from this menu: rotation of layers, rotation of images, and an alternative to both. The *Image->Transforms->Image* and *Image->Transforms->Layer* menus both offer the ability to rotate either 90 or 270 degrees. The alternative, *Image->Transforms->Rotate*, offers a dialog which allows you to specify rotations in increments of 90 degrees. By default, this feature will rotate only the currently active layer, but a toggle is provided in the dialog to allow rotation of the entire image. All of these menu options allow specific rotations in multiples of 90 degrees. Again, if you need more arbitrary rotation angles, you can use the Transform tool's rotation option.

Moving On

This chapter was short and to the point—transforms in the GIMP are powerful, yet fairly simple to use. The important thing to remember is that, except in the case of cropping, transforms will create floating layers from selections.

Next we move on to another powerful but fairly straightforward feature—gradients.

Tutorial

Transforms in the GIMP are fairly easy to use, but are not quite as sophisticated as I'd like. You generally can't specify exact rotation amounts (except via the Script-Fu interface which is not discussed in this text). Getting exact rotations of 20, 32, or any other arbitrary degree can be difficult.

One of the tricks you can use to get more exact rotations is with the Transform tool. Try dragging the mouse farther from the center of the selection to be rotated. When you do this, the rate of change in rotation is reduced to the point where the increment or decrement is less than 1/10 of a degree (usually closer to 6/100 of a degree). As you move closer to the center of the selection, this rate of change increases. So, in some sense, you have a greater degree of control in creating rotations of specific angles. Hopefully, future versions will provide more precise control.

One common use of the resize option for a layer is to add some space around text layers so that you can blur the text. When you create a text layer, you usually get a layer that fits the text exactly. Try adding a border around the text using the Border option in the Text tool dialog. You may want to add even more space later. Many text tricks require a blur layer to be combined with other layers to produce three-dimensional effects. If you blur a text layer in which the text runs up against the edges of the layer, you'll get hard lines instead of blurs where the text and layer edges meet. Resizing the layer allows some room for the blur to complete. If you use this trick, be sure to turn off the Keep Transparency option in the Layers dialog.

Try using the scale option to enlarge an entire image; you may find the quality of the image degrades a bit. The amount of degradation depends on the quality of the original image and the scale amount. In some cases, you can clear up some of the degradation by using a blur filter, followed by sharpening the image a little. Despeckling the image may also help. Both *Sharpen* and *Despeckle* are filters available under the *Filters->Enhance* menu. *Blur* filters can be found under *Filters->Blur*.

Chapter 10 - Gradients

A *gradient*, often referred to more generically as a *blend*, is a smooth transition from one color to another. Gradients can be used to produce background images, as when a painter primes a canvas, or to produce a smooth transition in a layer through application as a mask. They can also be used to create special effects of their own through the use of composite modes on new or existing layers. Note that the smooth appearance of a gradient on a display depends upon on your video hardware. Gradients look best on high color (65K or higher) displays. Gradients will work on lower-end displays, but the appearance of their smoothness suffers and they will appear speckled, at best.

The GIMP offers two main tools for dealing with gradients: the Blend tool and the Gradient Editor. This chapter discusses the use of both tools, as well as a few tricks for their general application in your images.

The Blend Tool

In the last column of the fifth row of buttons in the Toolbox, you will find the Blend tool. The icon looks like a square with the left side dark and the right side light. Double clicking on this button will bring up the Tool Options dialog for the Blend tool. We covered this dialog previously in **Chapter 4 - The Toolbox**, but let's review it.

When you select the Blend tool, the default settings in the Tool Options allow you to create a gradient that runs from the current foreground color to the current background color along a linear transition. That means the place where you first click in the image will become the foreground color and wherever you drag to and release the mouse button will become the background color. The straight line between these two points will be filled by the smooth transition between the two colors. If

Tool Options

Blend Options

Opacity: ———————— 100.0

Offset: ———————— 0.0

Mode: Normal

Blend: FG to BG (RGB)

Gradient: Linear

Repeat: None

☐ Adaptive supersampling

Max depth: ———— 3

Threshold: ———— 0.20

Close

Blend Tool Options

the gradient has not been applied to a selection, then the gradient appears to run through the nontransparent regions of the layer. If the layer does not have the Keep Transparency toggle enabled, then the entire layer will be modified by the gradient.

A gradient is applied by clicking once, holding the left mouse button down and dragging across the image to the end point, and then releasing the button. You can start a gradient from anywhere within the Image Window, but you can actually end it outside the window. The GIMP will determine the length of the drag operation and adjust the gradient appropriately. This is true of gradients applied to selections, as well. You can start and stop the gradient inside or outside of the selection and the GIMP will calculate how much of the gradient to apply within the selection region. All gradient operations must start inside the Image Window, as that's the only way the GIMP can recognize the initial mouse click.

Modes

The default settings in the Tool Options dialog specify that the pixels of the gradient will replace the current pixels in the layer. This is specified by the Normal option of the composite mode's options menu. This menu is simply labeled *Mode*. Other options include all the modes discussed previously. The Behind option of the brush modes is included in the gradient composite modes. The mode selected is used in computing new pixel colors as the gradient is applied.

Blend Types

The blend type can be chosen using the options menu labeled *Blend*, just below the Mode menu. There are currently four types of blends: RGB foreground to RGB background, HSV foreground to HSV background, foreground to transparent, and custom gradients from the Gradient Editor. The default is RGB foreground to RGB background. The difference between gradients using foreground and background colors as RGB or HSV types is subtle in most cases. HSV tends to produce slightly darker gradients. Foreground to transparent gradients are useful as masks when applied directly to a layer. Custom gradients are really the most versatile, since these can run a number of transitions of multiple colors, with or without transparency. We'll cover custom gradients more when we discuss the Gradient Editor.

Gradient Types

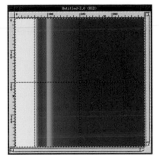

Gradient using Linear type and the Abstract_1 gradient from the Gradient Editor. The gradient was created by dragging from the right vertical guide to the left one along the horizontal guide.

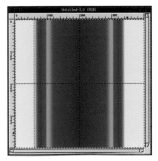

Same gradient except the type has been changed to Bi-Linear.

By default, a gradient makes a smooth transition from one color to another. This is a linear transition, and is specified by the *Gradient* options menu just below the Blend menu. This menu might have been labeled *Flow* or *Transitions* instead, since the options it provides determine how the gradient changes between end points. There are nine different types of transitions: Linear, Bi-Linear, Radial, Square, Conical symmetric, Conical asymmetric, and three forms of Shapebursts (angular, spherical, and dimpled). The first two, Linear and Bi-Linear, are the simplest. We've already covered Linear, and Bi-Linear is visually just about the same, unless the *Repeat* type is changed to *Sawtooth wave*. In that case, the Linear gradient will repeat in the direction you drag, including wrapping around to the other side of the Image Window. Bi-Linear does the same thing, but the gradient travels in both directions, meeting up at the end point of the drag. Although difficult to express in words, the effect is easy to see visually.

Select Sawtooth wave for the Repeat type and Custom for Blend type. The custom gradient should include a number of different colors, such as the Abstract_1 gradient (which should be part of the default distribution in what is referred to as the Extras[1] package). In a new Image Window, with the gradient type set to Linear, drag from left to right, across about three-fourths of the Image Window. The entire window is filled with the gradient, but you can see a sharp color change at the start and end points—for the Abstract_1 gradient this sharp edge occurs between the blue (start point) and yellow (end point) colors. These edges occur twice in the window. The gradient flowed from the start point to the end point, then started again. To the left of the start point you get the end of the gradient, as if the gradient repeated endlessly, and the Image Window was just a viewport on the gradient that included (specifically) the start and end points you supplied.

Now change the gradient type to Bi-Linear and apply the gradient the same way. This time the sharp edge occurs only once. With the Bi-Linear type, the gradient flowed in both directions from the start point, and spanned the distance to the end point. The difference is that Linear flows in one direction as it fills a layer, selection, or image, and Bi-Linear flows in two directions.

---

1. The GIMP distribution comes in three packages: the core programs, an extras package containing collections of gradients, patterns and brushes, and a set of unsupported plug-ins. Many binary distributions are likely to combine the first and last of these three. Some may combine all three, but most are likely to keep the extras package separate, simply due to its size.

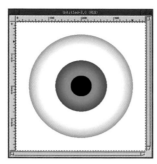

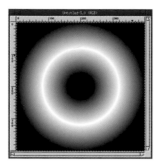

Radial gradient using the Radial_Eyeball_Green custom

Radial gradient, using default foreground and background colors (FG->BG type) with a Triangular wave

Radial transitions flow outward in all directions at the same time. The effect can be like creating an eyeball if you use the right kind of gradient. With the default foreground to background gradient, the effect produces three-dimensional spheres with very soft shadows (meaning the outline of the sphere is somewhat blurred).

Square transitions are just what they say—the effect radiates out in the shape of a square. The end point of the drag defines one-half the width of the square. The gradient actually looks a little like a four-pronged star, with the color between the prongs a smooth gradient. The square transition can produce some stunning effects when used in conjunction with the Repeat options.

Square gradient type, Blinds custom gradient, Triangular wave

There are two forms of the Conical gradient: symmetric and asymmetric. Both of these apply the gradient as if it were painted around the surface of a cone. *Conical symmetric* applies the gradient smoothly around the cone without showing any sharp edges (except at the point of the cone). It does this by applying the gradient equally in both directions around the cone. *Conical asymmetric* applies the gradient in one direction around the cone, so with the default gradient type (foreground to background) you will get a noticeable seam in the image.

The initial click point is the tip of the cone, and the end point simply determines the line down the slope of the cone from which the gradient will start. The length of the line has little effect on the application of the gradient. For Conical gradients it is the direction of the drag that determines the final effect. The first color applied (the foreground color or the first color in a custom gradient) starts where the line is between the start and end points (i.e., where you first clicked and where you dragged the mouse to). For symmetric conical gradients, the color (background, transparent or the last color of a custom gradient) is applied 180 degrees around from this line. For asymmetric conical gradients, the gradient is applied starting at this line, runs counterclockwise, and ends at the same line.

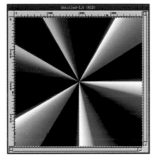

Conical symmetric gradient type, Blinds custom gradient, Triangular wave

Conical asymmetric gradient type, Blinds custom gradient, Triangular wave

Another gradient type with more than one form is the *Shapeburst*. This type, in all three forms, is similar to the square gradient. The three forms are angular, spherical, and dimpled. *Angular* looks very much like the Square gradient using the default foreground to background blend type, where the image appears like a four-pronged star. *Spherical* increases the size of the central star shape. *Dimpled* reduces its size. With custom gradients, the effect can become more obviously square-shaped, but the change in size of the central region is the same with the different forms of the shapeburst type. None of the shapeburst types can be used with the Repeat options; they become disabled when a shapeburst type is selected. Also, the shapeburst is unique in that it changes the gradient to fit the alpha channel or, if active, the selection.

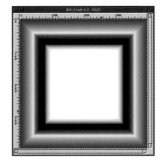

Angular shapeburst, Burning_Paper custom gradient

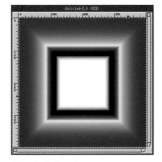

Dimpled shapeburst, Burning_Paper custom gradient

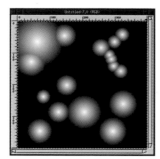

An array of balls. The first one was created using Radial gradient settings with a black foreground and white background (opposite of the default colors). The rest of the balls were created in the same way, except the Mode type was set to Lighten Only.

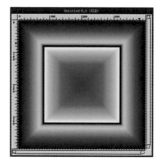

A Square gradient, Triangular repeats, using the Horizon_2 custom gradient.

Adaptive supersampling is turned on by using a toggle beneath the menus. When enabled, it activates the maximum depth and threshold sliders beneath it. Basically, adaptive supersampling provides antialiasing for the gradient. This is most useful in two cases: when you are using the repeat sawtooth option, or when you are using a custom gradient with abrupt color transitions.

Adaptive supersampling works by recursive subdivision. First, it calculates the color for a pixel. If the distance between this color and the colors of the surrounding pixels is more than the user-specified threshold, then it subdivides the pixel into four subpixels. This process is repeated until either the color difference between subpixels is less than the threshold, or the maximum recursion depth has been reached. Because of these calculations, adaptive supersampling will generally slow the process of applying the gradient. You may want to leave this toggle turned off while you experiment, and turn it on only when you're ready to apply the final gradient.

The Gradient Editor

The three basic Blend types offer a limited number of gradient effects. The real versatility of gradients is found with the use of custom gradients. A set of custom gradients is available in the default distribution of the GIMP, but there is no reason you can't create your own using the *Gradient Editor*.

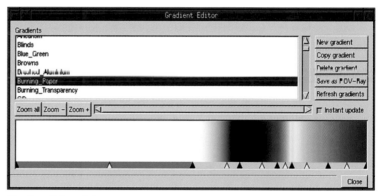

Gradient Editor dialog

The Gradient Editor is another dialog which is opened from the Image Window menu, *Dialogs->Gradient Editor*. The editor consists of a scrolled list of custom gradient names. Next to this is a set of five buttons. We'll discuss these in a moment. Beneath the scrolled list are buttons for zooming the preview window, which is the window below these buttons. Next to the zoom buttons is a scroll bar used to pan through the preview window when a zoom is in effect. Beneath the preview window is a set of indicators that look like small triangles. Finally, below this is a status bar that displays information when the mouse is in the preview window.

The first thing you might want to do is select an entry from the scrolled list of gradients. If this list is empty, then you either don't have any gradients installed, or you installed them in a directory that is not defined as one of the gradient directories in the gimprc file. See **Appendix A - The gimprc File** for details on the gimprc file.

New/Copy/Delete/Refresh

The buttons to the right of the list of gradients are used to manage the gradient files. The first button will create a new gradient with a standard black-to-white blend. A dialog is presented for naming the gradient. The gradient will remain available while the GIMP is running, but is not actually saved until you exit the program. Deleting a gradient is done with the *Delete gradient* button. A delete operation removes the gradient from the scrolled list, as well as deleting the gradient file on disk; however, you will be prompted for confirmation before the deletion is actually performed. Gradient files do not have specific suffixes, like brushes or patterns do. The file names used are the same as the names shown in the scrolled list. This could potentially cause problems if these files are accessed directly, so you should probably use the Gradient Editor to manage the gradients directory.

Copying a gradient to a new gradient entry is done with the *Copy gradient* button. The copied gradient will be given the same name as the original with the word "copy" appended to it.

Gradients are available from various places on the Internet. Collections from other GIMP users are starting to show up everywhere (you can probably find a few by starting at the main GIMP site, `http://www.gimp.org/`). If you download new gradient files and install them in your gradient directories[2] while the GIMP is already running, you will need to use the *Refresh gradient* button to update the Gradient Editor's scrolled list of gradients with these new files.

Save as POV

Gradients can be exported as POV-Ray files using the *Save as POV* button. POV-Ray, which is short for The Persistence of Vision Raytracer, is a three-dimensional ray tracer that uses text files to describe three-dimensional scenes. The text files can include descriptions of textures to use on three-dimensional objects. The GIMP exports a gradient as a POV-Ray file that can be included in any POV-Ray scene. For details on using these files and the POV-Ray renderer, you should visit the POV-Ray web site at `http://www.povray.org/`.

---

2. Again, check the `gimprc` file for details on where the GIMP will look for gradient files.

The Preview Window

The *preview window* is the long rectangular window in the bottom half of the dialog. This is where you view and edit the gradient. A gradient consists of one or more segments. Each *segment* is made up of a left end point, a right end point, and a midpoint. Below the preview window is a set of triangular controls, known as *handles,* which sit in the *handlebar.* The dark triangles define the end points of a segment in the gradient, and the light triangles are the midpoints. You can click on each point and move it left or right within the segment. In a gradient with more than one segment, the end points exist as left end points of one segment and right end points for another segment. Moving an end point makes the first segment smaller and the other larger or vice versa. The only exceptions to this are the end points at either end of the preview window. These handles cannot be moved.

Segment end points are assigned colors using the Preview menu, which we'll discuss in the next section. The midpoint of a segment determines the location from which the gradient begins to transform into the opposite end point's color. Moving the midpoint to the left will increase the range of the gradient to the right of the midpoint, and vice versa.

Between the midpoint and the end points is a blank region that you can click in to select a segment. You can click anywhere along the bar in which the control handles are set to select a segment, or you can click on a midpoint. You can't click on an end point to select a segment, since the end point exists for two different segments. Holding down the SHIFT key while selecting a segment allows you to group a selection of segments. Click on one segment to make it the first selection, then click in another segment while holding down the SHIFT key. All segments between the first segment and the one you just clicked in will be selected. Selected segments are recognizable by the darker shade of gray used in the segment space between end points.

Some gradients can be very complex, having a large number of segments. Attempting to adjust the control handles for these gradients can be difficult—the handles overlap, so finding the one you want to change can be a chance guess at best. The Gradient Editor allows you to zoom in on a section of the gradient using the *Zoom +* button just above the preview window. Click on the button a few times to zoom in. The slider bar just to the right of the button will resize itself as you zoom. Once you've zoomed a few times, use the slider to move to the segment you want to work on. If you find you haven't zoomed enough, you can zoom again, and the slider will keep you close to the segment of interest. You may want to click on a segment space close to the desired segment as a place mark until you've zoomed in far enough to accurately select the segment.

Two other buttons accompany the Zoom + button: *Zoom -* and *Zoom all*. The first of these steps you back out of previous zoom operations. The Zoom all button will return you back out to the full preview of the gradient.

The Preview Menu

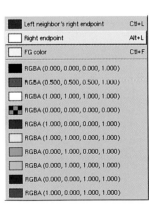

Gradient Editor's Preview menu

Clicking and holding the right mouse button in the preview window opens the *Preview* menu. Use this menu to edit a gradient. The menu has five sections:

1. Left end point color

2. Right end point color

3. Segment blending and coloring options

4. Segment management

5. Segment selection options

The first two sections are identical except for the end point on which they operate. Both operate on the currently selected segment (or segments). If more than one segment is selected, the left end point is that of the left-most segment and the right end point is that of the right-most segment.

Selecting a color for an end point can be done in one of two ways. The simplest method is to choose an existing color, either from another end point, from the foreground color, or from a set of ten predefined colors. Each of these options is available from the Preview menu's *Load from* menu option.

If you want a smooth gradient, then you will probably want to select the color of the closer end point of the adjacent segment's opposite end point. In other words, for a left end point, you select the color of the right end point of the segment just to the left of your selected segment. You make a similar selection for the right end point.

Alternatively, you can select an end point's color using the color selection dialog. This dialog is similar to the one opened for selecting the foreground and background colors, with a few minor differences. First, instead of a rectangular box with cross hairs showing the current

Load from submenu

color, this dialog has a circular color wheel window with a small circular outline at its center. Clicking the left mouse button in this window moves the small circle around the color wheel and selects the hue and saturation for each of the red, green, and blue levels of the new color. Below the color wheel is a rectangular window showing the original color on the left and the new color on the right. To the right of the color wheel is a vertical rectangle with a thin horizontal line running through it. You can use this line to adjust the value level for the new color. As with the other color selection dialog, this allows you to use sliders to adjust individual components of the color—red, green, blue, hue, saturation, value, and opacity—as well as to type in specific values. Unfortunately, the values you type in this dialog are different from the other dialog. In this dialog, the numeric values you can type in each field (except hue) must be between 0 and 1—they are effectively percentages. In the other color dialog, you use numbers from 0 to 255. This inconsistency is probably one of the few downsides to the GIMP and likely to be one of the areas addressed in the next release. Also, the Help button in the dialog is disabled in the 1.0 release.

Once you select the new color for the end point, click on the OK button in the color selection dialog, and the end point and gradient segment are automatically updated. You can watch the effect on the gradient as you adjust the colors in the dialog. The preview window will be updated as you make your color adjustments. The changes, however, are not made permanent until you click on the OK button. Choosing Cancel will cause the preview window to revert to its previous settings. Note that while using the color selection dialog, the rest of the Gradient Editor becomes insensitive to user input (i.e., all input features are "grayed out").

The color you just selected from the color selection dialog can be saved for future use. The *Save to* option in the Preview menu allows you to save the color to one of the 10 predefined colors. You simply select one of the existing entries in the set (a menu will open when you select the Save to option). The old entry is replaced by the new color. Each entry in the set shows the color and its RGBA settings. The Color Editor keeps track of the predefined colors and makes them usable with any of the available gradients, or for any new gradients you might create. The set consists of 10 entries—you cannot add to this list, nor can you delete entries.

Blending and Color Functions

There are submenus for the blending and color functions section of the Preview menu. The first applies to how the end point colors are blended, using various forms of mathematical functions. The other determines which color elements are used by the blending function. The choices include ordinary RGB and either clockwise or counterclockwise HSV. All of the options in these two submenus apply to the currently selected segment or segments.

Segment Management

With a new gradient, you start with a single segment—two end points and a midpoint centered between the end points. To add segments, use one of the segment management options in the Preview menu. There are two ways to add segments: splitting the current segment or segments uniformly, or splitting them at their midpoints. Either method will work on selections of multiple segments.

Splitting segments uniformly will open a small dialog box with a slider. The slider is used to determine the number of segments to create. You can create two or more new segments from the current selection of segments. Each segment selected is split the number of times you specify. If you have three segments selected and choose to split them each into three uniform segments, you end up with nine total segments. Splitting the segments at the midpoints is the same as splitting them uniformly with the slider set to two.

To delete one or more segments, you can use the *Delete segment* option in the Preview menu. Deleting a segment does not change the end point colors on the remaining segments. Deletions cannot be undone using CTRL-z, so be careful using this feature.

The other segment management options deal with positioning of the control handles. There are two menu options available here: recenter midpoints and redistribute handles. The first option will recenter the midpoints of all selected segments within their respective segments. This does not change the position of end points. The second option will redistribute all control handles evenly throughout the entire width of the combined selection. This option repositions both midpoints and end points.

Adjusting Segments Using the Handlebar and Handles

Segments can be resized not only by dragging the control handles, they can also be moved as a whole. By clicking and dragging in the empty space between an end point and a midpoint, you can move a selection left or right. This has the effect of moving the corresponding end points of the segments to either side of the segment you are moving. A segment can be moved left or right until the adjoining segment's end point meets its midpoint.

Segments can be moved independently or in groups. Clicking, holding and dragging a segment that is not selected will move only that one segment. Clicking, holding and dragging in a selected segment will move all selected segments. If you hold the SHIFT key before clicking in a segment, you will cause the segments on either side of the segment or segments to be moved to be *compressed*—the midpoint of the adjoining segments moves in proportion to the distance that the end point moves. In this way, you can move one segment to the left, for example, until the segment to its left is completely compressed. The compressed segment will have the two end points and the midpoint all in the same location. Note that the opposite side will be *decompressing*—the segment on that end will expand.

Moving and compressing segments can be done while the mouse is over either an end point or in the space between end points and a midpoint. Clicking and dragging on a midpoint has the same effect as just clicking, which is to select the segment. Pressing SHIFT-click on a midpoint will extend the selection, as discussed earlier.

Segment Selection Options

The four options in the *Selection operations* submenu consist of flipping or replicating segments and blending colors and opacities. A segment or a selected group of segments can be flipped so that the right end point becomes the left and the left end point becomes the right. Also, the segment or segments can be replicated two or more times. Each replicated segment is positioned to the right of the original, and the combined width of the original and all replications is the same as the width of the original segment.

Blending of end point colors and opacities works only when multiple segments are selected. Both options work by changing the gradient to start on the leftmost end point and run smoothly to the rightmost end point, removing all other gradients in between. In effect, you create a single gradient across the range of the selected segments.

Keyboard Shortcuts for the Preview Menu

Many features in the Preview menu are accessible via keyboard shortcuts. The following table summarizes these shortcuts. Keep in mind that the shortcuts work as long as the mouse is in the preview window.

Shortcut (case sensitive)	Function
l	Opens color selection dialog for left end point.
CTRL-l	Uses color from right end point of segment to left of left end point.
ALT-l	Uses color from right end point of same segment as left end point.
CTRL-f	Uses foreground color for left end point.
r	Opens color selection dialog for right end point.
CTRL-r	Uses color from left end point of segment to right of right end point.
ALT-r	Uses color from left end point of same segment as right end point.
ALT-f	Uses foreground color for right end point.
s	Splits segments at midpoints.
u	Splits segments uniformly (opens dialog with slider).
d	Deletes selected segment or segments.
c	Recenters midpoints of selected segments.
CTRL-c	Redistributes handles of selected segments.
f	Flips selected segments.
m	Replicates selected segments.
b	Blends end point colors of selected segments.
CTRL-b	Blends end point opacities of selected segments.

The Status Bar

As you work with the Gradient Editor, you should notice that the region along the bottom of the dialog window displays text at different times. This is the *status bar*, sometimes called the *hint bar*. Since the preview window offers so many functions, it can be confusing as to what will happen at a given time for a given mouse click. The status bar will display the effect of mouse clicks when the mouse pointer is over the handle bar, midpoints or end points, and will display the current color values when the mouse pointer is over the preview window itself. If you ever forget what action will occur at a particular moment, hold the mouse still over a spot and read the text in the status bar.

Gradients, Masks, and the Foreground Color

Gradients can be used for all sorts of visual effects. One of the most common uses is as a mask, blending two layers in a seamless way. A foreground to background gradient, using the colors of black for the foreground and white for the background, allows you to flow one image into another. Using more sophisticated grayscale gradients, you can blend two layers in even more creative ways.

Setting the foreground color can be done by clicking the left mouse button on the preview window. Clicking, holding and dragging will cause the foreground color to cycle through all colors the mouse pointer is run over. This is another way you can save colors for later use.

First, we have a layer of our heroes, edited to remove background pixels.

Next, we place a sunset background behind the guys.

Now we apply a gradient, using default settings, in a layer mask on the first layer. The guys now appear to meld into the background.

Moving On

In the last chapter in this part we'll take a look at one of the features which saw a tremendous advancement in the few months leading up to the 1.0 release of the GIMP: printing.

Tutorial

You've learned the basics now, except for some details about printing and scanning, which we'll cover in the next chapter. At this point, you're ready to do something really interesting. We're going to combine the use of gradients, selections, layers, filters (even though these haven't been covered in detail), transformations, and various other tools to

231

create a red three-dimensional letter "S" with a backdrop shadow over a conical gradient. Because this tutorial uses gradients, the best results will be seen on systems with lots of color available to them. Lower-end (256 color) displays don't allow full appreciation of the aesthetic value of this tutorial, but there is no reason those users can't follow this tutorial too.

The first thing we need to do is to create a new gradient using the Gradient Editor. This new gradient should have the same black end points on both ends, and a white center. We'll be using this gradient later to create some pipe shapes. Creating the gradient turns out to be quite easy. Follow these steps:

1. Open the Gradient Editor dialog.

2. Click on the New gradient button—name the new gradient "simple pipe".

3. Place the cursor over the preview window at the bottom of the dialog and press the "s" key. This will split the new gradient at the midpoint.

4. Click on the midpoint of the left segment in the preview window to select that segment.

5. Click in the preview window by holding down the right mouse button to display the Preview menu. Select the option directly beneath *Right end point's color*, the *Load from* option, and choose the white entry (RGBA all have values of 1.0).

6. Click on the midpoint of the right segment in the preview window to select that segment.

7. Place the cursor over the preview window and press the "f" key— that will flip the right segment so the white end point moves to the middle of the preview window.

8. Click in the preview window by holding down the right mouse button to display the Preview menu. Select the option directly beneath *Right end point's color*, the *Load from* option, and choose the black entry (RGBA has the values of 0.0, 0.0, 0.0, 1.0).

It may seem like a complicated process at first, but you'll be surprised how quickly these steps become second nature when you start to create your own set of gradients with many more segments than this. Be sure your new gradient is selected in the dialog.

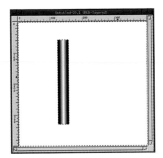

The selection with custom gradient applied.

The next step is to create a new Image Window. Make it 400x400, with a white background. Then add a new transparent layer to that window. Name the layer "pipe-1". What we want to do here is use the gradient we just created to make a tall, thin pipe. To do this, we make a selection in the pipe-1 layer that is rectangular and runs about three-fourths of the height of the window, centered vertically (it doesn't have to be exact—I'm just giving you approximate positioning and sizing at this point so your image will end up similar to mine) and just off to the left of center horizontally. Then select the Blend tool, making sure the Tool Options dialog Mode is set to Normal, the Blend is set to Custom and the Gradient is set to Linear. Drag the cursor from the left of the rectangular selection to the right. The selection should look something like the accompanying image when you've done this. Now deselect everything with SHIFT-CTRL-a.

Next, use a filter on this newly created pipe shape. You're going to apply the Polar Coordinates filter to the pipe-1 layer to make it curved. Select *Filters->Distorts->Polar Coords* to open the filter dialog. The dialog should be configured so that the pipe is curved and somewhat centered, like the next image.

The Polar Coordinates filter dialog showing how to configure the filter to get the desired results.

Once you've applied the filter to the pipe-1 layer, you need to make a duplicate of the layer. Click on the duplicate button at the bottom of the Layers and Channels dialog. Be sure the pipe-1 layer is selected first. Name the duplicated layer "pipe-2". Select the pipe-2 layer and then flip it, first vertically, then horizontally. Use the Flip tool in the Toolbox and its Tool Options dialog to accomplish this.

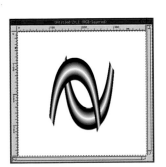

The Image Window after the duplicate layer has been flipped.

You now have the two ends to the S shape, except that the ends are not aligned properly, and the S is lying on its side. You'll fix the alignment first. Select the pipe-1 layer and move it to the left, so it's roughly constrained within the left side of the Image Window. Now move the pipe-2 layer so it's on the right side. The ends of the U shapes in each layer need to be lined up—just keep moving each layer until you get those ends to line up closely. You won't get an exact, smooth meshing of the two U shapes, but it should get close, and that's all you need for this example. In fact, the reason we created a new gradient with black ends and a white center was so that when you try to line up these two shapes, the outside edges would be more likely to match colors.

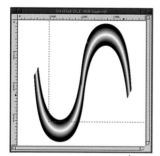

The Image Window after layers have been aligned.

Next, you'll want to merge the two pipe layers, but not with the background layer. Turn off the visibility of the background layer by clicking on its eye icon in the Layers and Channels dialog. Now open the Layer menu for one of the two pipe layers (right-click on that layer in the dialog) and select *Merge Visible Layers*. In this case, the merged layer is named "pipe-1", like the original layer. Rotate this new merged layer by 270 degrees, or you can rotate it by 90 degrees if you want. Since the two ends of the S shape are identical, it shouldn't matter. The rotations are found under *Image->Transforms->Layer*.

Now I'll explain how to add some of the three-dimensional effects. The first of these will be to Bump Map the S shape layer. Select *Filters->Map->Bump Map*. Set the dialog to roughly what is shown in the example shown here. After this is applied, the Image Window should look similar to the resulting image shown.

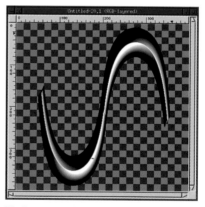

The Bump Map dialog settings you should use.

The Image Window after the Bump Map has been applied.

Now make the drop shadow for this layer. We need a copy of the S shape, so use *Layers->Alpha to Selection* on the pipe-1 layer (at this point, there should be only two layers—the background layer and the pipe-1 layer). Create a new transparent layer, and turn off Keep Transparency for it. Now fill the selection with a solid black color using the Bucket Fill tool. You may want to name this new layer "Shadow". Turn off the selection and blur the shadow layer using a Gaussian Blur filter of about radius five, both horizontally and vertically. Move the shadow layer to the left and down a bit, then lower the layer using the

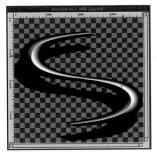

Drop Shadow for S shape

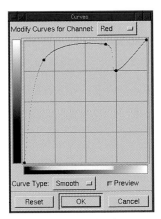

Curves dialog used for this tutorial

down arrow at the bottom of the Layers dialog. The drop shadow should now be behind the S layer, but above the background layer. Turn on the background layer's visibility now to see the shadow more obviously.

At this point, you have the basic shapes and three-dimensional effects. Now add some color. Open the Curves dialog (*Image->Colors->Curves*). Make sure the pipe-1 layer is selected. Set the *Modify Curves for Channel* menu to Red. Then adjust the lower end of the curve upward a bit. You can play with this until you get the colors you like, of course. The adjacent figure shows the curve I used for this tutorial.

Finally, let's add a more interesting backdrop to this image. Select the Greens gradient from the Gradient Editor's list of gradients. Then set the Blend tool to use a Conical symmetric gradient and a Blend type of Custom. Click on the background layer in the Layers dialog to make it the active layer. Now click on the upper left of the S shape in the Image Window and drag down to the lower right. The backdrop will look more interesting than the plain white we just had, but the colors don't really match the red of the S shape. Open the Hue-Saturation dialog (*Image->Colors->Hue-Saturation*). Increase the Saturation a bit and then adjust the Hue and Lightness sliders left or right until you find colors that match the red a little better. This is purely a matter of opinion—you are the artist.

Of course, you've probably noticed a few problems with this image: the S shape is not smooth in some places (for example, there is a stairstep effect along the top of the S), there appear to be some small white lines on the inside of the curves of the S shape, and the line where the two U shapes were joined is not a smooth gradient like the rest of the S shape. These problems can all be fixed using a combination of cloning, smoothing, and blurring. These techniques have already been covered; review those sections, and experiment on your own to improve this image.

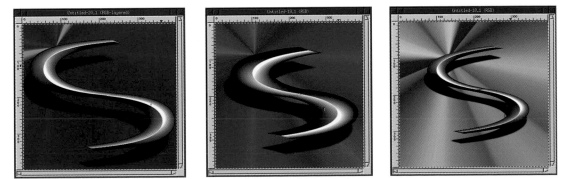

The author's variations of this image. Your version will differ in the width and height of the S shape and in the colors used.

Chapter 11 - Scanning, Printing, and Print Media

One of the most common tasks performed in preparation for creating digital works of art with the GIMP is scanning. Scanners can be used to import images of photographs, textured materials, three-dimensional objects, and other items for use in your GIMP projects. Proper scanning techniques are not hard to master, but do require a little thought and, as always, plenty of practice.

Another important part of the image development process is printing. The 1.0 release of the GIMP includes a print feature that supports PostScript, PCL and ESC/P2 printers, but there is more to printing an image than just having a supported printer. You need to know about paper types, how to avoid banding issues, and all those funny terms like dpi, lpi and halftoning.

This chapter explains the overall scanning process, including types of scanners supported under Linux, scan types, and methods to improve individual scans. This chapter also covers topics related to preparing and printing your images with the GIMP. By the end of the chapter, you should have a good feel for getting images into the GIMP and getting them out onto the printed page.

Types of Scanners

The great majority of this book's readers will be Linux or other PC-based UNIX users. Because of this, your familiarity with scanning is probably limited to hardware that works with personal computers. These devices are better known as flatbed scanners. A *flatbed scanner* is one with a glass top upon which you lay photos, documents, and other items to be scanned. These scanners usually have a cover to keep external light sources from interfering with the scanning system. Flatbed scanners come in various models, from low-end grayscale-only scanners that scan at no more than 150 dots per inch, to high-level scanners supporting 30 or more bits per pixel color scans at resolutions of 1200 dots per inch and higher. Flatbed scanners, although usually used to scan photos and other two-dimensional documents, can also be used to scan solid objects. This versatility allows for making quick "photos" without developing film. Flatbed scanners can use either their own interface cards, SCSI cards, or parallel port connections to connect to the computer. All versions require special drivers to make use of the scanner.

Another common type of scanner for personal computers is a *hand-held scanner*. These scanners are more portable but generally less powerful than their flatbed brethren. They are often used to scan smaller documents, such as 4x6 photos, due to the smaller scan width area (4" to 5"). Larger documents require multiple passes, and force you to manually combine the scans using software like the GIMP. Some hand-held scanners can be used with externally mounted guides to allow the user to scan along defined lines in the document. Using these scanners without the guides can lead to poor scans unless you have a very steady hand. The guides may be sold separately or can be built out of rulers, blocks of wood or other straight-edged materials that happen to be on hand.

Hand-held scanners come in both grayscale and color versions, although the color versions generally do not handle more than 8 bits of color total—not 8 bits per color channel. There are also high-end hand-held scanners that can capture up to 24 bits of color data. Hand-held scanners can require installation of an interface card and a special driver, or can connect directly to your PC's printer port.

Page scanners, also known as sheet-fed scanners, were popular for a short period of time prior to the radical price reduction of flatbed scanners. These scanners work somewhat like fax machines, where you feed the source document in one end and it is automatically scanned as it's pulled across the scan head. These devices run on various interfaces but are not currently supported by Linux.

Film and *slide scanners* are higher-end devices that permit scanning directly from film and slides. By scanning from the original negative or the positive (slide) film, the scan can produce much finer detail and more accurate colors. These devices can connect using their own interface cards or, more commonly, through standard SCSI interface cards. A *transparency scanner* (a cousin of the slide scanner) can often be connected to external ports on flatbed scanners. Transparency scanners that work with flatbed scanners are often much cheaper than slide scanners but generally offer lower quality scans.

Scanner Drivers

The GIMP does not support scanners directly in its core 1.0 distribution. However, integrated scanner support can be added through the use of the xscanimage Plug-In from the SANE project. This tool allows you to access a variety of scanners as long as the SANE drivers are properly installed. The SANE project is a separate project from the GIMP, although the two have been closely related since about the time the GTK toolkit (the windowing kit used for the GIMP) was made a separate package.

Once you've acquired and installed the SANE package per the instructions, make sure you have a link from the `/usr/local/bin/xscanimage` program to your `$HOME/.gimp/plug-ins` directory. This will allow the GIMP to see the plug-in at start time. The xscanimage program can actually run on its own or as a GIMP plug-in, so you probably want to leave it under `/usr/local/bin` and just make a symbolic link to your `.gimp/plug-ins` directory for it. To do this, run the following command:

```
% ln -s /usr/local/bin/xscanimge ~/.gimp/plug-ins
```

You will need to restart the GIMP for it to recognize the new plug-in or if you make changes to the SANE drivers that are configured. Configuration of SANE is beyond the scope of this book, but the most important thing you need to know is that the `/usr/local/etc/sane.d/dll.conf` file contains the names of the scanners configured for your system. Most people need only one entry uncommented here: the driver for their scanner, such as *umax* for UMAX scanners. Additionally, you can uncomment the *pnm* driver which is used to read in pnm files using the SANE interface, but this is mostly a debugging tool (you can read pnm files directly with the GIMP anyway). You might have problems if drivers other than these are listed in the `dll.conf` file but are not actually configured, so you may want to comment out the extra entries by inserting a pound sign (#) in the first column for unnecessary drivers. Also, check the configuration file specific to your scanner (for example, `umax.conf` for UMAX scanners or `mustek.conf` for Mustek scanners) in the same directory. This will contain the names of the devices necessary to access your scanner. Check the man pages for your drivers before making changes, of course.

Tip: the SANE package is included on the CD, but you can always retrieve the latest version from the SANE web site at `http://www.mostang.com/sane/`.

SANE-Supported Scanners

SANE, which stands for Scanner Access Now Easy, is a project to make adding scanner support to UNIX systems much simpler by using dynamically loadable drivers. The package contains a set of back-end drivers, along with a few front-end tools, such as xscanimage and the *xcam* program for QuickCam cameras. SANE is not Linux-specific. It has been ported to a number of UNIX platforms including FreeBSD, Solaris, DEC UNIX, and SGI IRIX.

The SANE package supports quite a few different scanner families, which in turn encompass a large number of individual scanners. Scanner brands supported include Artec/Ultima, Canon, Epson, Hewlett-Packard, Microtek, Mustek, Tamarack and ESCOM, and UMAX. However, not every model from each of these families is supported. You should check the SANE web site for more details on individual scanners. Beyond these families are a number of specific devices or models that have drivers available through SANE: Nikon Coolscan film scanners, the Polaroid Digital Microscope Camera, QuickCam cameras, Siemens 9036 scanners, and Agfa SnapScan scanners. There are also many scanner drivers under development, including Apple, Plustek, and Logitech scanners, and the SGI IndyCam. Some of these were in beta test at the time of this writing and may have a low level of support. Again, check the SANE web site for up-to-date details.

Scanner-Specific Drivers for Linux

Beyond SANE, a number of drivers are available for specific scanners. These include most of the same families listed above, plus A4 Tech scanners and a few Genius hand-held scanners. Like the SANE drivers, all of the standalone Linux drivers can be found on the CD.

TIP: when looking for up-to-date drivers for Linux, the place to start is the Sunsite archives. Check out `ftp://sunsite.unc.edu/pub/Linux/apps/graphics/capture/`. *If you need support for other platforms you should consider the SANE package instead of the stand-alone drivers.*

Using Scanners

Now that you know a little about what scanners are and how to find drivers for them, you need to learn what you can do with them. First, the basics: setup. We'll be talking about flatbed scanners at this point, since these offer the best price/performance range for the average user.

Flatbed scanners are simple to install, for the most part. They plug into parallel or SCSI ports. I prefer SCSI versions because I can connect more than one device to a SCSI adapter externally. That means I don't have to open my computer each time I want to add a new device. If you use a scanner connected to a parallel port, you may want to get an A/B switch box for the parallel port so you can run the printer off the same port. Just be sure you have the switch set to the right channel when you want to scan or print.

Many flatbed scanners on the market today come with their own proprietary version of a SCSI card. These cards are generally not designed to have many devices hanging off the SCSI cable. They are used to connect the scanner only. Avoid these cards. Get a good SCSI card that meets the latest SCSI specifications, such as one that supports Ultra Wide or SCSI-3. The reasons are twofold: the proprietary cards support only one device (which somewhat defeats the purpose of using SCSI to begin with), and the drivers for the scanners do not work with these cards. The latter is the bigger issue. Many of the scanner drivers available for Linux are expected to work with real SCSI cards. The UMAX drivers, for example, definitely do not work with the cards that come with the scanners. If you were to cut corners in hardware, the SCSI card would not be the place to do it. You should also be certain that the SCSI cable is not unshielded or too long—no more than 6 feet for SCSI-1 cards or 18 feet for SCSI-2 and SCSI-3 cards. SCSI cables that are too long or unshielded may degrade the data passing through them. Make sure all devices on the cable have unique SCSI IDs, and that the SCSI cable is properly terminated. Also be sure that any SCSI-1 devices are placed at the end of the cable if you also have SCSI-2 devices. Otherwise, the SCSI-2 devices may not function properly.

SCSI-1 cards are no longer sold by retailers, but plenty of SCSI-1 devices are available on the open market.

Another thing to keep in mind about using scanners with other devices on a single SCSI card: you won't be able to access the other devices while scanning. This is generally only a problem if the other devices are storage devices, such as hard disks or removable media such as Jaz drives. If you think you might want to access these devices during a scan, you may want to place the scanner on its own SCSI card and the other devices on a separate SCSI card. I find that I don't access my Jaz drive while scanning, so I have them both on a single SCSI card. The choice as to whether to use one or more SCSI cards depends on your own needs, and is not a hardware- or software-specific requirement.

Running xscanimage

Device dialog for xscanimage

Once you've got the scanner connected and the SANE drivers installed, it's time to take a look at xscanimage, the interface used to make scans. First, when the GIMP starts, it scans for plug-ins and queries them for where they should be placed in the various menus. The xscanimge installs itself in the *Xtns->Acquire Image* menu in the Toolbox. Select the *Device Dialog* option in the *Acquire Image* menu. This will open a small dialog showing the available devices. If you uncommented the pnm device in the dll.conf configuration file for the SANE drivers, there will be two pnm devices listed, along with the entries for any other drivers you configured. The first image is an entry for the UMAX driver. Double click on one of the drivers, preferably one which is a real scanner and not one of the pnm devices.

The dialog that opens will have the name of the driver and the device name it uses to access that device. The contents of the window depend on the features available for the scanner selected. The options described here are available for the UMAX driver. Also note that you should read the sane-<driver> man pages (such as sane-umax) to check which options arc potentially dangerous. In the case of the UMAX driver, the *Quality Calibration* option in the Enhancement frame will cause the SCSI bus to hang, so it shouldn't be used. This is noted in the sane-umax man page.

The main dialog for xscanimage and the UMAX driver contains a menu bar and two frame sections: Scan Mode and Enhancement. The *Scan Mode* section allows you to select a scan mode and a scan source, set the resolution of the scan and scan a color negative, if desired. The *Enhancement* frame shows a 10-bit mode, quality calibration and a custom gamma table option. Keep in mind that with other drivers, some options may be grayed out or possibly not even displayed, while other options not shown in these examples may be available.

Main dialog for xscanimage

The *Preferences* menu offers a few useful options. First, *Show Advanced Options* will expand the dialog to show two more frames—the Geometry and Advanced frames. Another option in the Preferences menu is a submenu for specifying the units to use in the Geometry frame. Some users in the United States will find the default use of centimeters to be a little confusing, and may want to switch to the more familiar inches. Any changes to the default settings can be saved using the *Preferences->Save Device Settings* option.

The *Geometry* frame is used to select the region of the scan surface to use in the scan. These sliders can be used visually with the Preview Window, which will be discussed after we talk about Scan Modes. The *Advanced* frame is left to expert users.

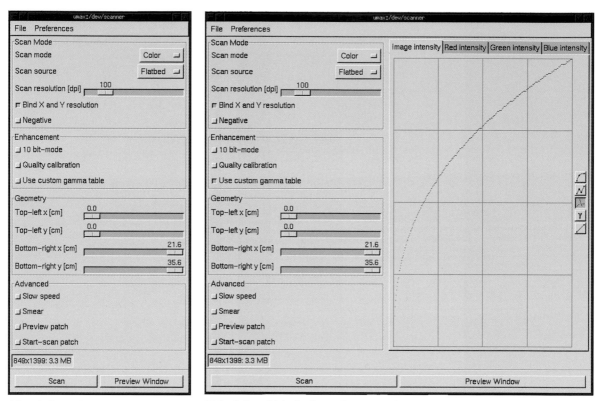

Main dialog with advanced options displayed.

Main dialog with both advanced options and custom gamma sections displayed.

Scan Modes - Line Art, Grayscale, Color, Dithered

The *Scan Mode* menu offers three standard options: Line art, Gray, and Color. *Color* refers to an RGB scan. This is what you'll use in many cases when you simply want to transfer an image from a print to the computer just as it is. *Gray* is short for grayscale and does the same thing, but the image is opened into a grayscale Image Window instead of an RGB Image Window. The *Line art* option causes a scan that is somewhat like applying a threshold on a grayscale scan, but does so during the scan itself. The Image Window opened for this scan holds a grayscale image that is actually just black and white—no shades of gray. The usefulness of this option depends on your needs: it can be very useful for scanning architectural and mechanical drawings, but it is limited in an artistic sense. In any case, not all scanners support all three modes.

A line art mode scan on the left vs. a grayscale scan on the right that has had its levels adjusted and a threshold of 127 to 255 applied to it. The images are very similar, but are not exactly the same.

When you select the Line art mode, the Enhancement frame changes. The 10-bit mode option is removed and replaced with a *Threshold* slider. This slider can be used to determine the level of brightness in the scan. Higher values reduce the range of bright colors, while lower numbers increase the range. If the scan preview is very dark (in grayscale mode), then use a lower threshold value. If the preview is very bright, try a higher setting. In order to use line art scans efficiently, you may want to run a few passes at only 100 dpi resolution first to find an optimal threshold setting, then make a final scan at a higher resolution.

Another mode that may be available for other scanner drivers is the *Dithered* option. This scan mode produces a halftone image[1] consisting of many small dots. This mode can be useful with a small image size when only a reasonably good quality scan is desired. Check your driver's man page to determine if the option is supported.

---

1. See discussion on halftones in the section on printing later in this chapter.

Getting the Right Geometry with the Preview Window

Preview window for xscanimage

At the bottom of the main dialog are two buttons: *Scan* and *Preview Window*. The first will start the scan using the settings you've made in the rest of the window. The latter opens another dialog, the Preview Window. This window can be used to provide a quick, low-resolution scan of the entire scan area, which can then be used to select a smaller section for the full scan. At the bottom of the Preview Window are two more buttons: *Acquire Preview* and *Cancel Preview*. Click on the Acquire Preview button, and wait for the scanner to grab the image. You should notice that as it scans, the image is partially displayed a piece at a time (at least it does for the UMAX driver; other drivers may not permit this). Wait for the scan to complete. The preview is a low-resolution, low-quality scan. Its purpose isn't to be a good scan, just a recognizable representation so you can quickly specify the region of interest. Cancel Preview is self explanatory.

Along the left side and top of the window are rulers which can help determine coordinates of a region to be scanned. However, unlike Image Windows, you can't drag guides into the preview from the rulers. You can use the sliders in the geometry frame of the main dialog to set an outline. As you move each of the sliders, a dotted line is moved from the left, right, top or bottom of the Preview Window. This makes selecting the scan area quite easy. A simpler method is to click and drag within the Preview Window itself, just as you would create a selection in an Image Window.

The Preview Window will cache the last preview acquired, even between GIMP sessions. This makes it easier to pick up from where you left off and saves some time in preparing for new scans. If you move the documents on the scanner's glass, you should reacquire the preview. The cached image is saved in a device-specific name under the user's $HOME/.sane directory. If you don't want xscanimage to cache the preview image, you can disable it from the dialog opened via the *Preferences->Preview Options* menu option.

Using the Custom Gamma Table

Now you should be ready to try a scan. Click on the Scan button in the main dialog and wait for the new Image Window to open with your scan. Notice at the bottom of the main dialog is a small box showing the dimensions of the scan and the amount of disk space it will use. These values change with the geometry settings and the scan resolution[2] you provide. Once the scan completes, examine the results. In many cases, the scan will be too dark or too light—not quite the same as the original image. This is easy to fix. Click on the *Use custom gamma table* option in the Enhancement frame of the main dialog. This opens another section of the main dialog, the *Image Intensity* section. This section shows a graph of the gamma curve, which defaults to a diagonal red line running from lower left to upper right. The five buttons along the right side allow you to adjust the curve. Changes in the curve affect how bright or dark the scan will be. The next to last button—the one with a Greek gamma character—will probably be of most interest. If you already know the gamma setting for your monitor, you can set it manually with this button. My system requires a gamma setting of approximately 2.6, which I discovered by using a trick provided by Larry Gritz, author of BMRT (see the tip on the next page). When you click on this button, a small dialog will open, allowing you to specify this value. Alternatively, you can do the same thing from the *Preferences->Preview Options* menu option.

Scan of a Linux Journal cover using the default gamma settings. This scan is darker than the actual cover.

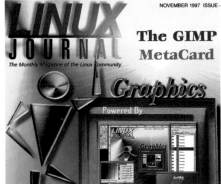

Same scan but with gamma set to 2.6.

---

2. The scan resolution is in dots per inch (dpi) and is discussed in the section on dpi later in this chapter. Setting the scan resolution often depends on your requirements for printing the image, which is why the dpi discussion is in the section on printing.

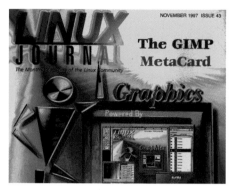

Same scan but with a hand drawn gamma curve.

The gamma curve can be manipulated by drawing directly in the graph, by adding control points that can be dragged within the graph, or by using one of the buttons to preset the graph to a particular setting. Often you will use a combination of the latter two options. To add control points, click on one of the first two buttons in the Image Intensity section. When either of these or the last button is selected, you can drag control points within the graph. Selecting the third button will allow you to simply draw the graph. Note that the graph must proceed from left to right, so any existing points on the graph directly above or below the points you draw are removed. Effectively, this means that there is a vertical line between this new point and the next point (to the left or right, depending on which direction you're drawing). This will lead to some harsh changes in light during the scan. It's probably not what you're looking for, but every artist can find something new in all of these tools, so experiment to see the possible effects.

If you're not sure what gamma setting is most appropriate for your monitor, experiment by using values between 1.0 and 2.8, working with low-resolution scans of small parts of the full scan area. These scans probably won't take very long, and will help you zoom in on a more reasonable gamma setting for your scanner.

There is an on-line description for finding the correct gamma setting for your monitor at `http://radsite.lbl.gov/radiance/refer/Notes/gamma.html`*. This is a slightly technical explanation, but the section on finding the gamma value to use requires only that you squint at an image and choose the value where two shades of gray appear to match. It's rather easy and quick to do, so give it a try. Your scans will benefit from this brief experiment!*

Finding the Sweet Spot

Desktop scanner technology has progressed a long way in the past five years. It used to be that the scanner would not get a clean scan of the entire surface, even if the glass was completely spot free. These conditions should not exist for newer hardware. However, if you have an older scanner or your scans seem to be less than optimal, here is a little trick for finding the best scanning region on your scanner's glass.

First, set the scan resolution to 100. To examine the entire surface of the scanner glass, set the geometry values to their minimums and maximums. For my UMAX 1200S the scan area is 8.5" by 14". Place a white cover over the glass or, if available and unmarked, just use the cover that comes with the scanner. Be sure the white area is solid white and clean. Now scan the surface. After the scan completes, run the Equalize filter (*Image->Colors->Equalize*) once and then adjust the brightness and contrast of the image to their maximums. The darker areas of the scan are likely to be poorer quality than you'd like. The areas that are solid (or near solid) white are the best. You can use a cardboard cutout of this region if you need to, so you can always place your prints in the right spot on the glass. Again, this technique is probably not necessary for newer desktop flatbed scanners, but may be useful if you have an older one.

Scanning Three-Dimensional Objects

Scanning photos or other printed images now seems less of a chore than it once might have. Still, what do you do when you need something quick and don't have time to pull out the camera, get the shot, take the film to be developed (don't forget using the whole roll—who wants to waste one roll of film for one shot?), and wait to get it back just to scan it in? In these cases, you should consider using your flatbed scanner to get "photos" of three-dimensional objects. The trick is to use objects that you can safely place on the scanner glass top, that won't move during the scan and, if necessary, add appropriate lighting to get the best view of the object.

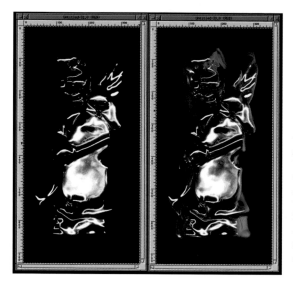

Sample three-dimensional scans of a gold plated angel figurine. The sample on the left was scanned in a darkened room without a cover over the scanner. The sample on the right was also scanned without a cover, but with two desk lamps used to light the scene. The reddish color comes from reflections off surrounding objects. Both images have had their levels adjusted and some brightness/contrast adjustments were made, as well.

The object won't fit snugly under the flat cover that your flatbed scanner provides. A cardboard box will work nicely in place of this. I find that the boxes in which printer paper is delivered to offices, the ones with two stacks of 500-sheet packs, fit nicely over my scanner's 8.5"x14" glass plate.[3] I cut this down a bit to a depth of about three to four inches tall, but that's personal preference. I also recommend painting the inside of the box a non-reflective black, so that the backgrounds of the three-dimensional objects and their depths show up more clearly.

When you scan three-dimensional objects, the scanner will cast shadows from its own light. This shadow may be enough to show the three-dimensional aspect of the scan, or you may want to add lights under the cover to show more detail in the object or cast shadows in a different way. The problem with this is finding lights which both fit under the cover (and possibly on the glass itself) and have enough of a light source to provide the effect you need. This may be the hardest part of the job, tantamount to the lighting issues you face when taking a decent photograph indoors. Small table lamps work well. Be certain not to shine the light toward the glass, or you may get unwanted reflections on the object. Remember: the preview window is your best friend when doing prep work for a scan like this.

---

3. Although I don't use the term here, the glass plate of the flatbed scanner is actually called the *platen*. I just find it simpler to call it the glass plate or glass bed.

Once you have the lights (if any) in place, the object positioned and the geometry of the scan set from the preview window, then you're ready to scan the image. After the scan is complete, you will most likely want to run the image through the Levels filter to adjust the range of lightness. Since you don't really want to use the background, you need to either cut it out or fill it with some other pattern or color. How you do this depends on the shape of the object you scanned. If it's a relatively simple shape with few curves, for example, you might try using the selection tools to outline the object itself. In this case, after the selection is made, you'll want to invert the selection before flood filling or cutting the background (or copy the object and paste it into its own layer). Alternatively, you can use the Fuzzy selection tool on the background around the image to make a selection. This will work only if the background is mostly the same solid color—thus the need for the black color on the inside of the box! You can also try using the Select by Color selection, although this is likely to include sections of the object as well. Any selections you make will probably look better with just a bit of feathering applied. Whatever you choose, chances are good that you'll want to use the selection again later. Be sure to save it to a channel before removing the selection.

Be careful when placing three-dimensional objects on the scanner's glass plate. You don't want to scratch it or drop something on it. Keeping the glass clean is an important part of scanner maintenance, whether scanning flat sheets or three-dimensional objects.

Textured Materials

Scanning textured materials is a great way to get a quick background image. Not surprisingly, scanning cloth or other textured materials is not unlike scanning a document. Just lay the material on the glass and place the flat cover over it. You can try variations much like you would with three-dimensional objects: using a box instead of the flat cover, and variations on lighting, including colored lights. With fabric, make sure it is wrinkle-free and lying flat on the glass, especially if the printed pattern on the material is the focus of your scan. Other materials, wrinkled paper for example, work better if they aren't flat. The rules and limits to scanning textures are only in your imagination.

Texture scans of the back cover of a black loose-leaf notebook, the back cover of an encyclopedia, and of material used for a window curtain.

Scanning Practice - What Every Scan Needs

Almost every scan you do, whether it's a photo, three-dimensional object or textured material, usually needs a bit of cleanup or sharpening. Textured materials may need this less than photos, since the materials often end up as out-of-focus backgrounds anyway. Most scans also need some color adjustment. This can easily be done with the Levels dialog. Here's a technique that works well for most photos and three-dimensional scans—start with an Auto-Levels adjustment in the Levels dialog, then lighten the image a little with the manual Input and Output Levels adjustments.

Scanning is an imprecise art at best. Some of your scans will require a bit of cropping, even though the preview window provided by xscanimage allows reasonably accurate alignment. All of your scans will require some fiddling with the physical alignment of the object to be scanned on the scanner glass. This means you are likely to become quite familiar with the preview window. Finally, most scans will require some level of gamma adjustment. Although xscanimage will save most device-specific settings, you may want to write this value down on a sticky note and place it on your monitor for quick reference, at least until you've finally memorized it. Many graphics programs benefit from proper gamma settings and not all of them are as easy to configure as xscanimage.

Alternatives to Scanning

There are a number of alternatives to scanning you can use to get photos into your computer. Not all of these provide the high quality that flatbed scanners do, but each will probably become another member of the resource list you use when working on images with the GIMP.

Digital Cameras

Digital cameras are one alternative method for getting images into the GIMP—one that bypasses scanning altogether. A digital camera stores images in memory or on magnetic media, often in JPEG format (although this is not a defined standard for these devices). The images are generally small, around 640x480 pixels. The advantage of digital cameras is the ease with which images can be transferred from the camera to the computer—no film developing or scanning is required. However, the quality of images from off-the-shelf digital cameras can be somewhat limiting for professional artists. Digital camera technology comes, at least in part, from the video camera world, where resolutions of 640x480 pixels work just fine. This resolution might suffice for web images but is insufficient for images intended for print media. This is not to say digital cameras cannot provide high quality images. On the contrary, if you have the means, there are plenty of high-end digital cameras for the professional graphic artist which are more likely to produce the image sizes you require. In any case, Linux users interested in using digital cameras should check the Sunsite archives before making a purchase to verify that the camera they are interested in has a driver available.

The Kodak PhotoCD Format

Another alternative to scanning your own images is the PhotoCD format from Kodak. This format provides five different image sizes, the largest with a resolution of about 2,000x3,000 pixels, on CD-ROM scanned from your photos. To get your photos onto a PhotoCD, you send the negatives or slides to Kodak via a local film developing lab or directly to a Kodak lab. The film is scanned and returned to you along with the CD of scanned images. Index prints are provided, so you can quickly check the images on the CD. Use the *hpcdtoppm* program available in the NetPBM set of tools to convert images on the CD to the ppm format. These ppm files can then be loaded directly into the GIMP.

CD-ROM Photo Collections

The explosion of the Web has brought about a plethora of multimedia solutions for both Macintosh and Microsoft Windows platforms that can be purchased from software retailers. Among these you will find catalogs of images on CD-ROM, all touted as including high-resolution images in TIFF and JPEG formats. Don't be fooled. The meaning of high-resolution is context-specific. For web-based artwork, these CD-ROMs offer some reasonably high-resolution images; however, these images are generally far too small to be used on their own for print media. At best, you could use them as small parts of a composite image built using the GIMP.

If you need higher-resolution stock images, you can search out true high-resolution images on CD-ROM from various resources. Use one of the on-line search engines using the search term "stock photo" to find collections of these available over the Internet and on CD-ROM via mail order.

Tip: Yahoo! maintains a category devoted specifically to stock photography at `http://www.yahoo.com/Business_and_Economy/Companies/ Photography/Stock_Photography/.`

The Cost of Going From Print to Computer

Scanners were once limited to the realm of artistically inclined computer jocks with money to burn. Economies of scale and advances in technology have brought the average price for flatbed scanners down in the past few years. Recent excursions to local computer chain outlets revealed SCSI-based 30-bit color flatbed scanners available for less than $100. That's a drop of nearly $100 in less than a year, and a drop of nearly $1,000 in five years. Consider that this is also a one-time purchase. There are no extra inks or papers that have to be refilled for scanners, and the quality of a 30-bit color scanner can last for the next two to five years before you might want to upgrade to a newer technology. After all, 30-bit scans at 8 1/2" by 11" and 300 dots per inch[4] will take up to 24MB of hard disk space. You'll need bigger disks long before you'll need a new flatbed scanner.

PhotoCD processing can cost about $1 to $3 per image scanned, plus shipping costs. This price is taken from a relatively old source, so it may have gone down a bit since then. Digital cameras are available for about $400 to $600 for an average consumer model. Hand-held scanners are hard to find these days. The low cost of flatbed scanners has made them fly off retailer's shelves.

Forget hand-held scanners if you don't already own one. Flatbed scanners will fit most users' needs, and PhotoCD scans will cover many more users. If you need to go beyond this, you should probably consider looking into using a service bureau, where film can be scanned on big, expensive drum scanners. With service bureau scans the quality goes up, but so will the price. Stay away from digital cameras unless you have serious time constraints in getting your images on the Web—at least until image sizes from digital cameras start to get over the 1000x1000 pixel resolution range at department store prices.

---

4. See discussion on dpi later in this chapter.

Printing

Scanning work comes in at the front end of your image processing work with the GIMP. On the opposite end comes printing. The 1.0 version for the GIMP provides an easy-to-use interface for printing. The Print Plug-In provides the user with a means to orient an image on the printed page, set paper types, scale and brighten an image before printing, and print in color or black and white. The plug-in supports a wide range of popular desktop printers and can be used in conjunction with Ghostscript to print to other printers.

Desktop inkjet printers are not continuous tone devices. That is, the images they create are more like television monitors than film. Televisions have many tiny red, green and blue phosphors—individual points of colored light. Film has no such set of individual points; it is a continuous tone image. A printed page is made up of huge numbers of tiny dots. Take a close look at one, a very close look. You can actually see the dots in some places, for example the front page of a newspaper. The dots are generally made up of Cyan, Magenta, Yellow and Black colors. Printers, therefore, deal with images in the CMYK color space. Using dots to create the printed image is referred to as *halftoning*.

If you remember from **Chapter 2 - GIMP Basics**, CMYK is a subtractive color space. That is, adding color takes away reflected light so the points get darker with more ink. This is the opposite of RGB, where adding color produces white light. The GIMP has limited support for dealing with CMYK images. You can decompose an image into its C, M, Y, and K components, but this produces four grayscale Image Windows. There is no CMYK Image Window, so you can't see a composite version of your image in the CMYK color space. Since the Print Plug-In will convert the image to CMYK before printing, the printed page may not look quite like the one on your screen. As suggested in **Chapter 2**, you will probably want to print small sections of the image first to check the output quality before trying to print the complete image.

Supported Printers

The Print Plug-In directly supports a wide range of printers. The following list comes from the on-line documentation (which is also available on the accompanying CD) for the Print Plug-In:

Printer Family	Models Supported
HP DeskJet	500, 500C, 520, 540C, 600C, 660C, 68xC, 69xC, 850C, 855C, 855Cse, 855Cxi, 870Cse, 870Cxi, 1100C, 1120C, 1200C, and 1600C
HP LaserJet	II, III, IIIp, IIIsi, 4, 4L, 4P, 4V, 4Si, 5, 5FS, 5L, 5P, 5SE, 5Si, 6L, 6P
Epson Stylus	Color, Color Pro, Color Pro XL, Color 400, Color 500, Color 600, Color 800, Color 1500, Color 1520, and Color 3000

The drivers for these printers are built directly into the Print Plug-In, so you don't need special printer configurations in the /etc/printcap[5] file. In fact, you should probably use the most generic printer configuration, at least for the Epson Stylus printers. Use one with no input or output filters configured. This allows the Print Plug-In to control the output quality directly.

Using Ghostscript

PostScript printers are supported by the Print Plug-In via the use of the Ghostscript interpreter. Ghostscript is a tool which takes PostScript input and converts it to an output format specific to a wide range of output devices. In general, Ghostscript can be used for accessing a large number of printers from the GIMP, including printers from HP, DEC, Tektronix, Xerox, Apple, Epson and Canon. It also supports a wide range of display devices, including a standard X11 device, VGA/EGA devices, and output to the PPM/PGM, TIFF, JPEG and PNG image file formats.

Configuration of Ghostscript can be a little confusing if you are trying to support only a specific printer, but there is quite a bit of documentation to walk you through the process. Fortunately, most UNIX and Linux vendors have already made versions of Ghostscript available to their customers. Users of commercial Linux distributions will find that Ghostscript is probably already installed on their systems, although the version may not be the latest and it might not support your particular printer. In that case, you will need to get the source and build and

---

5.   Or via lpadmin for SVR4-based UNIX systems.

install it yourself. Be warned: it's not the simplest free software around to build and install manually! Be sure to read all the files with the `.txt` extensions before starting to build the program.

An on-line version of the Ghostscript FAQ in HTML format can be found at `http://www.cs.wisc.edu/~ghost/`. *Links from here will lead you to the latest version of Ghostscript, which is now supported by Aladdin Enterprises. Ghostscript is free for personal use, but users should still read the accompanying license which can also be found via the on-line FAQ.*

The program name for Ghostscript is actually gs. Most Linux distributions will have installed this program under `/usr/bin` *or* `/usr/local/bin`. *Looking in these directories for the gs program is probably the quickest way to see if the package is installed. Then try running*

```
% gs -h
```

which will tell you what output devices are configured.

Once you have Ghostscript installed, you need to establish a printer entry in `/etc/printcap` that will allow you to funnel PostScript print requests through the Ghostscript interpreter. Although the syntax of the printcap file is a bit difficult to follow, there are a number of ways to edit it. First, Linux users will find that most distributions are now shipping with some version of a graphical printer management tool. Red Hat has been shipping its Printtool package with its distributions since about the 4.0 days. This package is fairly simple, but handles most basic printer needs and does all the editing of the printcap file behind the scenes for you. Non-Linux users who use the lpd printing system (.ie., those based on the BSD lpr tools) may want to take a look at the APS filter package, which includes a graphical interface for configuring the printcap file. Users who run a version of UNIX based on SVR4's lpsched or clones (such as LPRng) might not use `/etc/printcap` and will have other tools for configuring print services.

The Linux Printing HOWTO provides extensive information on configuring your lpd-based system's `/etc/printcap`. *Along with this document, the Linux Printing Usage HOWTO explains how to use the lpr tools (lpr, lpd, lpc, lprm). Both of these are available on-line at the Linux Documentation Project at* `http://sunsite.unc.edu/LDP/`. *Since the lpd tools originated on BSD systems, users of systems such as FreeBSD or BSD/OS will probably find these documents useful as well.*

You can also edit the `/etc/printcap` file by hand. The printcap(5) man page can help users who choose this route. A very simple printcap entry for a parallel printer connected to `/dev/lp1` that can be used with the HP and Epson drivers in the GIMP's Print Plug-In looks like the following:

```
gimp:\
 :sd=/var/spool/lpd/lp0:\
 :mx#0:\
 :sh:\
 :lp=/dev/lp1:
```

This entry would not work if you need to pass the output through the Ghostscript interpreter. The entry created for me by Red Hat's Printtool for use with Ghostscript and the same printer (connected to `/dev/lp1`) looks like this:

```
lp:\
 :sd=/var/spool/lpd/lp:\
 :mx#0:\
 :sh:\
 :lp=/dev/lp1:\
 :if=/var/spool/lpd/lp/filter:
```

The last line, prefixed with `:if=`, tells the print spooler to use a script that passes the PostScript file through Ghostscript as an input filter. Note that Red Hat recommends you not edit this entry by hand and instead let the Printtool facility do it for you. More information and links to an on-line version of the `/etc/printcap` man page are available from the Linux Printing HOWTO.

Keep in mind that if your printer supports PostScript files directly then you can configure a printcap entry like the first entry above and skip passing it through Ghostscript. In either case, whether you use Ghostscript or have a PostScript-ready printer, you need to configure the Print Plug-In to use the PostScript driver.

The Print Plug-In

As long as you have one of the supported printers, have installed Ghostscript, or you have a PostScript-ready printer, you can now configure the GIMP's Print Plug-In to use the printer. Open the Print dialog by selecting *File->Print* from an Image Window's menu (the Print dialog is available only from Image Windows—it's not available from the Toolbox's File menu). The first thing to do is select which printer to send the output to. The Printer options menu will list all printers configured in your printer configuration. For LDP users, this would be all the entries in the `/etc/printcap file`. For SVR4 lpsched users, this would be the printers listed by the `lpstat -t` command. Select an appropriate printer. Alternatively, you can select the print output to go to a file instead of a printer with this option.

Print dialog   *Setup dialog*

Now go into the Setup dialog by clicking on the button labeled *Setup*. Here you can select the driver to use and the command to use for printing. Selecting the driver is simple enough. If you have one of the supported printers, select it from the *Driver* options menu. If not, select *PostScript Level 2* if you are going to be using Ghostscript. You can use *PostScript Level 1* if Ghostscript is not configured for level 2 support (again, use the `-h` option to verify this). If you use a PostScript-ready printer, you will need to check its documentation to determine which PostScript level to configure in the Print Plug-In.

It's important that you select the Printer you will be using before going into the Setup option. If you don't, and have left the Printer set to File, you may not be able to specify the print command to use.

Below the Driver menu is the *PPD File* text entry field. You can use this field to specify the name of a PostScript Printer Description file, if you have one. This field is available only if you have selected either PostScript Level 1 or PostScript Level 2 as the driver. Its use is limited to those users who have PostScript-ready printers. This file provides a list of available media sizes, types, sources, and resolutions along with the commands needed to select them. If you use Ghostscript with the level 1 or 2 drivers, you probably won't need to use this and can leave the field blank.

The last field has the print command to use. The Print Plug-In will print to the printer selected using the command specified here. For LDP users (Linux and other PC-based UNIX users, for example), the command will be something like

```
% /usr/bin/lpr -Pgimp -l
```

where `lpr` is the name of the program which spools print requests. This command was generated by the plug-in itself and is presented here so you can specify other command line options if you need them. The Print Plug-In figures out which printer to use (the -P option) from the printer name you selected from the Printer options menu. When you are finished with the Print Setup dialog, click on the OK button.

The next option in the Print dialog is the *Media Size* options menu. This menu provides a number of options such as Letter, Legal, A4, Tabloid, A3, and 12x18. By default, images are printed to fit the page and are automatically rotated to fill the largest area possible The options actually listed will depend on the printer driver you selected in the Setup dialog. PostScript printers will have all of these options available. The Epson Stylus Color 500, on the other hand, only supports Letter, Legal and A4. Even though the Print Plug-In is likely to correctly understand what paper types work with the printer driver you selected, you should still check your printer's documentation to determine the paper sizes it supports. Most desktop inkjet printers will support Letter or Legal sizes at a minimum.

Media Type is available for only a few supported printers, such as the HP DeskJet 500 and 520. This menu allows you to choose the type of media you will be using in the printer. Options include Plain, Premium, Glossy, and Transparency. Like Media Size, you should double check that the option you select is actually supported by your printer before trying to use it.

Media Source is also available for a limited number of printers, such as the HP LaserJet 4V and 4SI. These printers have multiple paper trays and this menu allows you to choose the tray.

The *Orientation* menu offers three options for all printers: Auto, Portrait, and Landscape. *Auto* is the default and tells the Print Plug-In to automatically rotate images to fit the media selected. *Portrait* is the standard format. *Landscape* rotates the image 90 degrees.

Some printers allow you to specify different print resolutions. The options here are very printer specific. The HP LaserJet 4V offers resolutions of 150, 300, and 600 dpi. The Espon Stylus Color 500 has 360 and 720 dpi resolutions. The term dpi is discussed a little later in this chapter.

Prints can be either black and white or color. Although these options are available for all supported printers, the Print Plug-In will force the output to grayscale for printers that don't do color output and for images that come from grayscale Image Windows.

To the left of these options is a preview display of the orientation of the output. The black outline is the media and the solid black box will be the printed region. This preview can be modified in a number of ways. First, the Orientation menu will rotate the display as needed. Below the display are two sliders, one for Scaling and one for Brightness. The *Scaling* slider will change the size of the printed region. The size of this region cannot exceed the dimensions of the media's outline. Scaling can be done as a percentage of physical media space or in ppi, pixels per inch. The use of ppi is more of an advanced topic and beyond the scope of this text. For most home users, and even many professionals, the default percent setting will suffice.

Aside from scaling, you can also move the printed region within the media outline. To do this, click on the solid black box and hold the mouse button down. Now drag the box around inside of the outline. The box will always stay within the outline. This means you can't ask the Print Plug-In to print your image so that it hangs off the edge of the media, cropping it along the boundaries of the media. If you need to do this, you will need to manually crop the image first, then print it. Also note that if you scale the image down, then reposition it in the outline and try to scale it back up again, the Print Plug-In will catch when the scaling has reached the media's edge and do the appropriate thing. That means the scaling, which normally proceeds down and to the right, will fill up and to the left or right, whichever is most appropriate. In other words, the Print Plug-In is relatively smart. It won't allow you to go past those page boundaries!

The last feature of the plug-in is the *Brightness* slider. If your prints are coming out a bit dark, you can lighten them directly within the Print Plug-In by using this slider. The default setting of 100 sets the slider tab to the center of the slider bar, allowing you to move it down (darken) or up (lighten). According to Mike Sweet, the plug-in's author:

A brightness of 100 is usually good for most B&W (black and white) and Post-Script printers, while most inkjet printers need a brightness between 100 and 120 for acceptable results.

Experimentation with an Epson Stylus Color 500 showed values of 100 to 120 to be about right for most of the prints I tried.

The settings you use in the Print dialog are valid for the current session, even if you use the Print Plug-In from different Image Windows. The settings are not saved between GIMP sessions, however.

Preparing for Print Media

You've seen how to use the print services within the GIMP but there is much more to printing than just selecting the Print option. Print preparation requires an understanding of how printing works and what to expect when the printing occurs. Let's take a look at what dpi, lpi and halftoning, three terms you'll often see in relation to printing images, are all about.

dpi, lpi, and Halftoning

Raster images are always discussed in terms of *pixels*, the number of dots on the screen that make up the height and width of an image. As long as the image remains on the computer, there is no need to worry about converting this to some other resolution using some other terminology. Pixel dimensions work well for web pages, for example.

Many images aren't very useful if they remain solely on the computer. Their real usefulness lies in their transfer to film, videotape, or print media such as magazines, posters and even fabric. The trouble with this is that printing an image is much different than simply viewing it on the screen. There are problems related to color conversions (RGB to CMYK), for example. Printing also requires a different set of dimensions than the pixel resolution used for monitors because of the way printers work. In order to get the image to look the way you want it on the printer, you'll need to understand how printers work. First, some background information:

- Printer resolution is given in dots per inch, more commonly referred to as *dpi*. This is the number of dots the device can output in an inch.

- Lines per inch (*lpi*) relates to halftoning. Many devices (such as printers) have only bi-level channels. This means they either paint a colored dot or they don't—there are no smooth steps. *Halftoning* means using different patterns of very closely arranged dots to simulate a greater number of color shades. Obviously, several dots must be used in certain on/off combinations to simulate having more shades.

- lpi comes from the world of photography while dpi comes from the world of design. Whether it makes sense to speak of dpi resolution for a raster image or not depends on what you'll be using that image for. Most magazines, such as *Time*, are printed with 153 lpi or less. Newspapers such as the *Wall Street Journal* are printed at 45 to 120 lpi.

Halftoning masks are the patterns used to create the shades of color or levels of gray seen in the lines per inch on the printed media. Most masks are square. Let's say you have a printer which can print 300 dpi. If the halftoning mask is four pixels wide by four pixels high, then you'll have $300/4 = 75$ lines per inch (lpi) for the halftones. That is the effective resolution of the device since you are interested in nice shaded printouts and not in single bi-level dots. An ultra-expensive 1200 dpi typesetter will be able to do 300 lpi if you use the four pixel by four pixel halftone mask described above. Of course, the larger the halftone size, the more shades you'll get, but the lower the effective resolution will be.

If you are only going to display an image on your screen, then perhaps speaking of dpi in the image is pointless. You'll be mapping one pixel in the image to one pixel on your display, so the size of the image will depend only on the size of your monitor. This makes sense; when you create images for display on a monitor, you usually only think in terms of available screen space (in pixels), not about final physical displayed size (inches). For example, when you create a web page, you try to make your images so that they'll fit on the browser's window, regardless of the physical size of your monitor's screen.

The story is a bit different when you are creating images for output on a hard copy device. You see, sheets of paper have definite physical sizes and people do care about them. That's why everyone tries to print letter-sized documents on A4 paper and vice versa. The simplest thing to do is just create images considering the physical output resolution of your printer. Let's say you have a 300 dpi printer and you create an image which is 900 pixels wide. If you map one image pixel to one device pixel (or dot), you'll get a 3-inch wide image:

$$\frac{900 \text{ pixels in an image}}{300 \text{ dots per inch}} = 3 \text{ inches of image}$$

That is hardly what you want, because most likely your printer uses bi-level dots and you'll get very ugly results if you print a photograph with one image pixel mapped to one device pixel. You can get only so many color combinations for a single dot on your printer—if it uses three inks, cyan/magenta/yellow (CMY) and if it uses bi-level dots (spit ink or do not spit ink, and that's it), you'll be able to get only a maximum of 2*2*2 = 8 colors on that printer. Obviously, eight colors is not enough for a photograph.

This is where halftoning comes in. A halftone block is usually a small square of pixels which sets different dot patterns, depending on which shade you want to create. Each halftone block is mapped to an image pixel. Let's say you use the four pixel by four pixel halftone mask as in the previous example. If you map one image pixel to one halftone block, then your printed image will be four times as large than as if you had simply mapped one image pixel to one printer pixel. You end up with a print which more closely matches the image displayed on your monitor (disregarding issues about converting RGB images to CMYK for now).

A good rule of thumb for deciding at what size to create images is the following. Take the number of lines per inch (lpi) that your printer or printing software will use, that is, the number of halftone blocks per inch it will use, and multiply that by two. Use that as the number of dots per inch (dpi) for your image.

Say you have a 600 dpi color printer that uses 4-pixel halftone blocks. That is, it will use 600/4 = 150 lpi. You should then create your images at 150*2 = 300 dpi. So, if you want an image to be five inches wide, then you'll have to make it 300*5= 1500 pixels wide. Your printing software should take all that into account to create the proper halftoning mask. For example, when you use PostScript, you can tell the interpreter to use a certain halftone size and it will convert images appropriately. Unfortunately, most Linux software doesn't allow users to specify things like halftone mask sizes yet (at least not easily). You would probably have to either edit the PostScript document manually or use a filter file to do it for you. Either way, it's not a process for the average user who just wants to print and not program.

If you need to create an image destined for print, you should check the printer documentation to find either the lpi or, alternatively, the dpi and the number of pixels used in the halftone. You can then compute the number of pixels you'll need in your image and forget about trying to specify halftone masks yourself.

Keep in mind that most desktop inkjet printers are destined for MS Windows or Macintosh users and don't always include all the information you may need. If the printed documentation provided with the printer doesn't provide dpi, lpi and halftone information, you may need to check the technical specifications available from the manufacturer. For many manufacturers, this information is now available on-line via their corporate web sites. If all else fails, you can probably just use the available resolutions for your printer in the Print Plug-In to determine the size of your image. If the maximum resolution is 720, for example, and you know you'll be printing at the printer's maximum for your finished print, then use 720 dpi to calculate the size of the image to create.

File Sizes and Getting Images to the Printer

The sizes of images destined for print tend to be much larger than those of images destined for the Web. This is simple mathematics: a display monitor usually runs about 72 dpi, while a printer runs anywhere from 150 to 720 dpi or higher. A 720 dpi image that will be 5"x7" would require over 18 MB just for the raw data. The GIMP's XCF file format will use much more than that if you want to save layer information. Images destined for print will require lots of disk space.

Providing the additional disk space on your work system is not a big problem. Disk sizes are reaching the 7-10 gigabyte range at prices of around $300 retail. The problem, therefore, isn't getting space locally, but getting the images from your machine to your editor or print shop. Obviously, saving an 18 MB image as a TIFF file to a floppy disk isn't going to cut it. And unless you have some high-speed network connections—something like ADSL or maybe a cable modem— uploading via the Internet is going to take quite a bit of patience. You'll need some high-density off-line media.

Currently, there are a number of options for off-line media: removable disks, WORM drives, tapes, and CD-ROMs. Each of these is supported by Linux, and by other UNIX flavors to various extents. A good way to determine the best option is to find out what media the other guy is using. Right now, Zip disks are quite popular and fairly inexpensive.

Most of your final artwork will probably fit under the 100 MB capacity of these disks, although if you need to send the XCF files, you might be pushing it. The higher-end cousin of the Zip is the Jaz drive. These offer 1 to 2 GB of disk space, although there are reports that the earlier versions of these drivers would lock up if you used more than about 630 MB. If you choose either of these drives, chances are you'll need to use the DOS partition they come with instead of replacing it with a Linux partition. Most print shops and publishing houses are not likely to be using Linux. At least not yet.

Alternatively, you could burn your own CD-ROM with your artwork. The cost of blank CDs has recently gone down considerably, so this option is not as farfetched as it once was. The problem here is that burning a CD requires 650 MB of free disk space for a copy of the CD image. Still, if you have the time and hardware, it is a fairly well-supported alternative to Jaz/Zip disks.

If you're interested in learning how to write your own CDs, start with the Linux CD-ROM Writing Howto at `http://sunsite.unc.edu/LDP/HOWTO/CD-Writing-HOWTO.html`*.*

Jaz drives currently run about $250 to $300, with individual disks running about $120. Zip drives are getting to below the $100 range with media around $20 to $30 apiece. These prices should drop soon as competing products begin to make inroads in the off-line storage arena. You can probably forget tapes, since many tape archive programs package data in their own formats, and unless you have DOS/MS Windows or Macintosh tape software on your Linux/UNIX box, it's not worth the effort. The same goes with WORM drives (which is a more generalized category of media similar to, and including, CD-ROMs).

Banding

Since halftoning is used in printing and the use of more ink to get darker colors is common practice, it can take quite a bit of ink to get the right tones on the printed page. Images with lots of gradients are particularly troublesome because of the banding that can occur where the halftone dots are not smooth.

Banding is an abrupt color change where there should be a gradual transition. It can occur for a number of reasons, not the least of which is poor support in a printer driver or the printer itself. But you can take a few steps to reduce this effect. First, try using a lighter shade in dark gradients. Some banding occurs because of the color contrasts in gradients and the way that a printer handles those shades of color. Similarly, a different color gradient can be used. Be careful here. Banding can become more noticeable in lighter areas. Trying to lighten an already light gradient can make the problem worse.

Print Media Types

A number of types of print media can be used either directly or indirectly with inkjet printers. Standard laserjet plain paper is fine for text printing but useful only for sample prints, at best, when used with the GIMP. To get high quality output you need to use high quality paper.

Standard plain paper for inkjet printers, also referred to as laser print paper or copy paper, runs about $5 to $8 per ream, with each ream having about 500 sheets of 20 to 24 lb. paper. This paper is good for home use but you wouldn't use it for your resume. The reason is simple: plain paper allows the ink to spread more than other papers. Print ordinary text on it (you don't need to use the GIMP to do so, but you can) and take a look at how smooth and crisp the letters are. Print something big, to make it obvious. As you can see, prints on plain paper are low-quality, and an image from the GIMP uses a bit more ink than ordinary text would.

Coated papers are specially treated to help limit the amount of ink spreading. The better the coating, the less the spreading. These papers run slightly more than plain paper, but are good for printing rough drafts of your images. They hold up well with resolutions of 300 to 360 dpi, but can start to wrinkle badly under the weight of the ink from higher resolutions.

Premium papers are the next step up from coated papers. These papers are much smoother on their surfaces than the coated and plain papers, and ink spreading occurs to a much smaller degree. Images print well on these papers at resolutions as high as 720 dpi, possibly higher. This makes premium papers excellent for printing photographs and other high-color prints. Premium papers don't wrinkle much with 360 dpi prints, but can begin to show a little wrinkling with 720 dpi prints. It's best to let the ink dry on these higher-resolution prints before handling the paper and certainly before laying anything on top of the paper! Premium paper comes in packages of 100 to 500 sheets and runs roughly twice the cost of plain paper. The high availability of inkjet printers has increased demand for premium papers, and in turn has brought their cost down over the past few years.

High gloss paper is the paper of choice for final prints that need the highest quality finish. High gloss papers are specially coated on one side to allow the paper to take ink without letting it spread. This means that 720, 1200 and 1440 dpi printers can print cleanly on these papers. In fact, you probably won't notice the high quality of the prints from 1440 dpi printers unless you use a high gloss paper. Compared to the other paper types, high gloss papers are expensive, running anywhere from $12 to $15 for a package of 15 to 25 sheets of paper. Most home users have little need for the high quality you get from these papers since premium papers are far less expensive and work well with medium quality prints. High gloss papers are more for professionals who need to check the quality of the output of their digital works before sending them off to a high-end printer to be used on posters, magazines or book covers.

Ivory board is a type of paper used for business cards. Its paper acts much like premium paper or any other coated paper as far as ink spreading is concerned. Greeting cards, which usually come perforated and pre-scored for folding, are another form of specially coated paper. They are generally thicker than the ivory board used for business cards but with the same feel to the surface of the paper. Both types of paper can be purchased for use with inkjet printers from computer retailers and office supply companies.

Printing on Fabrics

You may have noticed prepackaged kits for creating iron-on transfers for T-shirts or other fabrics from your printer. The kits allow you to print to special papers which are the iron-on transfer sheets. When using these papers, you need to be certain to allow the paper to dry, per the instructions that come with the paper. For best results you should probably cut out the transfer from the sheet, leaving a small border except for one side. On that side you need to leave enough of an edge to use to pull the paper from the fabric after ironing. Keep in mind that you shouldn't use steam with the iron while doing the transfer.

One tip for using transfers is to flip the image in the GIMP right before printing; otherwise, any text in the image will be backward on the fabric. If no text is used, then flipping the image may not be necessary.

Pantone Colors

It is important to note that the GIMP does not currently support Pantone colors. Pantone is a system for insuring the color consistency of printed output. Unfortunately, Pantone's current licensing prohibits integration of the Pantone Matching System (PMS) directly into the GIMP; a future version of the GIMP may somehow avoid this by providing Pantone capability in an add-on, binary-only module.

Useful Resources on the Net

The Internet has plenty of useful resources related to scanning and printing. Always check your scanner and printer manufacturer's latest updates. Most of these can be found by starting your search at Yahoo!, AltaVista, Excite, Lycos or any of the myriad other web search engines. A few web sites and pages that were used in preparing this chapter include:

*   Sunsite's collection of Linux drivers for image capture devices: `ftp://sunsite.unc.edu/pub/Linux/apps/graphics/capture/`

*   Philip Greenspun's terrific resource for taking, scanning and otherwise dealing with photographs (including information on getting them into PhotoCD format): `http://photo.net/photo/`

*   One specific page on photo.net that discusses adding images to the Web, including tips on using ImageMagick to convert PhotoCD images to JPEG images: `http://photo.net/wtr/thebook/images.html`

Moving On

You should now be ready to begin experimenting with some of the more esoteric aspects of the GIMP—the Filters and Script-Fu scripts. The rest of this book is a quick reference to most of the Filters in the core distribution, and some of the Script-Fu scripts. A few filters that are included in the Unstable package are also shown, since they have not acted unstable on my system and I find them interesting. All of these are shown in the images in **Part 2**. Now that the details have been covered in **Part 1**, don't forget to take a peek at the CD-ROM. The CD-ROM includes a small Gallery of images and some tutorials to show what you can do with the GIMP.

All of the images you've seen in the book are on the CD-ROM. Some of the original photos, in fairly large scans, are also included. Plus, there are links to more information on the Web, on-line documentation, tips, tutorials, man pages, FAQs, a few XCF files from the Gallery images, and more.

Part 2 - Filters and Script-Fu Effects

The following pages have examples of many filters that are available for the GIMP. All of these are accessible from either the Filters or Script-Fu submenus in the Image Window menu. Most of these filters are included in either the core or Extras source distributions, while a very few may be in the Unstable source distribution. If you use a binary distribution it is highly possible that not all of these filters will be available. In that case, you may want to install from the source distributions instead.

Not all filters in the core distribution or the Extras package have examples here. Some filters don't lend themselves well to visual examples, and/or have very specific purposes, such as the digital signature filters. Also, most filters offer fairly complex sets of configurable parameters. Some filters could take up a chapter of their own just to explain their use. In future revisions of this book, I hope to cover a few of these in more detail. For now, just use these pages as a reference to find an appropriate filter for your image processing work.

Most of the images provided include the dialog settings for the filter that created that image. In a few cases, the filter has no configurable parameters and only the final effect is shown. In other cases, the dialog is so large that it didn't fit well next to the image, so the dialog is presented as a separate image. The original images used in these examples are included on the CD so you can try to reproduce some of the effects.

Chapter 12 - Artistic

The *Artistic* filters include Apply Canvas, Cubism, Oilify and Mosaic. The *Apply Canvas* filter can be used to make an image look as though it has been placed on a painter's canvas. You may want to apply this to a white background, blur it, and then combine this with your image. Otherwise the canvas effect may look too artificial. The *Cubism* and *Oilify* filters can turn an ordinary photo into something that looks much more like a painting, as the examples show. Finally, the *Mosaic* filter converts an image into a three-dimensional collection of tiles of varying sizes and shapes.

The time required for an Artistic filter to complete processing is highly dependent upon the settings used, the image composition, the computer's processor speed and the amount of memory available. In general, all of the Artistic filters can take a bit of time to complete processing, especially on large images.

Original image

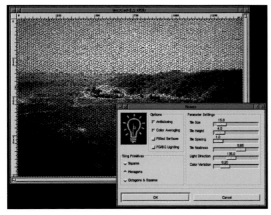

Mosaic

Oilify

Apply Canvas

Cubism

Chapter 13 - Blur

Each of the *Blur* filters takes an image and modifies it so that it appears to be out of focus in various ways. The simplest of these is the *Blur* filter. This filter can be used to smooth out rough spots, where colors are spotty and need to be made to appear to flow more smoothly from pixel to pixel. Similarly, the *Gaussian Blur IIR* and *Gaussian Blur RLE* use different methods to achieve basically the same sort of effect.

Motion blur can be used to make an image appear as if it were moving, either away from the camera or to the side. *Pixelize* blurs an image by creating small blocks of combined pixels similar to what you see when you zoom all the way in on an image. *Tilable* and *Variable* blurs offer variations on the Gaussian blurs.

Original image

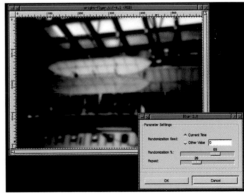

Blur

Gaussian Blur IIR

Motion Blur

Gaussian Blur RLE

Variable Blur

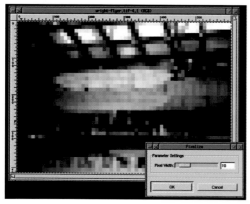

Pixelize

Tilable Blur

Chapter 14 - Colors

The *Colors* filters offer you the ability to modify the colormap for an image or selection. Most of these work only on RGB images, so be sure to convert indexed images to RGB before trying to use them. These filters can offer some powerful effects. Unfortunately, such versatility comes at the price of complexity. The *Filter Pack* filter, for example, has a number of preview windows showing what the current image is and what it can be changed to. It may take a little practice to understand that you need to click on the previews to move through color variations. Additionally, the *Saturation* toggle, which is off by default, can be enabled to allow access to even more preview windows. Such complexity is minor in comparison to the *Colormap Rotation* filter. For this filter, just remember that you can drag the arrows in the color wheels or type numbers in the *From* and *To* fields just below the wheels.

For each of these filters, you should plan to experiment with different images, alternating using the entire image with using selections of the image. Experimentation is the key—without it, you'll never completely understand the full extent of the Colors filters.

Original image

Alien Map

Colormap Rotation

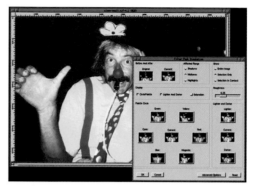

Filter Pack

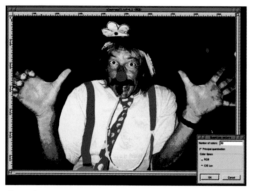

Quantize

Gradient Map

Scatter HSV

Colorify

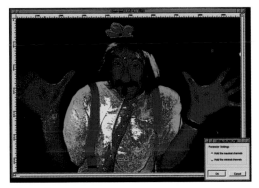

Max RGB

Value Invert

Chapter 15 - Distorts

Each of the *Distorts* filters offers attractive and obvious effects. The *Curtain*, *IWarp*, and *Polar Coordinates* filters can produce very eye-catching effects. The trick with these is to start with images having very distinct colors—bold yellows and browns or bright greens and reds, for example. I use these filters to produce backdrops for other images by taking colorful covers of magazines, scanning them, and then running them through the Distorts filters a few times until the original image is no longer recognizable. The key is that the original image was overflowing with a variety of bright colors.

Another filter which can produce some interesting effects is the *Waves* filter. The front cover of this book shows an example image for the Waves filter. Notice that, like the example above, the effect on the original image by using the Waves filter is to produce an image that is nearly unrelated to the original image, yet still visually appealing. It takes a little effort to recognize the faces of people from the original image on the left side of the example. Again, the original image had a good color mix. Applying the filter a few times—and perhaps running it through a few other Distorts filters—would make an interesting backdrop for another image.

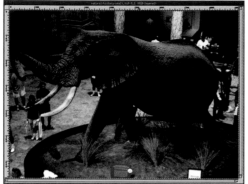

Original image

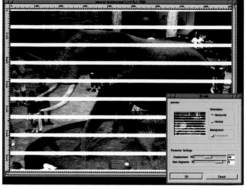

Blinds

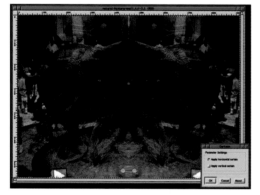

Curtain

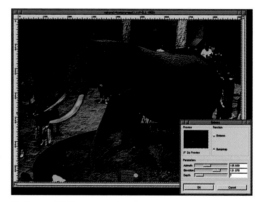

Emboss with Bumpmap toggle

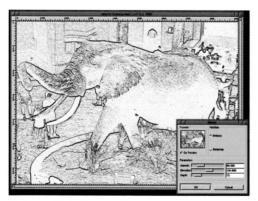

Emboss with Emboss toggle

Engrave

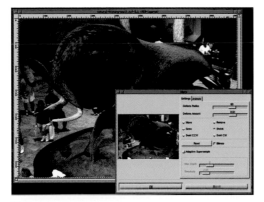

IWarp

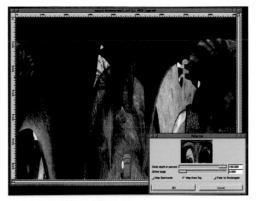

Polarize (Polar Coordinates)

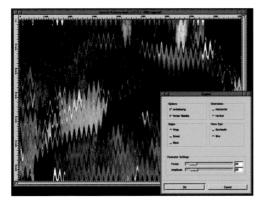

Ripple

Shift

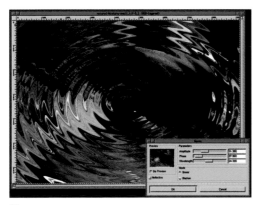

Waves

Whirl and Pinch

Chapter 16 - Edge-Detect and Combine

The *Edge-Detect* filters look for patterns in an image where straight lines of colors appear. The way they do this differs from one filter to another, and their effectiveness also varies. You may find that after running an Edge-Detect filter, the resulting image will need to be brightened or color-corrected using the Levels dialog. Remember: few filters will produce an acceptable final image all by themselves. Mix and match filters, especially with the Colors filters (*Filters->Colors* from the Image Window menu) to get the best results.

In these examples, you can see that the *Sobel* filter produces a more distinct, smoother set of lines than the other filters. However, don't let this fool you. The results can be a product of the complexity of the source image. Also, the final images shown here are all corrected for brightness and contrast, as suggested above. With a different source image, you could find that one of the other Edge-Detect filters is better suited.

Now I'd like to discuss one of my favorite filters: the *Film* filter, which is one of the *Combine* filters. I don't get to use this filter much, but it produces a rather unique effect. Unlike the Edge-Detect filters, this one doesn't operate on one image to find edges. Instead, it takes a series of images and connects them together as if they were each a frame in a roll of film. It isn't a terribly difficult effect to achieve, but it is an interesting one.

Original image

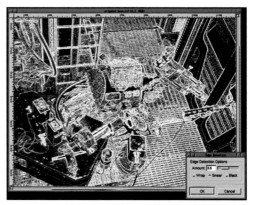

Edge

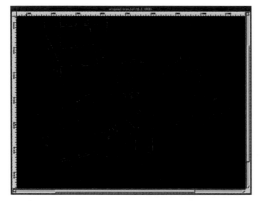

Laplace

Sobel

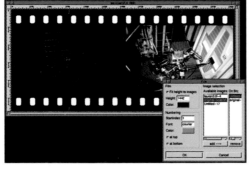

Film

Chapter 17 - Enhance

The only example from the *Enhance* filters given here is the *Sharpen* filter. You should use this filter fairly often if you scan your own images. Nearly all scanned images can be improved with some amount of sharpening. Each image in this book was scanned and sharpened at least once. Often each was sharpened more than that, depending on the image's quality.

Original image

Sharpen

Chapter 18 - Glass Effects

The *Glass Effects* filters are just what you'd expect—filters that make reflections of the image in one form or another. The examples show the effects better than words can describe. Fortunately, these filters are all rather easy to use. You may find these most useful when used with selections, with the selections feathered just a bit.

Apply Lens

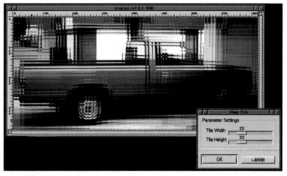

Glass Tile

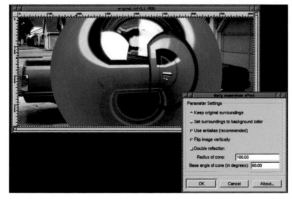

Conical Anamorphose

Chapter 19 - Light Effects

Some of the most visually attractive filters, the *Light Effects* filters, work without respect to existing images. They produce flares, either as a starburst or as a reflection from a camera, using variations in position and color. You should find these most useful when created in a separate layer, and then combined using one of the many layer modes available.

The *Sparkle* filter, unlike the other Light Effects filters, does work on an existing image, layer, or selection. It looks for the brightest points in the image, and turns them into multi-pronged flares. You will find that getting a single point in a selection to flare can be difficult and can take a number of attempts before you find the right filter settings. In general, if the filter is taking a long time to process the image, you probably won't get very distinct flares (you'll probably get a lot of flares right next to each other which overlap and cause big white blotches). If the progress bar for the filter appears to move quickly, then slows for a few moments occasionally, you should get more distinct flares. Like many filters, the Sparkle filter takes some practice and a lot of experimentation to learn to use it well.

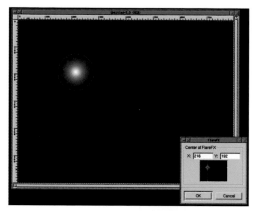

FlareFX

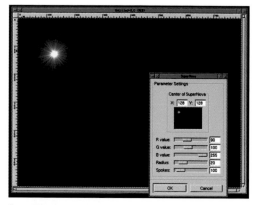

SuperNova

Sparkle

Chapter 20 - Map and Miscellaneous

Map filters can be subdivided into two different types: filters that use one image as a source for altering another image, and filters that tile images in one manner or another. The first set of filters include Bump Map, Displace, Coordinate Map, and Map to Object. The *Bump Map* and *Displace* filters both provide a means for adding depth to an image. *Coordinate Map* requires a 256x256 source image which is used to re-map the colors in your original image. The example here uses the original image scaled to 256x256 to produce the effect you see. Coordinate Map is included in the set of Unstable plug-ins. It's not part of the core distribution. I'm not sure why this one is considered unstable; I haven't had any problems using it. Finally, the *Map to Object* filter maps the source image to a plane or sphere, based on the orientation, lighting, and material characteristics you specify. An important point to note about the Map to Object filter is that the preview window displays in a ratio of 1:1, meaning that height and width are the same in that window. However, if your image does not have this ratio, then the effect will be stretched horizontally or vertically. This can be surprising when you try to create a perfect sphere and end up with a squashed one instead.

The other filters under Map all perform various forms of tiling, from the artistic-looking *Make Seamless* to the more traditional *Small Tiles*.

The other filter in this group is the *Video* filter, which is found under the *Misc* submenu in the Filters menu. This filter converts your image into something that looks like a somewhat distorted television image.

Original image

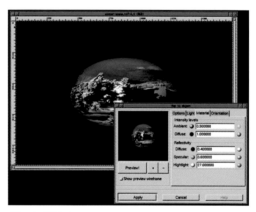

Make Seamless

Bump Map

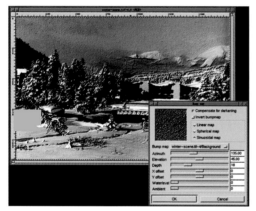

Map to Object

Coordinate Map

Displace

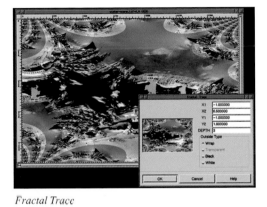

Fractal Trace

Paper Tile

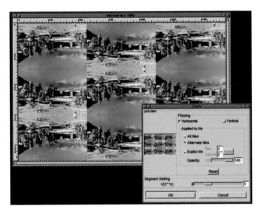

Small Tiles

Video

Illusion

Chapter 21 - Noise

All of the *Noise* filters effectively add a blur to an image by making the image "spotty". The filters use different methods of combining noise and the original image. This is like combining your image with the static you might see on a television which is set to a channel where there was no television signal broadcast.

Original image

Spread

Noisify

Randomize

Chapter 22 - Render

Along with the Artistic, Distort, and Map filters, the *Render* filters offer the most imaginative processing to be found in the GIMP. These tools provide everything from the square, semi-transparent pastel-colored blocks of the *Figures* filter to the bizarre shapes and colors of the *Qbist* and *Flame* filters. Qbist images are difficult to describe but the filter is very simple to use. Simply select one of the nine preview windows. The selected preview then becomes the middle preview and all the previews are updated based on that one. Continue to do this until you find a design that fits your intentions. Similarly, the Flame filter, using the default gradient given, provides images that can roughly be described as images of flames. But experimentation shows that you can go far beyond these simple flames to roaring explosions and raging solar flares, just using the default gradient.

One of the most important Render filters is the *GFig* filter, which is the GIMP's drawing tool. The interface is a bit confusing and will take some practice to master (future versions will probably change this interface to make it easier to use and extend). However, if you need to draw circles, curves, or complex outlines, GFig will be your best tool. Detailed examples of this filter can be found in **Chapter 8 - Drawing and Painting**.

All of the Render filters are worth exploring, but the *Plasma* filter's usefulness may not be immediately obvious. Start with this filter if you wish to create clouds of any sort. The general procedure for clouds is to create a plasma layer, desaturate it, add a layer mask, and copy the plasma image into that layer mask. At this point, you will want to adjust the brightness and contrast of both the desaturated plasma image and its layer mask to get the effect you really want. Also, stretching the layer horizontally or vertically is a common trick for making clouds with the Plasma filter.

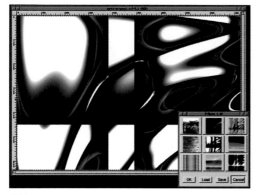

Qbist

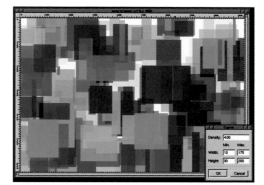

Figures

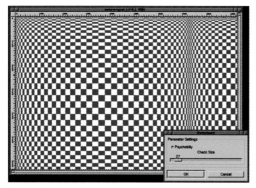

Checkerboard

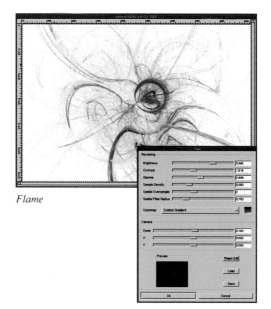

Flame

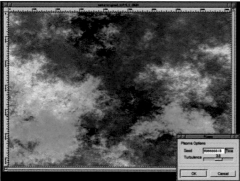

Plasma

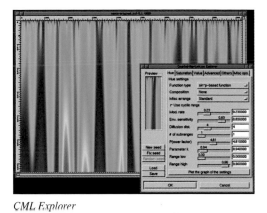

CML Explorer

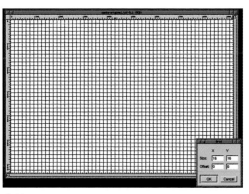

Grid

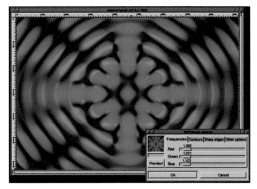

Diffraction Patterns

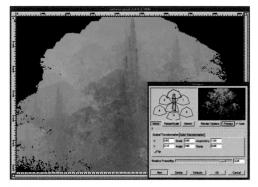

Ifs Compose

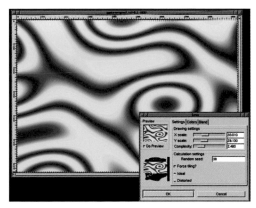

Sinus

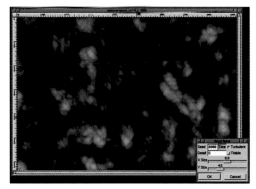

Solid Noise

303

Chapter 23 - Script-Fu

Script Fu effects are slightly different from filters in that they are not compiled programs that perform specific functions. Instead, they are text files that use the Scheme scripting language to access features found in other filters. Using Script-Fu scripts, you can mix and match filters to make reproducing a given effect a breeze.

The Script-Fu submenu in the Image Window menu has a number of different categories. Like the filters, not all scripts have visual or visually impressive effects. Some, like the *Selection* scripts, are simply quick ways of doing tasks that otherwise would take a number of steps if done by hand, and are not designed for producing final effects in and of themselves. Most scripts create a new layer, or at least allow you to specify that you want a new layer created for the given effect. Since scripts may run many commands to create their effects, chances are you won't be able to use the Undo feature of the GIMP to remove those effects—Undo will remove only the last command, not the entire script that was run. Therefore, you'll usually want to create a new layer when dealing with scripts so that you can simply delete the new layer to remove the script's effect.

Original image

I've included some of the more interesting effects in the examples here. The animation scripts are not included, as animations don't carry over well to print media.

Alchemy

You can produce interesting effects with the *Alchemy* scripts. *Clothify* produces an effect similar to the *Artistic->Apply Canvas* filter, but does so with a less obvious tiling of the effect. *Weave* is very creative—it produces what looks like woven pieces of reeds or bamboo with the original image overlaid on the individual strands, a very interesting effect.

Clothify   *Weave*

Decor

These scripts produce fairly obvious effects. One of the more impressive of these is the *Old Photo* script, which does a fairly good job of aging an image, as if it had faded and yellowed over time.

Old Photo

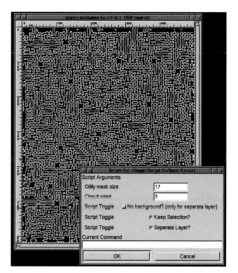

Circuit

Fuzzy Border

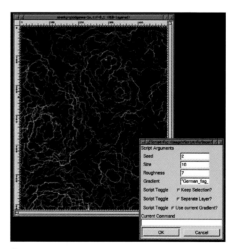

Lava

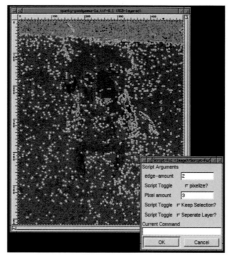

Predator

Modify

The only sample given here is the *Add Border* script, the effect of which is obvious.

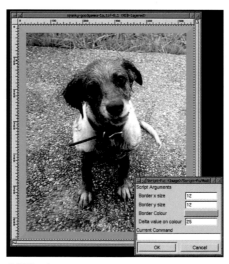

Add Border

Render

Again, only one sample is provided here: the *Line Nova* script. When the default settings are used, the effect looks a little like flares of light shooting from the center of the original image.

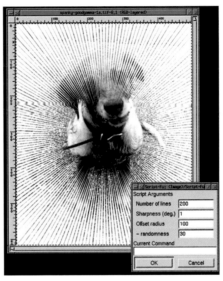

Line Nova

Shadow

As discussed in **Chapter 10 - Gradients**, the *Shadow* scripts take an image and add a shadow behind it, as if the image were floating above a flat surface. There are two of these scripts: *Drop-Shadow* and *Perspective*. Only the former is shown here. The latter gives the effect that the original image is not parallel to the surface beneath it, where the shadow exists.

Drop-Shadow

Glossary

A

Alpha Channel - The transparent channel in an image.

Anchor Icon - The fluer icon in the Layers and Channels dialog, used to associate multiple layers.

Anchor Layer - Composites a floating layer with an existing layer, using the mode set for the floating layer.

B

Banding - Visible lines running through a gradient blend that generally occur during printing. They can also be noticed when the blend is viewed on low-end (256 colors or less) displays.

Brightness - Similar to lightness, brightness is the perceived intensity of a self-luminous object.

Blend Modes - The set of options available to layers, bucket fills, brushes, and gradients, that determines how pixels are blended together.

Blend Tool - See Gradient Fill.

C

Channels - The separate pieces which comprise the color makeup of a pixel. For example, in an RGB image, there are three channels: Red, Green, and Blue. Adding an Alpha (transparency) channel would make it an RGBA image. Grayscale images have a single channel. Indexed images have three channels. Each of these latter two has an additional channel if an alpha channel is added.

CMY/CMYK - Cyan, Magenta, Yellow, and Black. An alternative color space used for digital images. Most commonly used in printing systems.

Color Models - Color models describe the composition of colors in a three-dimensional coordinate system. For RGB images, the coordinate system is a unit cube subset of the three-dimensional Cartesian coordinate system.

Composite/Composite Modes - To combine, as in "compositing two layers" or "compositing the red, green, and blue channels". Modes determine the method of the composite.

Continuous Tone Image - An original image such as a photo or painting.

Cross hair - Two lines that bisect each other perpendicularly. Used by various tools as an icon for the cursor.

D

Drawable - Another term for the displayed area in a layer. The drawable is needed by plug-ins to know which pixels to work on.

E

Edit Buffer - Storage used to save cut and copy operations, and from which paste operations get their data.

F

Flatten Image - Compose layers so that the Image Window will have a single layer containing the combined, visible portions of the original layers.

Floating Layer/Selection - Pasted selections become floating layers, also known as floating selections. A floating layer can either be anchored to an existing layer or turned into a new layer.

Fluer - Two double-ended arrows that bisect each other perpendicularly. Used as the cursor to represent the ability to perform a move operation.

G

Gradients - A granulated blend of colors.

Gradient Fill - The tool used to apply a gradient. Sometimes referred to as a Blend Tool. Makes use of the Gradient Editor dialog to select the gradient type, mode, and various other aspects of the fill operation.

Grayscale - A color model where all pixels are made up of varying intensities of gray.

Guides - Horizontal and vertical lines which run from the rulers in an Image Window to the opposite side of the window. They are used as guidelines for drawing, selecting, and a host of other tasks. The guides are not part of an image, they simply provide straight-line reference marks for the artist.

H

Halftone - An image created using a series of very small dots of various sizes and densities from a continuous tone image such as a photo.

Hue - The distinction between colors, such as red, green, and blue. Used in conjunction with the HSV color model.

HSV - Hue, Saturation, and Value. Sometimes called HSB, with B representing Brightness. A color model based on a user's perception of tint, shade, and tone.

I

Indexed - A type of image with a limited palette of colors, usually no more than 256 separate colors.

K

Kern - A measurement of the space between letters in text.

Keyboard Accelerators/Shortcuts - Keystrokes that allow access to tools, filters, and menu options.

Keyboard Modifiers - Keystrokes that modify the way a tool, filter or other feature operates. The CTRL, ALT, and SHIFT keys are considered keyboard modifiers.

L

Leading - The space, measured in points, between consecutive lines of text.

Layers - The parts of an image in the GIMP similar to a stack of translucent sheets which make up the viewable area in an Image Window.

Layer Modes - See Blend Modes.

Lightness - Similar to brightness, lightness is the perceived intensity of a reflecting object.

M

Marching Ants - The dashed line that moves around the perimeter of a selected region.

Merge Visible Layers - Similar to flattening, but composites only layers whose visibility is turned on.

Modes - See Composite/Composite Modes.

N

Named Buffers - A way of saving multiple cut or copy operations for retrieval at arbitrary times during a GIMP session.

O

Opacity - The amount of an image or pixel which is visible, that is, cannot be seen through.

P

Pantone Colors - A color matching system used to match spot colors and process colors. Pantone colors are not supported under the GIMP.

Pica - A unit of measurement equal to one-sixth of an inch, or 12 points.

Pixel Depth - The number of bits used to describe the color components of an image. Monochrome images have a 1-bit pixel depth. RGBA images have a 24-bit pixel depth.

Point - A unit of measurement equal to 1/72 of an inch.

Procedural Database/PDB - A database maintained by the GIMP of the routines, scripts, and filters available to external tools. Plug-ins and scripts use the PDB to process images. Plug-ins and scripts register their functions with the PDB so that other tools can call them via the PDB interface.

R

Redo - Reapplies the last change that was undone with the Undo menu option.

RGB - Red, Green and Blue. A common color model used for digital images.

S

Saturation - The measured amount a color deviates from a gray of equal intensity.

Scheme/SIOD - Scheme is a LISP-based scripting language. SIOD is a subset of this language. SIOD is the native scripting language used with the GIMP.

Script-Fu - The native scripting interface in the GIMP, which uses SIOD as its scripting language.

T

Tileable Image - An image whose edges can wrap seamlessly. A tileable image, when placed next to a copy of itself, will not display a distinct edge where the two copies meet.

Transparency - The amount of an image or pixel which is invisible, that is, can be seen through.

U

Undo - Takes back last applied change.

V

Value - A mode used for compositing layers, brushes or other image effects.

Appendix A - The gimprc File

The gimprc file is the file used by the GIMP at startup to determine where to look for other files, where to place temporary files, and various other run-time configuration items. The file contains numerous comments and is fairly easy to follow. The default gimprc is provided below for reference, with explanatory comments.

```
# Lines that start with a '#' are comments.
# Blank lines are ignored.

# The variable gimp_dir is set to either the
interned value
# .gimp or the environment variable GIMP_DIRECTORY.
If
# the path in GIMP_DIRECTORY is relative, it is
considered
# relative to your home directory.

(prefix "/usr/local")
(exec_prefix "${prefix}")
(gimp_data_dir "${prefix}/share/gimp/0.99.11")
(gimp_plugin_dir "${exec_prefix}/lib/gimp/0.99.11")
```

The prefix variable is the top-level directory under which the GIMP was installed. The gimp_data_dir tells the GIMP where system-specific patterns, brushes, gradients, and so forth are installed. The directory gimp_plugin_dir serves the same purpose for plug-ins. These values are used to find system-installed versions. They do not point to user-specific versions of these data and plug-in files. User specific copies are stored under the directory pointed to by either gimp_dir or GIMP_DIRECTORY.

```
# Set the temporary storage directory...files will appear here
# during the course of running the GIMP. Most files will disappear
# when the gimp exits, but some files are likely to remain,
# such as working palette files, so it is best if this directory is
# not one that is shared by other users or is cleared on machine
# reboot, such as /tmp.

(temp-path "${gimp_dir}/tmp")
```

```
# Set the swap file location. The gimp uses a tile-based memory
# allocation scheme. The swap file is used to quickly and easily
# swap files out to disk and back in. Be aware that the swap file
# can easily get very large if the gimp is used with large images.
# Also, things can get horribly slow if the swap file is created on
# a directory that is mounted over NFS. For these reasons, it may
# be desirable to put your swap file in "/tmp".

(swap-path "${gimp_dir}")
```

Notice that the default location for swap files is the top level directory pointed to by the gimp_dir variable. You may want to place these under a swap directory beneath gimp_dir to keep them separate from other files.

```
# Set the brush search path...this path will be
searched for valid
# brushes at startup.

(brush-path "${gimp_dir}/
brushes:${gimp_data_dir}/brushes")
```

The former location is the user-specific brushes, the latter the system-specific brushes. If the same brush file exists in both places, you will get two copies in your brushes dialog.

```
# Specify a default brush. If none is specified it defaults to the
# "1circle.gbr" brush which is just a single pixel sized brush.
# The brush is searched for in the brush path.

(default-brush "19fcircle.gbr")
```

19fcircle.gbr is part of the base GIMP distribution.

```
# Set the pattern search path...this path will be searched for valid
# patterns at startup.

(pattern-path "${gimp_dir}/patterns:${gimp_data_dir}/patterns")
```

Like brushes, the former is user-specific and the latter is system-specific.

```
# Specify a default pattern.
# The pattern is searched for in the specified pattern paths.

(default-pattern "wood2.pat")
```

wood2.pat is part of the base GIMP distribution.

```
# Set the palette search path...this path will be searched for valid
# palettes at startup.

(palette-path "${gimp_dir}/palettes:${gimp_data_dir}/palettes")

# Specify a default palette.
# The pattern is searched for in the specified pattern paths.

(default-palette "Default")

# Set the gradient search path...this path will be searched for valid
# gradients at startup.

(gradient-path "${gimp_dir}/gradients:${gimp_data_dir}/
gradients")

# Specify a default gradient.
# The gradient is searched for in the specified gradient paths.

(default-gradient "German_flag_smooth")

# Set the plug-in search path...this path will be searched for
# plug-ins when the plug-in is run.

(plug-in-path "${gimp_dir}/plug-ins:${gimp_dir}/plug-ins/script-
fu:${gimp_plugin_dir}/plug-ins")

# Set the path for the script-fu plug-in. This value is ignored by
# the GIMP if the script-fu plug-in is never run.

(script-fu-path "${gimp_dir}/scripts:${gimp_data_dir}/scripts")
```

Script-Fu is the plug-in that runs the Scheme-based scripts.

```
# The tile cache is used to make sure the gimp doesn't thrash
# tiles between memory and disk. Setting this value higher will
# cause the gimp to use less swap space, but will also cause
# the gimp to use more memory. Conversely, a smaller cache size
# causes the gimp to use more swap space and less memory.
# Note: the gimp will still run even if 'tile-cache-size' is
# set to 0. The actual size can contain a suffix of 'm', 'M',
# 'k', 'K', 'b' or 'B', which makes the gimp interpret the
# size as being specified in megabytes, kilobytes and bytes
# respectively. If no suffix is specified, the size defaults to
```

```
# being specified in kilobytes.

(tile-cache-size 10m)

# Speed of marching ants in the selection outline
# this value is in milliseconds
# (less time indicates faster marching)

(marching-ants-speed 300)

# Set the number of operations kept on the undo stack

(undo-levels 5)

# Set the color-cube resource for dithering on 8-bit displays
# The 4 values stand for shades of red, green, blue and gray
# Multiplying the number of shades of each primary color yields
# the total number of colors that will be allocated from the
# gimp colormap. This number should not exceed 256. Most of the
# colors remaining after the allocation of the colorcube
# will be left to the system palette in an effort to reduce
# colormap "flashing".

(colorcube 6 6 4 24)

# Install a GIMP colormap by default -- only for 8-bit displays
# (install-colormap)


# Specify that marching ants for selected regions will be drawn
# with colormap cycling as opposed to redrawing with different
stipple masks
# this color cycling option works only with 8-bit displays

# (colormap-cycling)

# Tools such as fuzzy-select and bucket fill find regions based on a
# seed-fill algorithm. The seed fill starts at the initially
selected
# pixel and progresses in all directions until the difference in
# pixel intensity from the original is greater than a specified
# threshold
# --> This value represents the default threshold

(default-threshold 15)

# There is always a tradeoff between memory usage and speed. In most
# cases, the GIMP opts for speed over memory. However, if memory is
# a big issue, set stingy-memory-use
# (stingy-memory-use)

# When zooming into and out of images, this option enables the
```

```
# automatic resizing of windows
# (allow-resize-windows)

# Context-dependent cursors are cool. They are enabled by default.
# However, they require overhead that you may want to do without.
# Uncomment this line to disable them.
# (no-cursor-updating)

# Layer preview sizes:
# none:  no previews in layers dialog/layer selector
# small:  32x32
# medium: 64x64
# large:  128x128
# #:     #x#

(preview-size small)

# Controlling ruler visibility
# The default behavior is for rulers to bc ON
# This can also be toggled with the View->Show Rulers command
# or shift+control+r

# (dont-show-rulers)
```

Rulers are visible across the top and left sides of Image Windows. See **Chapter 3 - GIMP Windows.**

```
# Ruler units
# The units of rulers can be one of: (pixels
inches centimeters)
# The default is pixels

(ruler-units pixels)

# Disable auto saving
# Just uncomment the line below...
# (dont-auto-save)



# Disable confirmation before closing an image without saving
# Just uncomment the next line
# (dont-confirm-on-close)

# Setting the level of interpolation
# Uncommenting this line will enable cubic interpolation.
# By default, the GIMP uses linear interpolation, which is faster,
but has
# poorer quality
# (cubic-interpolation)

# Set the gamma correction values for the display
```

```
# 1.0 corresponds to no gamma correction. For most displays,
# gamma correction should be set to between 2.0 and 2.6
# Run the utility "gamma_correct" to determine appropriate values
# for your display.

#

# One important item to keep in mind: Many images that you might
# get from outside sources will in all likelihood already be
# gamma-corrected. In these cases, the image will look washed out
# if the gimp has gamma correction turned on. If you are going
# to work with images of this sort, turn gamma correction off
# by removing this line, or setting the values to 1.0.
# gamma-correction 1.0
# gamma-correction 2.0
#           ___

(gamma-correction 1.0)

# Set the manner in which transparency is displayed in images
# Transparency type can be one of:
#   0: Light Checks
#   1: Mid-Tone Checks
#   2: Dark Checks
#   3: White Only
#   4: Gray Only
#   5: Black Only
# Check size can be one of:
#   0: Small
#   1: Medium
#   2: Large

(transparency-type 1)

(transparency-size 2)

# gfig pattern directory

(gfig-path "${gimp_dir}/gfig")

#- Next line modified by GIMP on 1998-04-14 02:17:15

(last-tip-shown 11)
```

The last entry is an example of a line automatically added to the gimprc by the GIMP. In this case, it shows the last Tip of the Day displayed. Whenever you use the Preferences dialog to change configurable settings, the changes will be marked by a comment line similar to the last one shown here.

Appendix B - Keyboard Shortcuts

The following tables give the default keyboard shortcuts as they are supplied with the standard GIMP distributions and available on the CD-ROM included with this book. These settings are user-configurable, and distributions from other sources may have different defaults. Information on how to change them is given below.

The following abbreviations are used for keyboard modifiers:

- CTRL - Either Control key on the keyboard

- ALT - The Alt key, generally on the lower left side of the keyboard

- SHIFT - Either Shift key on the keyboard

The case of the letters used in the keyboard shortcuts is significant.

Tools

Keystrokes	Tool
m	Enable the Move tool
= or -	Zoom In or Zoom Out, respectively
SHIFT-c	Enable the Crop tool
SHIFT-t	Enable the Transform tool
SHIFT-f	Enable the Flip tool
t	Enable the Text tool
o	Enable the Color Picker tool
SHIFT-b	Enable the Bucket Fill tool
l	Enable the Gradient Fill (Blend) tool
SHIFT-p	Enable the Pencil tool
p	Enable the Paintbrush tool
SHIFT-e	Enable the Eraser tool
a	Enable the Airbrush tool
c	Enable the Clone tool
v	Enable the Convolver tool

Selections

Keystrokes	Tool
r	Enable the Rectangular selection tool
e	Enable the Elliptical selection tool
f	Enable the Free-hand selection tool
z	Enable the Fuzzy selection tool
b	Enable the Bézier selection tool
CTRL-a	Select All
CTRL-SHIFT-a	Select None (turn off any current selection)
CTRL-SHIFT-l	Float selection
CTRL-SHIFT-h	Sharpen selection boundaries
CTRL-SHIFT-f	Feather selection
CTRL-t	Toggle selection
CTRL-i	Invert selection

Modifiers Before Mouse Click

Selection Tool	CTRL	SHIFT	CTRL-SHIFT
Rectangular, Elliptical, Free-hand, Fuzzy and Bézier	Subtract from current selection	Add to current selection	Intersect with current selection

Modifiers After Mouse Click

Selection Tool	CTRL	SHIFT	CTRL-SHIFT
Rectangular	Creates new selection using click point as center of selection	Constrains new selection	Constrains new selection and centers it on initial click point
Elliptical	Creates new selection using click point as center of selection	Constrains new selection	Constrains new selection and centers it on initial click point
Free-hand and Fuzzy	No effect	No effect	No effect
Bézier	Moves control points	Moves splines (handles)	No effect

All selections can be moved, without moving the image or layer contents, by pressing and holding the ALT key while clicking and dragging with the left mouse button.

Image Menu Functions

Keystrokes	Function
CTRL-x	Cut
CTRL-c	Copy
CTRL-v	Paste
CTRL-k	Clear
CTRL-. (CTRL-period)	Fill
CTRL-z	Undo
CTRL-r	Redo
CTRL-SHIFT-x	Cut to named buffer
CTRL-SHIFT-c	Copy to named buffer
CTRL-SHIFT-v	Paste from named buffer
CTRL-SHIFT-o	Offset layer by specified amount
CTRL-d	Duplicate entire Image Window, including all layers and masks

View Options

Keystrokes	Function
=	Zoom In
-	Zoom Out
1	Zoom 1:1
CTRL-SHIFT-i	Show Window Info
CTRL-SHIFT-r	Toggle Image Window ruler
CTRL-SHIFT-t	Toggle Image Window guides
CTRL-e	Shrink Wrap

Dialog Windows

Keystrokes	Function
CTRL-SHIFT-b	Brush Selection dialog
CTRL-SHIFT-p	Pattern Selection dialog
CTRL-p	Palette dialog
CTRL-g	Gradient Editor
CTRL-SHIFT-t	Turns on Tool Options dialogs
CTRL-l	Layers and Channels dialog

Filters

Keystrokes	Function
ALT-f	Repeat last
SHIFT-ALT-f	Re-show last

By default, none of the filters available from the Image Window menu have keyboard shortcuts.

Layers and Channels

Keystrokes	Layer Function
CTRL-t	Toggles the yellow dashed line around the edge of a layer
CTRL-n	Opens the new layer dialog to create a new layer
CTRL-f	Raises the currently selected layer by one layer, if possible
CTRL-b	Lowers the currently selected layer by one layer, if possible
CTRL-x	Deletes active layer
CTRL-s	Scales active layer
CTRL-r	Resizes active layer
CTRL-h	Anchors floating layer
CTRL-m	Merges visible layers

Keystrokes	Channel Function
CTRL-n	Opens the new channel dialog
CTRL-f	Raises the currently selected channel by one layer, if possible
CTRL-b	Lowers the currently selected channel by one layer, if possible
CTRL-x	Deletes active channel
CTRL-s	Copies channel to selection

Other Menu Options

Keystrokes	Function
CTRL-n	Opens a new Image Window
CTRL-o	Opens an existing image file
CTRL-s	Saves image
CTRL-q	Quits completely from the GIMP
CTRL-w	Closes Image Window

Changing Defaults or Adding Your Own Shortcuts

GTK, the windowing toolkit upon which the GIMP is built, gives applications the ability to let users install their own keyboard shortcuts in any menu. To use this feature, simply move the cursor over the menu item you wish to change (or to add a keyboard shortcut if it doesn't already have one) and press the keys you wish to use for that menu item.

For example, by default there is no keyboard shortcut to access the Print dialog. Click on the Image Window once to open the Image Window menu. Click on the File menu option to open the file submenu. Move the cursor over the Print option so the option is highlighted—leave the mouse there, but don't click on the option. Now press SHIFT-ALT-p. The menu will resize itself to allow the keyboard shortcut to be added to the right of the Print option. From now on, you can use SHIFT-ALT-p to access the Print dialog. That's all there is to it!

Once a menu option has a keyboard shortcut assigned to it, you cannot explicitly remove the shortcut. However, you can always change it to a different shortcut simply by repeating the steps you used to create it originally, just like we just did for the Print dialog.

Keyboard shortcuts are global, meaning that only one feature within the GIMP can have a given keystroke combination. If the shortcut you enter is already in use, the option that originally used that shortcut will no longer have one. You can see this happen by changing the Mail Image option to the Print option shortcut. Just highlight the Mail Image option and use the SHIFT-ALT-p keystrokes again. The Print option loses its shortcut, and it is given to the Mail Image option.

Appendix C - Adding Fonts To Your System

The GIMP is based on Xlib, and therefore has access to the font-rendering engines within the X server on your UNIX host. This normally means that the GIMP will have access to up to three types of fonts: Bitmap, PostScript Type 1, and TrueType. Bitmap fonts are not widely distributed (not being readily available on commercial CD-ROMs that can be purchased from a software store like CompUSA or Egghead Software). My experience has been that you shouldn't bother with these unless you happen to be given some. Conversely, PostScript Type 1, usually referred to simply as Type1 fonts, are quite common. I've purchased at least four different CD-ROMs with thousands of Type1 fonts on them for use with Linux and X Windows applications. TrueType fonts are not commonly supported by most X servers without additional, commercial font servers. Discussion about adding fonts, therefore, will focus on Type1 fonts only. In order to make use of these fonts, you need to install them on your system and let the X server know about them.

First, a little background: nearly all X applications accept the -fn and/or -font command line options. This is a feature built into the X Windows Xt Toolkit API. Other toolkits, such as GTK or Qt, may not accept this command. Also, these options may sometimes be specified with two dashes (--) instead of one (-). How these options are used depends on the application. For xterms, just use -fn to specify the font used in the xterm window. This does not specify what font to use for the xterm title bar. That is controlled by the window manager's X resources. Specifying a font with the -fn or -font options generally only affects specific buttons, tables, lists, and so forth. In the GIMP, this option is handled through the use of the gtkrc file. A detailed discussion of this file is beyond the scope of this book. However, you will be using fonts within the GIMP to create images, and the underlying mechanisms for accessing them (whether for graphics or buttons), although meaningless to an ordinary user, are still very similar.

To find out what fonts are already available on your system, look under the font directories for `fonts.alias` files. There should be one of these in each directory under `/usr/X11R6/lib/X11/fonts`,[1] but whether there is or not depends on the distribution you're using. This file maps an alias name to the fully specified font name. The syntax for the fully qualified font name is given in the X Logical Font Description, which is available in Volume Zero, *X Protocol Reference Manual* from O'Reilly & Associates, Inc. **Chapter 7 - Colors and Text** briefly discusses this definition, although only with respect to using the Text Tool dialog.

The alias name for the font is the name on the left on each line of the `fonts.alias` file. For example, under `/usr/X11R6/lib/X11/fonts/misc`, in the file `fonts.alias` is the following line:

```
5x7 -misc-fixed-medium-r-normal--7-70-75-75-c-50-iso8859-1
```

To use this font with xterms, I would use:

```
xterm -fn 5x7
```

You can actually use the fully qualified font name on the right, but unless you understand how fonts are defined, you probably don't want to do this. Since the X server is being used to handle the fonts, adding fonts to your system is the same whether you use them for graphics or as resources for X application labels, buttons, and so forth.

Adding a New Font

Suppose you had a font called *westerngoofy* that you wanted to use in the GIMP as the start of some neat title graphic for a web page. By default, there isn't an entry in any of the `fonts.alias` files for westerngoofy, so when you use the text tool in the GIMP it won't show up in the list of available fonts. There are three steps to making this font available for use with the GIMP:

---

1. This is the standard location on most PC-based UNIX systems. Sun Solaris puts them under `/usr/openwin/lib/X11`. HP and AIX have their own locations as well, although there should probably be symbolic or hard links from `/usr/X11/lib` to wherever the files are actually located.

1. Grab the fonts and place them in a local directory

2. Configure that directory for use as a font directory

3. Tell the X server about this new font directory

The first part is simple—grab a copy of the font file and put it in some directory. Make sure you've uncompressed it—some archives provide fonts in compressed format. Most X servers don't understand compressed fonts (some do, but all understand uncompressed fonts). The directory you place the font file in can be owned by anyone. It does not have to be a directory under the system fonts directories (generally these are under `/usr/X11R6/lib/X11/fonts`). On my system, I have an `src/X11` directory under my home directory. Under this, I created a "fonts" directory where I put new fonts. If you are the owner of your system and have root access, you might want to put the fonts under `/usr/local/fonts` or someplace similar.

Since TrueType fonts are not supported by default by most X servers, we won't concern ourselves with them here. The font format you should be using is Type1. There are plenty of places to get these, including numerous CD-ROMs available from any decent computer software store. Some on-line resources are listed in the Linux Graphics mini-HOWTO under the "Other Topics" section.

The Linux Graphics mini-HOWTO is available at:
`http://www.graphics-muse.org/linux/lgh.html`

Next, you need to configure your new fonts directory so that the X server can provide fontname-to-file mappings. To do this, you need to get ahold of a little Perl script called `type1inst`, which is short for "Type 1 Install". This script is easy to use and comes with documentation explaining what you are about to do. Be sure to read the documentation first, of course. Basically, you run the script to create a couple of files, `fonts.alias` and `fonts.dir`, which the X server uses to associate a font's name to the actual font file. You can also use `mkfontdir`, but I like `type1inst` better. `mkfontdir` doesn't always seem to be available on all platforms, and finding a binary version (or even source) has never been easy for me. (I think it's buried in the X11 source tree, which I really don't want to download just for one program.)

`type1inst` is available from `http://goblet.anu.edu.au/~m9305357/type1inst.html`

The last step is to let the X server know about the new font directory. The `xset` command allows a user to configure a number of options for the X server. One of these options is the path to search for font files. The format of the command is as follows:

```
xset fp+ <path>
```

The `fp` option is used to modify the font path. The plus sign is used to add a directory to the font path. Because the plus sign is after the `fp`, the directory specified will be appended to the current list of paths, if there are any. Using `+fp` would prepend the new path to the front of the current list.

There are other possibilities. Running

```
xset -?
```

will provide a thorough list of options. The man page for `xset` also contains good descriptions of the options.

Now that the server knows where to look, it has to be told to go ahead and check for fonts in the new directories. The `rehash` option to `xset` does this. Simply run

```
xset fp rehash
```

and your new fonts are ready to use!

Of course, once you've installed the fonts in a directory and run `type1inst`, you can put the `xset` commands in your `.xinitrc` file so they are run every time you start up your X environment (such as with the `startx` script). This is what I do so that I always have access to the set of fonts I've installed from CD-ROMs or from font archives on the Net.

That's all there is to it. You should now be able to use your fonts with tools like the GIMP or any other X application in order to create lots of interesting images and graphical interfaces.

Index

Notes

Notes

Notes

Notes

Notes

Notes

Notes

Notes

Notes

Notes

Every month *Linux Journal* brings subscribers the most complete news and information on what the powerful Linux operating system can do. This includes Linux news, tips, features and reviews which you cannot find anywhere else. Our coverage of kernel changes, programming tools, and product releases is unparalleled.

- ■ Keep up on the latest Linux technology news
- ■ Read comprehensive reviews on Linux merchandise
- ■ Find answers in our Best of Technical Support column
- ■ Get involved with the Linux community
- ■ Increase your technical knowledge

SPECIAL OFFER

Return this coupon and you will automatically receive a free issue of Linux Journal, compliments of

The Artists' Guide to the GIMP

By subscribing today, you will save over 60% off cover price.

	2 YEARS	1 YEAR
US	❏ $39	❏ $22
CAN/MEX	❏ $49(USD)	❏ $27(USD)
Elsewhere	❏ $64(USD)	❏ $37(USD)

Please allow 6-8 weeks for processing

NAME _____

COMPANY _____

ADDRESS _____

CITY _____ STATE _____ POSTAL CODE _____

COUNTRY _____ E-MAIL _____

TELEPHONE _____ FAX _____

❏ Visa   ❏ MasterCard   ❏ American Express   ❏ Check Enclosed

CREDIT CARD # _____ EXPIRES _____

SIGNATURE _____

Detach and return this coupon:

**Linux Journal
PO Box 500
Missouri City, TX 77459-0500**

**http://www.linuxjournal.com/
888-66-LINUX [888-665-4689]
FAX 281-261-5999**

Notice

By opening the CD-ROM packaging, you are agreeing to be bound to the following terms:

This software is provided "as is", without warranty of any kind, either expressed or implied, including, but not limited to, the implied warranties of merchantability and fitness for a particular purpose. Neither the publisher nor its dealers or distributors assume any liability for any alleged or actual damages arising from the use of the contents of this CD-ROM. (Some states do not allow for the exclusion of implied warranties, so the exclusion may not apply to you.)

About the CD-ROM

All of the tools needed to get started with the GIMP are available on the CD in source format, with much of it in binary RPM and Debian formats. This includes both the GIMP core plug-ins and unstable distributions and the stable 1.0 version of GTK known to work with the 1.0 version of the GIMP. All of the images from the text can be found on the CD, as well as tutorials, general graphics documentation, links to important sites, and much more. Additionally, a Gallery of images from the author's collection is included exclusively on the CD. These images help illustrate some of the GIMP's many capabilities and also serve as inspiration for the reader.